Das LERNSTOFF
Übungsbuch

Roland Zimmermann

Basiswissen Englisch

Band 1: Die Zeiten

Lösungen

LERNSTOFF
SKG-VERLAG

The present progressive

Seite 14 – Exercise 1
1. is leaving
2. are (We're) writing
3. are (You're) doing
4. is carrying
5. is sitting
6. are dying
7. are travelling
8. are (They're) tasting
9. are (You're) watching
10. are not (aren't) running
11. is putting
12. are not (aren't) coming
13. are playing
14. is making
15. are repairing
16. is not (isn't) cleaning
17. is doing
18. are not (aren't) listening
19. are (We're) having
20. Is Judy writing
21. is (She's) waving
22. are (They're) hiding
23. is she going
24. is learning
25. is reading
26. are having
27. is working
28. are (We're) waiting
29. is singing
30. is sleeping
31. am (I'm) writing
32. are playing
33. are (We're) painting
34. is carrying
35. are looking

Seite 15 – Exercise 2
1. Jack is doing his homework in the classroom now.
2. My parents are working in the garden today.
3. The pupils can't see the worksheets on their desks at the moment.
4. Judy is in her room now.
5. Where are our books?
6. Jack's ruler is in his pencil-case now.
7. I can't (cannot) see my parents' car at the moment.
8. Tom is swimming in the pool now.
9. The pupils are writing an essay in their classroom at the moment.

Seite 15 – Exercise 3
1. Where are you playing?
2. Is Judy a boy?
3. Where is he at the moment?
4. Who is repairing the car?
5. What is Jim writing today?
6. What's the time?
7. How old are you?
8. What are you watching now?
9. What is Jack painting?
10. Where are you playing?
11. What are you cleaning?
12. Where are the parents sitting?
13. How many pets have you got?
14. Are you a good pupil?

Seite 16 – Exercise 4
1. Where are you going?
2. Where is he lying?
3. What is he doing?
4. What are you playing?
5. How are they working?
6. Who is singing terribly?
7. Is he paying attention?
8. Where are you lying?
9. What is he checking?
10. When are they driving?
11. Where are you going?
12. Who is running?
13. What is he watching?
14. Where are they driving?
15. What is he weighing?
16. Who is crying?
17. What are you reading?
18. Who is spelling the word?
19. What is he giving you?

Seite 16 – Exercise 5
1. David's hamster is playing the trumpet at the corner of our garden (now).
2. Because it is (it's) raining, he is (he's) standing under an umbrella.
3. David's penguins fetch four broken pots because they haven't got (have not got/ don't have) any drums.
4. There is a terrible noise, and his mother is frightened.
5. Now the music is over and the pets are going into their cages.

Seite 17 – Exercise 6
1. are reading
2. is (It's)
3. is doing
4. can't (cannot) go
5. is going
6. is (It's) – are not (aren't)
7. is helping
8. are (We're) coming
9. is (She's) trying
10. is carrying
11. are waiting
12. are learning
13. are you doing

Seite 17 – Exercise 7
1. My brother and my mother are buying a CD player (now).
2. Look, Jack is working in his room.
3. What are you doing (now)? — I'm (I am) writing a dictation.
4. How many pupils can you see in the classroom now?
5. We can't (cannot) repair our bikes now because we're (we are) having English.
6. My mother is watching TV (at the moment).
7. We are sitting in our rooms and are doing our homework (now).

Seite 18 – Exercise 8
1. My son Peter, my daughter Mary and her friend are at home and are making music today.
2. They are (They're) in the living-room and are practising.
3. I can't (cannot) read because they are (they're) so noisy.
4. But that is not (isn't) a problem because I haven't (have not) got anything against loud music.
5. Peter is playing the drums with his brother (at the moment).
6. His sister Betty is singing and her friend is playing the trumpet.
7. Peter is banging two pots together.
8. They are (They're) making a terrible noise.
9. The drums are standing in front of the door of his parents' room.
10. They can't (cannot) go out because the weather is bad.
11. It is (It's) raining.
12. So (That's why, Therefore) we can't (cannot) go into the garden.
13. We can't (cannot) ride our bikes and can't (cannot) play with our dog Oliver.
14. Because our parents are at home, we can't (cannot) make any noise.

Seite 19 – Exercise 9
(1) are sitting
(2) are
(3) are having (They're having)
(4) are waiting (They're waiting)
(5) is coming (he's coming)
(6) is carrying (he's carrying)
(7) is
(8) is
(9) are reading
(10) is not (isn't)
(11) can't (cannot) understand
(12) is
(13) are
(14) is shining
(15) are (they're) playing
(16) are sitting
(17) are watching
(18) is
(19) are cleaning

Seite 19 – Exercise 10
1. My friend's father is cleaning his car (now).
2. The sun is shining and it isn't (is not) raining.
3. My brother is sitting downstairs in my mother's room and is reading the newspaper.
4. My three sisters are in the garden and are playing cards.
5. My father's dogs are playing with their football.
6. Mary is opening the window now and is watching the dogs.
7. They are (They're) sitting on chairs and are looking at Mary.
8. Now the dogs are jumping onto a tree.

Seite 20 – Exercise 11
1. Mary can't write English.
2. My father is reading the newspaper in the garden now.
3. What is Jack doing at the moment?
4. David is playing tennis with Mr Hill in front of our house now.

Seite 20 – Exercise 12
1. Hello Peter. What are you doing?
2. I'm sitting in my room and I'm looking out of the window.
3. I can see my sister Betty (now). She's jumping onto a wall.
4. Where's her dog now?
5. He's sitting in front of his basket and is listening to the birds.
6. Can you hear the birds, too?
7. No I can't. The window isn't open.
8. Are Betty's cats jumping onto the wall, too?
9. They can't jump onto the wall because it is too high.

10. Are you sitting in (your) bed? – No I'm not. I'm not sitting in (my) bed because I'm standing on the window.
11. Can you call me later?

The simple present

Seite 26 – Exercise 1
1. goes
2. do
3. buy
4. carries
5. catches
6. watches
7. read
8. flies
9. wishes
10. don't learn (do not learn)
11. doesn't play (does not play)
12. don't do (do not do)
13. begin
14. likes
15. does
16. finishes
17. enjoys
18. do not (don't) study
19. do not (don't) stay
20. arrive
21. don't like (do not like)
22. kills
23. doesn't go (does not go)
24. buys
25. go
26. doesn't do (does not do)
27. cries
28. play
29. carries
30. don't go (do not go)
31. doesn't like (does not like)
32. do you normally spend
33. meets
34. go

Seite 27 – Exercise 2
1. My father doesn't (does not) go to work at six o'clock in the morning.
   When does your father go to work?
2. I don't do (do not do) my homework in the afternoon.
   What do you do in the afternoon?
3. The Jacksons aren't (are not) at home at the weekend.
   Where are the Jacksons at the weekend?
4. The pupils haven't got (have not got) to learn every day.
   Who has got to learn every day?
5. My father doesn't (does not) play chess in the evening.
   When does your father play chess?
6. Jack's sister can't (cannot) speak Japanese.
   Who can speak Japanese?
7. My mother doesn't (does not) always do the washing up after dinner.
   When does your mother always do the washing up?
8. I haven't got (have not got) to go to school on weekdays.
   When have you got to go to school?
9. Tom doesn't (does not) work in the garden.
   Who works in the garden?
10. I don't like English.
    What do you like?

Seite 28 – Exercise 3
1. When do you play tennis?
2. Who cleans his room?
3. Where do you do your homework?
4. When do you have tea?
5. When does school begin?
6. When is your first break?
7. Is there an assembly here?
8. What is (What's) your favourite subject?
9. Who(m) does he see quite often?
10. Where do they go?
11. What do you like?

Seite 28 – Exercise 4
1. When do you go to school in the morning?
2. I don't (do not) meet my (girl)friend at half past seven but at nine.
3. When is (have you got) your next English lesson? (When do you have …)
4. Do you like sport?
5. How old is your religious education teacher?
6. We don't have (do not have/haven't got) a biology lesson on Mondays.
7. Who plays football with you every Saturday?
8. Do you go out every Friday?
9. Jack never plays football on Sundays.
10. Francis always does his homework in the afternoon(s).
11. When does your mother wash the dishes?

Seite 29 – Exercise 5
1. What does Peter like?
2. What do you see?
3. Who goes to school at 8 o'clock?
4. Do you have flowers in the garden?
5. What has Mike got?
6. Where does your pen-friend live?
7. When do you watch TV?
8. Where are you?
9. Who does not (doesn't) play chess?
10. Where do you go?
11. How many books have they got?
12. What do they like?
13. What does he do?

Seite 29 – Exercise 6
1. Judy never goes to school on Sundays.
2. Tom and Jerry don't (do not) like cats for breakfast in the mornings.
3. Mike doesn't (does not) do his homework in his room after school.
4. Norman doesn't (does not) often play the guitar in a band.
5. Teachers sometimes work on Sundays.
6. Jill never sleeps in the garden.
7. We don't (do not) go out when it rains.
8. We never sing Christmas songs during the year.
9. My friend doesn't (does not) like French songs.
10. The orchestra never plays German music.

Seite 30 – Exercise 7
1. What do you hate?
2. When do you go out?
3. Who does the washing?
4. Where does he do his homework?
5. What does she put into the cupboard?
6. What have they got?
7. Where are the pupils?
8. Where would you like to live?
9. Who comes home every night?
10. Where do the mechanics work?
11. What does Mary do?
12. Where are you?

Seite 30 – Exercise 8
1. Mary: Frank, switch on the radio, please, the news about the football match between England and Germany comes at half past three.
2. Frank: Your watch is slow. It's already seven minutes to four – much too late. It's already over.
3. Mary: What a pity. I like listening to the news.
4. Frank: Is there a football match on TV tonight?
5. Mary: I don't want to watch it there because uncle George always plays the drums with spoons and forks in the living-room.
6. Frank: Don't grumble. After dinner he doesn't play there, but in his room.
7. Nary: But one (you) always hears (hear) him. It's really terrible.
8. Frank: I'm sorry, but I can't do anything about it.

Seite 31 – Exercise 9
1. Peter and Mary are always on holiday abroad in autumn.
2. They are (They're) on a caravan site in America.
3. They like spending their holidays there because the beaches are very nice.
4. Sometimes they drive into town and see the sights there.
5. There are many old castles and churches there.
6. Sometimes Peter's parents rent a fantastic apartment at the French coast.
7. It's got (It has got) nice furniture and a big garden.
8. This year the children want to go without their parents and want to stay in a lively youth hostel at a lake in Scotland because they want to see the monster there.
9. They want to take photos of it and want to sell the photos (them) to a magazine.
10. They always go to England by train and then they hitchhike to Scotland.
11. They often stay the night in youth hostels because it's (it is) cheaper there than in hotels.
12. And in these youth hostels it's (it is) more interesting, too because one (you) can meet many young people there.

Vergleich: Simple present – Present progressive

Seite 33 – Exercise 1
(1) are sitting
(2) is telling
(3) are listening
(4) tests
(5) is
(6) can't (cannot) pronounce
(7) can't (cannot) read
(8) gets
(9) goes
(10) is (She's) opening
(11) can see
(12) are (They're) playing
(13) are reading
(14) have (They've) got
(15) are

(16) are (they're) playing
(17) is making
(18) is not (isn't) listening
(19) is
(20) are
(21) are
(22) is (He's) carrying
(23) is (He's) putting

Seite 33 – Exercise 2
1. Because the weather is bad, Kermit must stay in the classroom today.
2. He is (He's) playing the drums with his legs and is making a terrible noise (now).
3. But Kermit cannot (can't) sing because he has got (he's got) a sore throat.
4. But Kermit always sings badly even if he has not (hasn't) got a sore throat.
5. He is (He's) not singing now, but is listening to a programme on the radio.

Seite 34 – Exercise 3
1. goes
2. are taking
3. gets up – is (he's) getting up
4. has got
5. is
6. get
7. have (We've) got to buy
8. wears – is (she's) wearing
9. does – is (she's) doing
10. cannot (can't) go – is (he's)
11. carries
12. watches – is (he's) sitting – is watching
13. can't do – are
14. play –   are – are training
15. have (We've) got – are (We're) sitting – are doing
16. do not (don't) work – are – are preparing
17. are you doing? – am (I'm) waiting
18. is watching – watches

Seite 35 – Exercise 4
1. does
2. is carrying
3. have
4. is sitting – is watching – plays
5. cooks – help
6. cleans – is – is washing
7. can come
8. is – goes
9. watches – is (she's) listening
10. is coming
11. isn't (is not) watching
12. goes – is (he's) going
13. is (She's) cleaning
14. is (He's) helping

Seite 35 – Exercise 5
1. My dog Eugen is in his room now and is writing a letter to me.
2. He must post it today because it's (it is) my birthday.
3. In my opinion Eugen is rather (quite/fairly/pretty) stupid: He always sticks the wrong stamp on the envelope and sometimes forgets the postcode.
4. But he often helps me and does the washing in the bathroom of our terraced house.

Seite 36 – Exercise 6
1. is playing
2. never watches
3. don't (do not) go
4. cannot (can't) go – is (it's) raining
5. are (We're)
6. gets
7. is playing
8. are (We're) doing

Seite 36 – Exercise 7
1. We always begin (start) our English lessons with a dictation.
2. Our teacher gives us a lot of (much) homework every day.
3. I drive to school by car every day, but today I'm (I am) walking because I've got (have got) a puncture.
4. In the afternoon I play the guitar or practise the piano.
5. My brother collects stamps and penguins.
6. I never usually watch TV in the evening(s), but today I'm (I am) sitting in my room and am watching Tom and Jerry.
7. I am not (I'm not) going home after school today because we've (we have) got lessons in the afternoon.
8. I don't (do not) go to bed before half past nine.
9. My parents don't (do not) drink coffee in the morning, but tea.
10. Do you wear uniforms at school?

Seite 37 – Exercise 8
1. is sitting – is playing
2. must practise – isn't (is not)
3. is – is listening
4. goes – is
5. is leaving
6. goes
7. buys – is (she's) standing
8. works
9. arrives

Seite 37 – Exercise 9
1. Pupils wear school uniforms at many schools in Great Britain.
2. They must stay at school from half past eigth till (a) quarter to four.
3. But today they can go home already at one o'clock because it is (it's) the Queen's birthday.
4. Tom is sitting in his room and is doing his homework (now).
5. He always starts with German, but today he is (he's) doing English.
6. Because his sister Susanna isn't (is not) at school today, she's (she is) sitting in her room and is eating a pizza.
7. Susanna has got many hobbies: She collects penguins and crocodiles and plays the guitar and the piano.

Seite 38 – Exercise 10
1. lives
2. is (He's) – has got
3. sees
4. is giving
5. are doing
6. have (They've) got
7. do – are
8. do – are not (aren't) doing
9. forget (tells)

Seite 38 – Exercise 11
1. There aren't (are not) any nice dresses in the girls' department today.
2. Mary is standing in front of the shelves and is looking at some expensive pullovers.
3. But she is not (isn't) buying anything because she hasn't (has not) got any money.
4. She always wants to have expensive things, but her parents have not got (haven't got/don't have) enough money, and so she often looks at cheap clothes only.
5. That's why she often finds nothing at all.
6. Then she is (she's) always very disappointed and runs around all over town to find something suitable.

Seite 39 – Exercise 12
1. have (We've) got
   We (We're) having
2. are (We're) sitting – are waiting
3. is
4. comes
5. are
6. do – study
7. is standing – is asking
8. sets – are
9. likes – are
10. goes – is

Seite 39 – Exercise 13
1. Tom's family has got a big garden behind their house.
2. There is (There's) a balcony with many flowers, too.
3. Tom has breakfast with his parents and his sisters in the dining-room every Sunday.
4. Father always reads the newspaper then.
5. But today he is (he's) watching TV because there is an interesting football match.
6. Tom is sitting in his room and is reading a magazine.
7. He also is listening to music.
8. On Sunday afternoons he sometimes goes to the disco because he likes loud music.

Seite 40 – Exercise 14
1. Tom usually gets up at five o'clock in the morning.
2. I cannot (can't) work in my room at the moment.
3. My mother never carries anything for my father in the supermarket on weekends.
4. What is Jack doing at the moment?
5. My father sometimes works on Sundays.
6. Judy is running down the hill now.
7. My brother is putting the books onto the shelf at the moment.
8. The teacher never prepares any lessons.

Seite 40 – Exercise 15
1. Jane is in the kitchen and is drying up at the moment.
2. My brother is standing in the bathroom now and is getting dressed because he must (has got to) go to school at half past seven.
3. I normally do the shopping, but today I'm (I am) doing the washing.
4. I am (I'm) standing in the bathroom now and am looking at my face.

5. Sometimes I get up at half past seven in the morning, but sometimes already at half past six.
6. I can't (cannot) help you now because I must dry up.

Seite 41 – Exercise 16
1. Janet and Peter must get up very early today because they can't (cannot) go to school with their father.
2. He has got (He's got) a bad headache and can't (cannot) go to work.
3. He normally works as a shop assistant in a supermarket.
4. He sells eggs, lemonade and orange juice.
5. In the evening(s) his work always finishes at half past six, and then he goes home.
6. He always drinks coffee with his supper and eats ham and eggs.
7. But today he is (he's) only eating milk and cornflakes.
8. After dinner his wife clears the table and does the washing up.
9. Janet and Peter are helping her: Peter is drying up and Janet is putting the dishes into the cupboard.
10. They sometimes read or play games together in the evening.
11. But today they are (they're) all sitting in front of the TV-set and are watching a boring film about ducks and cats.
12. It is (It's) about Donald Duck and his duck family.
13. Donald Duck has always got problems with his rich uncle and his little nephews.
14. They very often get on his nerves because they don't (do not) do what he says.

Seite 42 – Exercise 17
1. Tom and Jerry are at a popular school in London.
2. Their classrooms are very modern with CD players, and so they can always listen to CD's.
3. There are many nice pictures, lights and radiators there.
4. But today Tom and Jerry are tired of (are fed up with) the terrible school.
5. They can't (cannot) go on a bike tour because they are doing a stupid English test.
6. (That's) That is not (isn't) funny.

Seite 42 – Exercise 18
1. does – is (he's) learning – is
2. have (I've) got to go – is waiting
3. am (I'm) writing
4. is sitting

Seite 42 – Exercise 19
1. One of our teachers looks like a penguin, but he is (he's) quite nice.
2. He doesn't (does not) like our class at all because we often talk in his boring lessons and because we sometimes don't (do not) do our homework.
3. It always takes him a long time to correct our tests, and sometimes he doesn't (does not) do it at all because he's (he is) not interested in them.

Seite 43 – Exercise 20
1. When (How often) do you repair your bike?
2. What are they buying now?
3. When does Jill watch TV?
4. What are you listening to?
5. Who sleeps in the evening?
6. What does she buy?
7. Who answers questions?
8. Where do you do your homework?
9. Who speaks French?

Seite 43 – Exercise 21
1. My friend Tom plays football every day because he wants to play in the Premier League some time.
2. He's (He is) standing in the field today and is practising free-kicks all the time.
3. He's (He is) very disappointed because he never scores.
4. Although this is getting on his nerves, he knows that he must do it if he wants to get better.
5. Every Saturday he plays with his friends against a team of pupils in his class.
6. They mostly win because they can play much better.
7. Then Tom dreams about being the centre forward of Bayern Munich.

Seite 44 – Exercise 22
(1) are (We're)
(2) are visiting
(3) isn't (is not)
(4) is (he's) seeing
(5) must be
(6) has
(7) is (She's) cooking
(8) is (She's) tasting
(9) sees
(10) tastes
(11) is (She's) smelling
(12) smell
(13) doesn't (does not) matter
(14) have got
(15) are (they're) having
(16) have
(17) have
(18) is sitting
(19) is reading
(20) deals
(21) stops
(22) is
(23) explains

Seite 44 – Exercise 23
1. My grandfather is quite (rather) well-off. He has got (He's got) five detached houses, some dogs, fourteen secretaries and a wife.
2. On Thursdays he often goes to the cinema although he mostly hates the films there.
3. But today he is (he's) sitting in the living-room and is sticking stamps on the letters to his girl-friends.
4. He can't (cannot) find the addresses. Then he gets dressed and leaves the house.
5. He goes to a restaurant and eats a nice big cheeseburger.

The simple past

Seite 49 – Exercise 1
1. was
2. were
3. wanted
4. didn't (did not) want
5. began
6. went
7. was
8. braked – was
9. fell
10. flew
11. cut
12. broke
13. didn't (did not) like
14. got – was
15. drank – didn't (did not) eat
16. wasn't (was not)
17. fell
18. dreamed (dreamt)
19. woke – felt
20. didn't (did not) get – stayed
21. decided – didn't (did not) know
22. took
23. got – arrived
24. flew – didn't (did not) have
25. was – was
26. went – fell
27. did not (didn't) wake up

Seite 50 – Exercise 2
1. was
2. were
3. was
4. didn't (did not) ride
5. had
6. didn't (did not) have
7. started
8. took
9. tried – was
10. was
11. braked – was
12. was
13. crashed
14. fell – broke
15. started
16. took
17. was
18. had
19. crashed
20. helped
21. didn't (did not) want
22. didn't (did not) like
23. cleaned
24. repaired
25. were – went
26. got – felt
27. had
28. recovered – went
29. began

Seite 51 – Exercise 3
1. drove
2. didn't (did not) watch
3. happened
4. didn't (did not) have
5. found
6. saw
7. took
8. didn't (did not) learn
9. didn't (did not) give

Seite 51 – Exercise 4
1. What did you see?
2. Where did you play?
3. When did he go to bed?
4. When did she buy a book?
5. Who cleaned his bike?
6. Who(m) did Jim see?
7. Who taught English?
8. What did Judy cross?
9. Where did he swim?

Seite 51 – Exercise 5
1. I got a new BMX bike from my father yesterday.
2. I was in a bend and suddenly had to brake.
3. I crashed into a tree and fell off my bike.
4. The ambulance men took me to hospital at once.
5. I was in bed there all day long.
6. This wasn't (was not) a very nice experience.

Seite 52 – Exercise 6
1. Where did you see Jimmy?
2. What did Tim buy two days ago?
3. Why did you write a letter?
4. What did you feed?
5. Who got a new car?
6. When did school begin in Africa?
7. Where were you?
8. Did you do your homework?
9. How many sandwiches did he eat?
10. Who fought against the king?
11. How did they really feel?
12. What did he have?
13. Where were you?
14. What did Jack not (didn't Jack) find?
15. Where did you leave the bags?
16. How many sandwiches did they have?
17. Who went to London?
18. When did your parents see Tom?
19. What did Kate forget?
20. What did the pupils watch?
21. What were they interested in?

Seite 52 – Exercise 7
1. Three months ago we were in England because we wanted to learn English.
2. We were on holidays in London last year.
3. It was very nice although the weather there is often worse than in Germany.
4. The hotels were expensive, so we slept in youth hostels.
5. We didn't (did not) eat in restaurants, but bought hamburgers at McDonalds.

Seite 53 – Exercise 8
1. Janet left school at five o'clock yesterday.
2. We met him in London last year.
3. She didn't (did not) write a letter last week.
4. Two years ago they always went to the cinema on Sundays.
5. The band played a pop song at the party yesterday.

Seite 53 – Exercise 9
1. When did you buy this car?
2. What did Tom read?
3. Who wore a dress a week ago?
4. Did you get a good grade in English?
5. What fell into the water?

Seite 53 – Exercise 10
1. It was a strange day yesterday (Yesterday was a strange day) because our teacher didn't (did not) give us any worksheets.
2. He decided to show us something interesting about English bathrooms.
3. The showers in England are much smaller than in Germany.
4. We wrote down something about the country, too.
5. You can eat fish and chips or fantastic roast beef with fresh beans there, but you don't (do not) get any German sausages.
6. Before the lesson was over, our teacher was very angry with us because we played a trick on him and had a lot of fun.

Seite 54 – Exercise 11
1. I often worked in the garden.
2. It was Sunday yesterday.
3. He carried the wardrobe downstairs.
4. I did my homework in the dining-room.
5. Did he go to school every day?
6. She had a new dress.
7. They recognized him at once.
8. They felt tired.
9. He spoke English fluently.
10. They did not (didn't) like biology.

Seite 54 – Exercise 12
1. Last summer Mr Smith had a dangerous adventure.
2. He took a taxi to London.
3. Suddenly there were five penguins on the road.
4. The driver stopped at once and Mr Smith fell out of the taxi.
5. The ambulance took him to hospital.
6. Mr Smith didn't (did not) like being there at all.
7. Now he doesn't (does not) like penguins any more.

Seite 55 – Exercise 13
1. When did the race start?
2. Who fell off the bike?
3. What did the fathers clean?
4. Who(m) did the starter help?
5. Did the pupils like the track?
6. Who had an accident?
7. Where was the track?
8. What took place in the woods?
9. What did the teachers watch?
10. What were the mothers afraid of?
11. What didn't they like?
12. When did they go home?
13. Who did they take with them?
14. What did they repair?

Seite 55 – Exercise 14
1. Frankenstein jun. lived in a Celtic museum 212 years ago.
2. He always hid behind some Egyptian mummies and read boring books.
3. He liked playing football with the heads of the mummies very much and imagined becoming a famous football player, but he was worse than David Beckham.
4. When the visitors saw him and ran away, Frankenstein stopped walking around.
5. He bought an even more fantastic building, the ruins of an old castle in the capital of Scotland, and is writing books about his past at the moment.

Seite 56 – Exercise 15
1. threw – smashed
2. broke – was
3. came – tried – wasn't (was not)
4. noticed – tried
5. ran – followed – caught
6. made
7. got – hid – was
8. got – ran – went

Seite 56 – Exercise 16
1. When Judy was eleven, she had polio and so always has to (must) sit in her wheelchair.
2. She likes doing sports and is almost as fast as all the other children with her wheelchair.
3. Last year she lost two races, but the day before yesterday she took part in a race successfully and was first because she did 100 metres in 22 seconds.
4. She trains very hard at school regularly.
5. But she learns carefully for the most important subjects, too, because she wants to be better than her friends.

Seite 57 – Exercise 17
1. The pupils were in the zoo two days ago.
2. The farmers fed the cows every day last year.
3. Judy lost her bag yesterday.
4. We drank five bottles of coke the day before yesterday.
5. The pupils read many books in the lessons last year.
6. My parents never got up before eight o'clock three years ago.
7. The mechanics left the car in the garage last night.
8. John forgot his homework twice last week.
9. We didn't (did not) understand the grammar rules last year.

Seite 57 – Exercise 18
1. Tom and Jerry organized a race last Saturday.
2. Jerry rode a cat, Tom rode his BMX bike.
3. Because it was too boring round their houses, they took the more dangerous path through the woods with its high hills and bends.
4. Tom was much faster than Jerry, but suddenly there was an accident: Tom's pedal broke and he crashed into a tree.
5. Because he didn't (did not) wear a helmet, his head fell into the mud.
6. (He's) He is in hospital now and is waiting for a new head.

Seite 58 – Exercise 19
(1) had
(2) explained
(3) were
(4) paid
(5) didn't (did not) have
(6) got
(7) were

Seite 58 – Exercise 20

1. Peter had to take his driving-test four weeks ago.
2. He got his driving-licence and was allowed to drive his new car in the afternoon.
3. No experienced driver had to go with him.
4. But already after a few metres he had an accident.
5. He had to brake because five stupid ducks crossed the street and lost their eggs.
6. Because of the eggs the street was wet, and Peter slipped straight into some traffic lights.
7. But he was lucky because he was wearing a seat belt.
8. His car was o.k., too, – it was only a bit yellow, and so he had to wash it in the afternoon.
9. For the next two weeks he was not (wasn't) allowed to drive his car any more and so had to ride to school with his old scooter.
10. And the moral of the story: Do not (Don't) drive over ducks eggs!

The past progressive

Seite 62 – Exercise 1

1. was sleeping
2. were having
3. were writing
4. was waiting
5. were watching
6. were cleaning
7. was making
8. was sitting
9. were you talking
10. were running
11. wasn't (was not) overtaking
12. Were you really listening
13. was doing
14. were painting
15. were putting
16. weren't (were not) listening
17. Were you really paying
18. was watching
19. were cleaning
20. was looking
21. were driving
22. were interviewing
23. was shining
24. wasn't (was not) coming
25. were you waiting
26. were discussing
27. were feeding
28. were translating
29. were they not (weren't they) listening
30. were playing
31. was watching
32. were running
33. was crossing
34. were discussing
35. was studying

Seite 63 – Exercise 2

1. Who was he watching?
2. Who was running across the field?
3. Where was Sandy sitting?
4. Were you paying attention?
5. Who was driving the car?
6. What were you doing?
7. What was your father cleaning?
8. What was he explaining?
9. What were they learning?
10. Who was carrying the luggage?
11. What were they discussing?
12. Who was he looking for?
13. Who was she taking care of?

Seite 63 – Exercise 3

1. My brother was reading his newspaper all morning two weeks ago.
2. I was learning the irregular verbs all yesterday morning.
3. Last week we were writing essays during the lessons every day.
4. The children were watching TV the whole day two days ago.

Seite 63 – Exercise 4

1. Two days ago we were having breakfast for two hours.
2. Yesterday our teacher was explaining the past progressive to us for three hours.
3. I was waiting for the bus for more than 30 minutes the day before yesterday.
4. My brother was watching TV all evening yesterday.

Vergleich: Simple past – Past progressive

Seite 65 – Exercise 1

1. was doing – phoned
2. were sitting – began
3. were you doing – saw
4. was driving – crashed
5. were – went – went – stayed
6. were talking – told
7. came – were already waiting
8. decided – began – sat – were already sitting
9. was waiting (waited) – left
10. didn't (did not) play (weren't playing/were not playing) – was raining
11. was overtaking – appeared

Seite 65 – Exercise 2

1. Yesterday we flew to Scotland.
2. We were sitting in the plane all morning – it was really terrible.
3. Before we got out, there were (we got) some old potatoes and some strange sausages.

Seite 66 – Exercise 3

(1) was reading
(2) rang
(3) was
(4) was talking (talked)
(5) went
(6) was sleeping (slept)
(7) got
(8) were waiting
(9) didn't (did not) come
(10) was
(11) were sitting (sat)
(12) didn't (did not) know
(13) were learning
(14) were playing
(15) were
(16) came
(17) told
(18) started
(19) were only working (only worked)
(20) left

Seite 66 – Exercise 4

1. Tom: What were you doing all yesterday afternoon, Judy?
2. Judy: I was watching something funny, something about flying saucers and little green men from Mars.
3. Tom: I read an ad(vertisement) about it in the newspaper, but I decided not to watch the film because I wanted to study.
4. Judy: It was rather boring. The people from Mars were playing some silly tricks on other people the whole time.
5. Tom: Bad luck. Do you want to visit me?
6. Judy: I don't know yet. Perhaps later. See you.

The present perfect + (simple)/ Since – for

Seite 74 – Exercise 1

1. for
2. for
3. since
4. since
5. since
6. since
7. for
8. since
9. since
10. since
11. for
12. for
13. since
14. since
15. For
16. for
17. since
18. for
19. since
20. for
21. for
22. for
23. since
24. for
25. for
26. since
27. for
28. since
29. since
30. since
31. for
32. for
33. since
34. since

Seite 75 – Exercise 2

1. have (We've) learned
2. has just come
3. have never visited (I've never visited)
4. has collected
5. has tried
6. has happened
7. Have you guessed
8. has taught
9. have shouted
10. has cut
11. have (We've) jumped
12. hasn't (has not) brushed
13. haven't (have not) decided
14. have (They've) needed
15. has wanted

16. have played
17. have tried (We've tried)
18. Have you forgotten
19. haven't (have not) cleaned

Seite 75 – Exercise 3
1. We have (We've) learned a lot in the English lessons this year.
2. Have you ever collected penguins?
3. Our teacher has just entered the room.
4. We have (We've) often played football in physical education this week.
5. We have (We've) learned the irregular verbs once a week for two months.
6. She has (She's) bought a new dress.

Vergleich: Present perfect – Simple past

Seite 77 – Exercise 1
(1) have (We've) been
(2) have (We've) learned
(3) have (We've) had
(4) were
(5) have become
(6) have (We've) had
(7) had
(8) were
(9) have (we've) been
(10) haven't (have not) done
(11) haven't (have not) been
(12) haven't (have not) done
(13) had
(14) was
(15) was
(16) has (he's) given
(17) have (we've) worked
(18) has been
(19) found
(20) has been
(21) have (We've) done
(22) has become
(23) have (we've) been
(24) decided
(25) have (we've) been

Seite 77 – Exercise 2
1. Our government has had an energy crisis for five years.
2. Since that time we haven't (have not) been able to go abroad because petrol has been too expensive.
3. Last year we wanted to go on a journey to sunny Spain, but we had to spend our holidays at home because we didn't (did not) have enough pocket money.
4. We have (We've) spent our holidays in the garden since (then).

Seite 78 – Exercise 3
1. John and Mary flew to Munich last Easter.
2. My father has been in hospital since his accident.
3. Has Jack ever been to London?
4. Michael Jackson sang pop songs at his last concert.

Seite 78 – Exercise 4
1. How long (Since when) have you been here?
2. What did Tom drink last night?
3. Have you unloaded the van yet?
4. What has happened to Jim?

5. What were you worried about?
6. What have they pulled down?
7. What did your parents buy?
8. Who got the worst test result?

Seite 78 – Exercise 5
1. Two days ago the pupils of 6d were frightened of school because they had a test about the present progressive.
2. They sat there during the whole lesson and thought about the difficult sentences.
3. Since then they have (they've) been worried about their marks.
4. They haven't (have not) got back their tests yet because the teacher hasn't (has not) corrected them yet.
5. They have (They've) often done difficult exercises and the other teachers have given them strange worksheets, too.

Seite 79 – Exercise 6
(1) have (We've) been
(2) have (We've) had
(3) have been
(4) has tasted
(5) was
(6) didn't (did not) have
(7) were
(8) was
(9) have (I've) gone
(10) have not (haven't) flown
(11) think
(12) is
(13) have (I've) gone
(14) rode
(15) didn't (did not) enjoy

Seite 79 – Exercise 7
1. Where were you yesterday, Tom? – I was in town and bought exercise-books for school.
2. Have you ever learned anything for English? – So far I haven't, but this hasn't (has not) been necessary because I'm (I am) so clever.
3. Open the door, Tom, somebody has just knocked.
4. (Unfortunately) I'm afraid I haven't (have not) done my homework. Do I have to do an extra translation now?
5. Where have you been? – I haven't (have not) been anywhere.
6. Have you already invited Sandy to your party? – Yes (I have). I did it yesterday.
7. Two days ago I bought five very expensive books. That's why I don't (do not) have any more pocket money today.

Seite 80 – Exercise 8
(1) has worn
(2) bought
(3) went
(4) said
(5) hasn't (has not) gone
(6) has (she's) spent
(7) took
(8) didn't (did not) want
(9) haven't (have not) seen
(10) tried
(11) didn't (did not) answer

Seite 80 – Exercise 9
1. Yesterday Judy bought a nice dress, but she hasn't (has not) paid for it yet because she did not (didn't) have (hasn't got) any money.
2. She has (She's) got £10 pocket money for three years, but she hasn't (has not) saved anything so far.
3. For some time she's (she has) been worried because she is getting fatter and fatter.
4. Her trousers are too tight now and her blouses don't (do not) suit her any more; that's (that is) why she must throw away several things now.
5. Although she has (she's) eaten less since last Wednesday, she still doesn't (does not) look prettier.
6. But she has (she's) had this problem all her life. Poor Judy.

Seite 81 – Exercise 10
1. Mary hasn't (has not) seen John since October.
2. Peter left school five years ago.
3. Friedhelm has ridden a motorbike since Monday.
4. Susan wore a nice dress yesterday.

Seite 81 – Exercise 11
(1) told
(2) have (we've) had
(3) have been
(4) had
(5) was
(6) hasn't (has not) had
(7) has (he's) given
(8) got
(9) gave
(10) had
(11) has become

Seite 81 – Exercise 12
(1) got
(2) had
(3) was crossing
(4) appeared
(5) crashed
(6) was
(7) fell
(8) took
(9) hasn't (has not) been
(10) hasn't even (has not even) eaten
(11) had to bring

Seite 82 – Exercise 13
1. Three weeks ago we arrived in Scotland to spend our holidays there.
2. We have been to some museums since then and have seen many other sights.
3. At the beginning of the holidays the food in the hotel was very good, but for one week we have (we've) only had terrible things.
4. That is (That's) why we have (we've) only gone to McDonald's this week.
5. When we were in Italy last year, the food was much better.
6. We had so much spaghetti and so many pizzas there that we haven't (have not) wanted to eat things like that any more since that time.
7. But now we are in Scotland and would like to have pizzas and spaghetti again although we were so tired of them last year.
8. That's why we are happy that we can go home tomorrow.

Seite 82 – Exercise 14
(1) Since
(2) for
(3) since
(4) since
(5) since

Seite 83 – Exercise 15
1. What have you hated?
2. When did they buy the book?
3. What did the Romans found?
4. Who taught French last year?
5. Where have you been?
6. When did you buy the book?
7. What has she just finished?
8. Could you go to the disco yesterday?
9. Why didn't you (did you not) hear him?
10. When did he find his bag?
11. How often have you seen him?
12. Where has he gone?
13. How much (What) have they translated?
14. What did Judy eat?
15. Where has your brother gone?

Seite 83 – Exercise 16
1. Two weeks ago I got worked up because I had an accident.
2. A Swiss helicopter with five injured ducks couldn't (could not) brake in a bend any more and crashed into my dirty old motorbike.
3. I fell off my motorbike and haven't (have not) been allowed to get up any more since that time (since then).
4. Yesterday I was watching TV all day (long). Suddenly there was Donald Duck. As I have hated ducks since my accident, I left hospital at once and have (I've) been at home since.

Seite 84 – Exercise 17
1. for
2. Since
3. since
4. Since
5. for

Seite 84 – Exercise 18
1. When did you do your homework?
2. Where has Jack lived for two years?
3. Where has Jill been?
4. Who bought a dress two days ago?
5. When did Mr Jack teach children?

Seite 84 – Exercise 19
(1) was sleeping
(2) got
(3) looked
(4) saw
(5) was raining
(6) hasn't (has not) eaten
(7) has (He's) been
(8) wasn't (was not) worried
(9) was behaving

Seite 84 – Exercise 20
1. for
2. since
3. since
4. for
5. since
6. since
7. for
8. for
9. since
10. since
11. since

Seite 85 – Exercise 21
1. My brother has never drawn any pictures.
2. Last year the Jacksons didn't (did not) feed the animals in the cowshed in the mornings.
3. Has John done his homework yet?
4. Jill's dog didn't (did not) hide in the cupboard last week.
5. Kate fell into the water yesterday.

Seite 85 – Exercise 22
1. I have (I've) been worried about form 8a for some time.
2. For two weeks many pupils haven't (have not) paid attention and haven't (have not) learned anything.
3. The day before yesterday they had to do a really easy dictation about ambulances and petrol stations, but nobody got a top grade.
4. So I have (I've) decided to have a test today.
5. But that isn't (that's not/that is not) the end of the world for my pupils.

Seite 85 – Exercise 23
(1) have (We've) gone
(2) flew
(3) spent
(4) has become
(5) have not (haven't) had
(6) have (we've) done
(7) have not (haven't) been
(8) got

Seite 86 – Exercise 24
1. What has Tom collected?
2.. When did you choose maths?
3. Who had five tests last year?
4. What did they leave in the bus?
5. When did Tom catch a penguin?
6. Where has Judy lived?
7. Who sold their house?

Seite 86 – Exercise 25
1. Yesterday my friend invited me to a party although I haven't (have not) seen him for weeks.
2. We have (We've) been at the same school for three years, but so far we haven't (have not) been lucky: we have (we've) always been in different classes.
3. Unfortunately I can't (cannot) go to his party because I must (have (got) to) take my grandpa to the station.
4. He lives south of London and has to go by train because he hasn't (has not) had a car of his own for years.
5. Five years ago he had one, a nice green one, but the people in his street broke it because it was much too loud.

Seite 86 – Exercise 26
1. saw
2. haven't (have not) seen
3. has (He's) had
4. stole
5. have (We've) had
6. have (I've) done

Seite 87 – Exercise 27
1. We have (We've) been in England for three weeks.
2. Yesterday the weather was nice for the first time.
3. We went on a trip to the coast.
4. For many years there have been many tourists at the south coast of England.
5. But for some time not so many visitors have come from abroad any more.
6. 14 days ago we visited the museum in Colchester.
7. We didn't (did not) have to pay anything (for it) because our teacher's uncle is the director of the museum.
8. He has (He's) been in this museum for 35 years and looks almost like an ancient Egyptian.
9. But he is (he's) a bit mad and has ridden a motorbike for three years.
10. Yesterday he had an accident because he didn't (did not) pay (wasn't paying) attention to the traffic but was thinking about a Roman statue.

Seite 87 – Exercise 28
1. for
2. since
3. since
4. for
5. since
6. for
7. since

Seite 88 – Exercise 29
1. Judy has been worried for some weeks because she hasn't (has not) had any good marks in English any more.
2. She is frightened of her teacher because he has only given her bad marks this year.
3. The day before yesterday he threw her out of the classroom because she was very untidy during the lesson once again.
4. She hasn't (has not) been to school since (then), but has stayed at home all day long.
5. Unfortunately this doesn't (does not) help her at all: She can't (cannot) listen to her teacher and so she only learns a bit.

Seite 88 – Exercise 30
(1) have been
(2) has been
(3) went
(4) spent
(5) had
(6) tasted
(7) looked
(8) haven't (have not) eaten
(9) are (we're) eating
(10) wants
(11) have (I've) never travel(l)ed
(12) drove
(13) liked
(14) hasn't (has not) been
(15) doesn't (does not) know
(16) tells
(17) haven't (have not) been

Seite 89 – Exercise 31
1. She went to school two days ago.
2. We have been here for ten hours.
3. The Bells have lived in Manchester since last year.
4. Tom passed his driving test in 1978
5. Jim went to the dentist yesterday.

Seite 89 – Exercise 32
1. Not long ago I visited a safari park with my parents for the first time.
2. I have (I've) always been frightened of wild animals and that's why I wasn't (was not) very happy when a lion jumped from a rock down onto our car.
3. But it was quite young – probably only one year old, and so I wasn't (was not) worried.
4. We asked the zookeeper: "Is that yours?" – "No, that isn't mine, that is a lion from another zoo. Mine are in their dens."

Seite 89 – Exercise 33
1. Where have you been?
2. When was Tom in London?
3. How long has he had his job?
4. Since when has he lived in Leeds?
5. What did she buy two days ago?
6. Who has just come into the room?

Seite 90 – Exercise 34
1. I got a BMX bike three weeks ago.
2. Since that time all my friends have wanted to have a race with me.
3. We can ride in the woods because we've (we have) got special tyres, excellent brakes and very good handlebars.
4. When we fall off our bikes, our helmets protect us from bad head injuries.
5. Our favourite track has got a lot of bends and after rain some parts even with deep mud.
6. Last Saturday there was a terrible accident.
7. I was riding towards a bend and wanted to brake when suddenly my brake broke.
8. Dave was riding in front of me, and I crashed into him.
9. He fell off his bike and lost his helmet.
10. His face was full of mud, his foot was broken and both his arms hurt terribly.
11. The ambulance took Dave to hospital and he has been there since (then).

The present perfect progressive

Seite 94 – Exercise 1
1. have been working
2. has not (hasn't) been learning
3. have (I've) been repairing
4. have (They've) been thinking
5. have been unloading
6. has not (hasn't) been cooking
7. has been doing
8. have been living
9. have been practising
10. have been playing
11. have not (haven't) been doing
12. have (I've)been waiting
13. have been sitting
14. have been doing
15. has not (hasn't) been talking
16. have been singing
17. has been practising
18. have (We've) been discussing
19. have (They've) been organizing
20. have not (haven't) been learning
21. has (She's) been going
22. has been explaining
23. have not (haven't) been discussing
24. has (He's) been sitting
25. have been cleaning
26. have been redecorating
27. has been listening
28. have been carrying
29. have you been doing
30. have (They've) been practising
31. have they been waiting
32. have (I've) been looking
33. has (She's) been helping

Vergleich: Present perfect progressive – Present perfect simple

Seite 97 – Exercise 1
1. have (I've) been working
2. has worked (has been working)
3. have (I've) been repairing
4. has received
5. has forgotten
6. has repaired
7. has been working – has not (hasn't) become
8. have (We've) never been – has told
9. have you been doing – have (I've) been repairing
10. has not (hasn't) understood – has (he's) been looking
11. has not (hasn't) arrived – have (I've)been waiting
12. have (you've) watched – have not (haven't) learned
13. have (you've) been watching – have not (haven't) learned
14. has been telling
15. have (we've) worked (have (we've) been working)
16. have (I've) been looking – have not (haven't) found
17. have (They've) been working
18. has (She's) finished
19. have (We've) been redecorating

Seite 98 – Exercise 2
1. has done
2. have been decorating
3. have (We've) been working
4. has been getting
5. have been checking – have not (haven't) found
6. have you seen – haven't – haven't seen
7. have been thinking – have not (haven't) reached
8. have (I've) always thought
9. has forgotten
10. have – gone
11. have (I've) been thinking
12. have bought
13. has (She's) been trying – has changed
14. has (he's) been looking – has not (hasn't) been
15. have (We've) been having
16. have (I've) never liked
17. have (They've) left – have not (haven't) been able to understand
18. has (She's) had

Seite 99 – Exercise 3
1. We have (We've) had problems with the English tenses for years.
2. This year we have (we've) been doing (have done) exercises for it again and again, but we have not (haven't) learned anything at all.
3. Our teacher has not (hasn't) explained the problems very well and has given us much too difficult translations.
4. So we have (we've) tried to learn from English TV programmes.
5. We have (We've) been sitting in front of the box for weeks and have been watching boring films.
6. But we have not (haven't) made any progress at all.
7. The films which have been on in this time have been much too difficult for us and so we have (we've) understood almost nothing.
8. We have (We've) bought several English books and have read them, too, but the vocabulary was too complicated and that's why we have (we've) understood only very little.
9. So I have (I've) tried (I've been trying) to learn together with my sister for weeks, but as she has (she's) had problems with the English grammar for years, too, not very much has come out of it.
10. I have realized that it depends on me alone whether I get good marks.

The past perfect (simple)

Seite 102 – Exercise 1
1. You had (You'd) stayed in a youth hostel.
2. Peter had gone swimming.
3. We had (We'd) got away from it all.
4. They had not (hadn't) climbed mountains in the winter.
5. We had (We'd) been here for ten months.
6. Our teachers had corrected our tests quickly.

Seite 102 – Exercise 2
1. had (I'd) confused (confused)
2. had (he'd) hit
3. had happened
4. had (he'd) seen (saw)
5. had (I'd) seen (saw)
6. had (I'd) been (was)
7. had said (said)

Seite 102 – Exercise 3
(1) (had) finished
(2) became
(3) had (He'd) been
(4) got
(5) had (He'd) been
(6) didn't (did not) like
(7) got

Seite 103 – Exercise 4
(1) came
(2) saw
(3) had stolen
(4) had (she'd) phoned (phoned)
(5) came
(6) asked
(7) had got (got)
(8) wanted
(9) had had
(10) had had
(11) found
(12) had (they'd) been looking

Seite 103 – Exercise 5

1. Although I had (I'd) told Peter where to find Northern Ireland on the map, he had to ask his sister once again.
2. He has wanted to go there for three years, but he has (he's) needed his money for more important things time and time again.
3. Two days ago he bought a record player, which he had (he'd) seen in a suburb of his hometown and which he is very proud of.
4. He would (He'd) like to go to one of the Welsh islands in the winter season now although he doesn't (does not) know where to stay there and although it is often 15° below zero there.
5. Yesterday he got a passport, which he doesn't (does not) need, because he's (he is) a citizen of the United Kingdom and because Wales isn't (is not) separate from Great Britain.

The past perfect progressive

Seite 107 – Exercise 1

1. had been living
2. had (I'd) been living
3. had you been studying
4. had been repairing
5. had (she'd) been telling
6. had (He'd) been doing
7. had (they'd) been drinking
8. had (they'd) been studying
9. had (he'd) been consulting
10. had (they'd) been discussing
11. had been driving
12. had (he'd) been living
13. had (They'd) been walking
14. had been trying
15. had (we'd) been discussing
16. had been taking
17. had you been learning
18. had just been reading

Seite 108 – Exercise 2

1. had been waiting
2. had (We'd) been listening
3. had (I'd) been working
4. had (They'd) been talking
5. had (I'd) been sleeping
6. had (We'd) been watching
7. had been doing
8. had been carrying
9. had (He'd) been climbing

Seite 108 – Exercise 3

1. After we had (we'd) been playing all afternoon, we went home again because it started to rain.
2. John had been practising for two hours before he went on stage.
3. We had (We'd) been cleaning the windows for two hours before our mother told us that she had (she'd) already done it the day before yesterday.
4. He (He'd) had been working on his computer for two days before he found the mistake.
5. The politicians had been discussing unemployment for hours before they reached an agreement.

Vergleich: Past perfect (simple) – Past perfect progressive

Seite 110 – Exercise 1

(1) went
(2) had (they'd) spent (spent)
(3) (had) arrived
(4) wondered
(5) hadn't (had not) gone
(6) was
(7) didn't (did not) shine (was not shining)
(8) had (they'd) been
(9) had been
(10) weren't (were not)
(11) didn't (did not) like
(12) had seen (saw)
(13) went
(14) was born
(15) (had) spent
(16) flew
(17) left
(18) was raining
(19) swam
(20) was raining
(21) didn't (did not) mind
(22) were
(23) showed
(24) had (they'd) been telling (were telling)
(25) visited

Seite 110 – Exercise 2

1. We had (We'd) been working at our computer for three hours when our teacher came into the room (entered the room) and told us that he had (he'd) found a mistake in the program.
2. Although we had (we'd) been using the program for years, we hadn't (had not) found that out.
3. We had found out that there were problems with our printers, but we didn't (did not) think that this had anything to do with our software.

Seite 111 – Exercise 3

(1) left (had left)
(2) wanted
(3) was raining
(4) was looking (had been looking)
(5) saw
(6) was shining
(7) went
(8) took
(9) came
(10) was raining
(11) didn't (did not) know
(12) arrived (had arrived)
(13) were
(14) went
(15) didn't (did not) want
(16) arrived
(17) found
(18) had (he'd) forgotten
(19) climbed
(20) fell
(21) took
(22) was lying
(23) was
(24) was
(25) had been waiting
(26) sacked
(27) has been looking
(28) hasn't (has not) found

Seite 111 – Exercise 4

1. Last year my brother and I hitchhiked through England.
2. After we had (we'd) been (were) in London, we went on a trip to Liverpool.
3. As we didn't (did not) like this town very much, we went away again quickly.
4. When we arrived in Dover, we found out that the hovercraft had already left the port.
5. After we had (we'd) been waiting for more than three hours, my brother had an excellent idea.
6. He jumped into the water and swam over to the Continent.
7. Since then he has (he's) been telling everyone how well he can swim.

Seite 112 – Exercise 5

(1) was
(2) had
(3) was
(4) loved
(5) had
(6) danced
(7) told
(8) were
(9) (had) found
(10) didn't (did not) want
(11) didn't (did not) know
(12) was sitting (sat)
(13) was talking (talked)
(14) had been (was)
(15) decided
(16) smiled
(17) looked
(18) (had) behaved
(19) changed
(20) began
(21) was
(22) was
(23) ran
(24) was
(25) wasn't (was not)
(26) have
(27) end

Seite 112 – Exercise 6

1. As we had (we'd) been sitting in our room for hours, we wanted to go out.
2. But because it had been raining non-stop the day before, the grass was wet.
3. So we went back into the house although the fresh air would have done us some good.
4. We waited till the grass was dry.
5. After we had (we'd) been playing (were playing) outside for two hours, we went back into the house again.

The going to-future

Seite 115 – Exercise 1
1. is going to wash
2. are going to clean
3. are you going to do
4. is he going to buy
5. is going
6. are not (aren't) going to do (We're not)
7. are going to buy
8. are you going
9. is going to drive
10. are not (aren't) going to learn
11. is not (isn't) going to watch
12. are you going to do
13. are not (aren't) going to have
14. Are they going to sing
15. She is (She's) not going to get
16. are (they're) going to leave
17. Are they going to sell
18. is not (isn't) going to paint
19. is going to write
20. are you going to do
21. is going to be
22. is going to watch
23. are going
24. is going to visit
25. are not (aren't) going to eat
26. is going to do
27. are going to have
28. Is he going to forget
29. are going to see
30. are not (aren't) going to repair
31. is going to bring
32. is going to be
33. is going to be

Seite 116 – Exercise 2
1. What is he going to buy?
2. Who is she going to visit?
3. Who isn't going to celebrate his birthday?
4. Who is going to arrange the wedding?
5. What isn't he going to pay for?
6. Who are they going to listen to?
7. What are they going to talk about?

Seite 116 – Exercise 3
1. Gilbert is not (isn't) going to paint his room.
2. The Jacksons are not (aren't) going to buy a new house.
3. We are not (We aren't) going to the match.
4. They are not (aren't) going to repair their bikes.

Seite 116 – Exercise 4
1. I'm (I am) going to take part in a chess tournament at our school because I'm (I am) better than all the others.
2. Are you going to buy the green or the red car? – I'm (I am) going to take the red one because I like it best.
3. Where are you going this afternoon? – Nowhere. I'm (I am) going to watch a film on TV.
4. Are you going to the cinema or to the theatre tomorrow? – I don't (do not) know yet.

The will-future

Seite 120 – Exercise 1
1. will set
2. will be
3. will probably have
4. will (we'll) go
5. will not (won't) pay
6. will (I'll) leave
7. will your father say
8. will have
9. will be
10. will (they'll) have
11. will not (won't) rain
12. will (We'll) go
13. will take
14. will not (won't) be

Seite 120 – Exercise 2
1. We will (We'll) perhaps travel (go) to Italy next year.
2. I think that the weather will be nice there.
3. We will probably stay in a youth hostel if there are any vacancies.
4. The youth hostels have always been very cheap so far, but next year they will probably become a bit more expensive.
5. If it is too expensive in Rome, we will go to one of the islands off the Italian coast.
6. I'm (I am) sure that we will enjoy our stay there very much.

Seite 121 – Exercise 3
1. When will he be back?
2. What will you have soon?
3. When will you go shopping?
4. Who will take the job?
5. Who will set the text?
6. Who will Mary pay?
7. Who will probably find the way?
8. What will you get on in time?
9. What will TV be like in the future?
10. What will you buy?
11. What will the sky be like?

Seite 121 – Exercise 4
1. We will (We'll) probably go to Rome in the summer, since we have always spent (we always spent) our holidays in northern Europe in the last few years.
2. We don't (do not) know how we'll (we will) get there, but that doesn't (does not) matter.
3. I hope that we can hitchhike (will be able to hitchhike.)
4. Although the weather will probably be very nice in Italy, we will (we'll) take an umbrella although I doubt if we will (we'll) need it.
5. I don't (do not) know where we'll (we will) stay either, but I hope that there will be a vacancy somewhere.
6. Unfortunately we will (we'll) meet a lot of German tourists there, too.
7. They will (they'll) queue in front of the museums and will want to see all interesting sights just like us.

The future progressive

Seite 124 – Exercise 1
1. will (They'll) be working
2. will not (won't) be cooking
3. will be feeding
4. Will the band be playing
5. will (He'll) be cleaning
6. will not (won't) be raining
7. will be having
8. will (We'll) still be sleeping
9. will be taking
10. will (They'll) be talking
11. will be training
12. Will you be working
13. will (You'll) decorating
14. will not (won't) be listening

Seite 124 – Exercise 2
1. What will Michael be talking about?
2. What will your sisters be cleaning?
3. What will the boys be watching?
4. Who will be riding in the morning?
5. Who will you be helping all day long?
6. Who will be opening Parliament?
7. Where will they be dining?
8. Who will be rehearsing?
9. What won't you be playing?
10. Where will the men be working?
11. Who will be watching the play?
12. What will the soldiers be attacking?
13. Who will be paying attention?

Seite 125 – Exercise 3
1. What will you be doing when we visit you?
2. The children will not (won't) be sitting in their classrooms when you come to school during the break.
3. If you call me at nine o'clock, I will (I'll) be doing my homework.
4. I'm sure my uncle will be working in the fields again all day long when we visit him in the summer.
5. You don't (do not) have to (needn't) go shopping today. I'll be (I will be) going into town anyway.
6. You don't (do not) have to come over today because I will (I'll) be learning anyway.
7. The pupils will be writing a dictation when the fire-alarm takes place in the 3rd lesson.
8. You must not disturb us tomorrow afternoon because we will be discussing our problems with our headmaster then.
9. We will (We'll) be having breakfast when you arrive at twelve o'clock.
10. The students will be taking their final exams all tomorrow morning.
11. You can visit me tomorrow although I will (I'll) be repairing my car all the time.
12. Will you really be working all day tomorrow?

The future perfect

Seite 128 – Exercise 1
1. will (We'll) have finished
2. will (They'll) have informed
3. will have put
4. will have unloaded
5. will (You'll) have come
6. will not (won't) have corrected
7. will (he'll) have arrived
8. will (they'll) have repaired
9. will you have left

Seite 128 – Exercise 2
1. The children will have cleaned their bikes when the parents come back from their trip to Wales.
2. Before they leave for England, they will (they'll) have got the necessary information from our travel agency.
3. He will have stayed with us for three months by next week.
4. Although I have (I've) been telling him again and again, I am (I'm) sure that he will not (won't) have finished the work by this afternoon.
5. I think that she will (she'll) have spent all her money by next week.
6. I will not (won't) take any measures before we will (we'll) have reached an agreement.

The future with …/ Überblick: The future tenses/mixed tenses

Seite 131 – Exercise 1
(1) will (you'll) visit
(2) won't (will not) be
(3) are you going to take
(4) am (I'm) going
(5) are you going to do
(6) will probably be
(7) will (you'll) enjoy

Seite 131 – Exercise 2
1. We will (We'll) perhaps go to Italy next year.
2. I think the weather will be very nice there.
3. The hotels have always been very cheap so far, but next year they will (they'll) probably be a bit more expensive.
4. So we are (we're) going to stay in a youth hostel on the outskirts of Rome because the rooms are always cheaper there.
5. We already booked our flight at the travel agency in our shopping precinct yesterday.
6. I'm (I am) going into town tomorrow and am going to buy two pairs of shorts and five T-shirts.
7. With a bit of luck I will (I'll) find something cheap because I have (I've) to save my money for the holiday.
8. But I think that will not (won't) be too difficult because there have been special offers for some weeks.

Seite 132 – Exercise 3
1. am (I'm) going to spend (am spending)
2. leave
3. will (We'll) probably have
4. will not (won't) rain
5. does the train leave
6. are you going to do (will you be doing)
7. are you going to buy
8. will (he'll) find
9. are (We're) celebrating (are going to celebrate)
10. will be working
11. is
12. will (I'll) have finished
13. are not (aren't)
14. will last (lasts)
15. is (He's) going to buy
16. going to be
17. am (I'm) going to take
18. will (I'll) do – will (I'll) drop
19. arrive
20. will be
21. will give
22. are going
23. will (you'll) miss

Seite 133 – Exercise 4
1. will (I'll) have finished
2. will you do
3. does the hovercraft leave
4. am (I'm) going – Are you coming
5. is celebrating (is going to celebrate)
6. will be watching

Seite 133 – Exercise 5
1. It is (It's) going to rain in a minute.
2. We are meeting in front of the town hall.
3. Do you already know where you will (you'll) go (are going) in your summer holidays?
4. We will (We'll) have already discussed the problem before he arrives.
5. Look out of the window. There are clouds everywhere in the sky. It's (It is) going to snow soon.
6. When do your holidays start?
7. I have (I've) got a bad headache. I'm (I am) going to see the doctor now.
8. Don't give away the book, please – I'll (I will) read it tomorrow.
9. Will you have finished the work when the bell rings?
10. We decided yesterday that we are (we're) celebrating (going to celebrate) my birthday on the last weekend in April.

Seite 134 – Exercise 6
1. I think we will (we'll) enjoy ourselves very much on our class trip next week.
2. We have to get up very early because our train leaves already at twelve minutes to four.
3. Our teacher has told us that we must be there on time.
4. We arrive in Scotland not before seven o'clock the next morning.
5. I hope that the wardens in the youth hostels will not (won't be) as unfriendly as last year.
6. But we will (we'll) be walking around the island the whole day anyway.
7. I hope it will not (won't) be raining (won't rain) all the time again.
8. But everybody will have bought a raincoat by the beginning of our trip anyway.

9. I am (I'm) going to buy my coat with my mother in town tomorrow.
10. I think it will (it'll) be cheaper there than in our little village.
11. There will probably be terrible spiders in our rooms again, which the girls will complain about.
12. We have agreed with our teachers that on the last day we will finish our holiday with a farewell party.

Seite 135 – Exercise 7
(1) are you going to do (are you doing)
(2) don't (do not) know
(3) will (I'll) go
(4) bought
(5) didn't
(6) are
(7) haven't (have not) bought
(8) is
(9) was running
(10) didn't (did not) find
(11) has been
(12) don't you try
(13) is
(14) have (I've) never been
(15) will (I'll) go
(16) will (you'll) be
(17) have (you've) got
(18) haven't
(19) have
(20) gave
(21) didn't (did not) want
(22) has (He's) been
(23) was
(24) Don't be
(25) is
(26) will (I'll) go

Seite 135 – Exercise 8
(1) John: I suppose I'll (I will) get my blue camel tomorrow.
(2) Jack: Really? I've (I have) always thought that you've (you have) already got a green one.
(3) John: You're (You are) wrong. The green camel in our living-room isn't (is not) mine but my parents'.
(4) Jack: You're (You are) lucky. I've (I have) wanted a real animal for years, but so far I've (I have) only had boring parrots .
(5) John: And the kangaroo in your garden, isn't that yours?
(6) Jack: No, that's (that is) the pet of our zoo's keeper. I have to take care of it in the winter.

Seite 136 – Exercise 9
(1) has just told (has just been telling)
(2) flew
(3) wanted
(4) has seen
(5) wanted
(6) slept
(7) had
(8) was
(9) hadn't (had not) had
(10) got
(11) was walking (walked)
(12) happened
(13) was
(14) came
(15) was beating (beat)
(16) began
(17) had (He'd) never been
(18) phoned

(19) arrived
(20) checked
(21) didn't (did not) find
(22) rose
(23) wasn't (was not)
(24) is
(25) will find
(26) I'll (I will) go
(27) don't (do not) think

Seite 136 – Exercise 10
1. After the Romans (had) defeated the Celts, they founded many Roman settlements in England.
2. Many leaders of the native tribes fled to the mountains as they were safer from the persecutions of the Romans there.
3. Even today you can see many relics of the Roman times.
4. At the moment many of them are being restored in order to give the people a better picture of their historical past.

Seite 137 – Exercise 11
(1) know
(2) are going
(3) haven't decided
(4) weren't you discussing
(5) was
(6) haven't been able to reach
(7) will have decided
(8) won't go (am [I'm] not going)
(9) got
(10) had spent (spent)
(11) wanted to have
(12) had seen (saw)
(13) had to go
(14) wasn't
(15) didn't like
(16) won't do

Seite 137 – Exercise 12
1. After the pupils (had) got back their tests, they were very disappointed with their marks and complained about the difficult sentences.
2. They had (They'd) been practising the difference between the past perfect and the past perfect progressive for weeks before they wrote the test.
3. But many pupils still don't (do not) know how to apply the tenses correctly
4. That's why they have been (they've been) practising difficult sentences since last Monday.
5. Since that time they haven't (have not) been bored any more.

Seite 138 – Exercise 13
(1) have you been
(2) have (I've) been looking
(3) look
(4) have (I've) been trying
(5) didn't you do
(6) did
(7) talked
(8) have (I've) forgotten
(9) Do you think
(10) will give
(11) am (I'm) not
(12) has (He's) only given
(13) was
(14) was
(15) were writing
(16) rang
(17) was
(18) had to stop writing
(19) did not (didn't) give

Seite 138 – Exercise 14
1. I have (I've) wanted (intended/planned) to go to Scotland for two years, but so far I haven't (have not) had enough money.
2. After my girlfriend had shown (showed) me photos of the Scottish islands, I wanted to book a trip at once.
3. I loved the variety of the scenery, the lonely lakes and the green forests.
4. But I really don't know how to get there (how I'll get there), and I doubt whether my mother will give me any money.

Seite 139 – Exercise 15
(1) has lived (has been living)
(2) don't (do not) like
(3) want to live
(4) have (I've) spent
(5) has been (is)
(6) was
(7) milked
(8) fed
(9) slept
(10) was
(11) was
(12) rode
(13) are (We're) going to spend
(14) are (We're) making
(15) are (We're) sitting
(16) are talking
(17) have (We've) planned (have been planning)
(18) has come
(19) wants
(20) has been
(21) discussed
(22) went

Seite 139 – Exercise 16
(1) came
(2) had lived (had been living) (lived)
(3) arrived
(4) were
(5) have changed
(6) needed
(7) pushed
(8) have destroyed
(9) don't (do not) have
(10) to live
(11) have become
(12) is
(13) takes
(14) isn't (is not)
(15) will treat
(16) will probably not happen (won't probably happen)

Seite 140 – Exercise 17
(1) went
(2) was
(3) haven't (have not) had (hadn't [had not] had)
(4) went
(5) have been living (have lived)
(6) were watching (watched)
(7) were jumping
(8) (were) playing
(9) was
(10) went
(11) fed
(12) threw
(13) caught
(14) hadn't (had not) seen
(15) began
(16) was raining
(17) got
(18) went
(19) are
(20) live
(21) will (I'll) never meet (I never meet)
(22) won't (will not) go
(23) went
(24) wrote
(25) will go
(26) is

Seite 140 – Exercise 18
1. Lately my pronunciation has become worse and worse although I have (I've) read (have been reading) so much.
2. I don't (do not) read the sentences thoroughly enough, and that's why everything sounds wrong.
3. As I want to get better marks, I must change this soon.

Seite 141 – Exercise 19
(1) drove
(2) had (he'd) overtaken (overtook)
(3) crashed
(4) phoned
(5) took
(6) has been
(7) will (he'll) be able to leave (can leave)
(8) is (He's) watching
(9) hasn't (has not) done

Seite 141 – Exercise 20

1. Some time ago we started to talk about a new aspect of grammar.
2. For years we have not (haven't) done anything as difficult as that.
3. Although our teacher explained everything to us, we have not (haven't) understood (didn't understand) anything at all.
4. That's why he has (he's) given us a lot of worksheets in the last few weeks.
5. Yesterday we did a translation, but we did not (didn't) know how to do it at all.
6. But that's (that is) nothing new (But that isn't anything new): We have (We've) always had our problems with it.
7. And that's why we have (we've) had to work a lot for some time in order not to get bad grades.
8. Yesterday we were not (weren't) even allowed to watch TV only because we did not (didn't) know the irregular verbs.
9. We all hope that the test will be very easy tomorrow.

Seite 142 – Exercise 21

(1) had
(2) was shining
(3) wasn't (was not) raining
(4) were
(5) had been
(6) went
(7) has (he's) taught (has been teaching)
(8) has shown (has been showing)
(9) taught
(10) had (He'd) just returned
(11) didn't (did not) understand
(12) were listening
(13) were
(14) was
(15) told
(16) is
(17) is going to give
(18) are
(19) haven't (have not) paid
(20) won't (will not) like

Seite 142 – Exercise 22

1. Three days ago Bayern Munich lost its football match against Manchester United.
2. During the whole match the Munich players were playing very badly and weren't (were not) running after the ball very successfully.
3. They have (They've) been running very slowly for weeks and haven't (have not) won very many matches in this time.
4. Although Bayern Munich has bought the best players for years, it hasn't (has not) always been very successful and hasn't (has not) won the European Cup for some time.
5. They have (they've) taken part in every European tournament since 1972, but the last time they won the Cup was in 1980.

Seite 143 – Exercise 23

(1) went
(2) spent
(3) hadn't (had not) seen
(4) were
(5) looked
(6) told
(7) invited
(8) had
(9) were sitting (sat)
(10) went
(11) wrote
(12) are
(13) are talking
(14) have done
(15) have written
(16) are correcting
(17) will give
(18) always sets
(19) will stay

Seite 143 – Exercise 24

1. Not long ago I went shopping in our town.
2. As some of my old jeans did not (didn't) fit any more, I wanted to buy two new pairs.
3. I went into Judy's fashion shop and tried on seven different pairs of trousers, but not a single one really suited me.
4. I have (I've) always had problems finding the right size because I'm too fat.
5. That's why I have (I've) never worn tight clothes.
6. For weeks I have (I've) been trying to find something nice, but so far I have not (haven't) been lucky.
7. I have (I've) often ordered something from a catalogue, but that has mostly been even worse.

Seite 144 – Exercise 25

(1) is
(2) has (He's) been working
(3) since
(4) will (they'll) have
(5) has (He's) known
(6) for
(7) began
(8) has been
(9) did
(10) have (they've) been talking
(11) for
(12) has not (hasn't) understood
(13) has (He's) been studying
(14) for
(15) since
(16) left
(17) has (she's) spent
(18) doesn't (does not) know
(19) since
(20) has (she's) read
(21) has become
(22) will not (won't) have

Seite 144 – Exercise 26

1. Many wild animals have become extinct on our planet because we have not (haven't) taken care of them.
2. Some people think that soon there will not (won't) be any polar bears, sea-lions and penguins any more.
3. For years we have (we've) been continually talking about these problems on TV, but almost nothing has happened so far.
4. Can you imagine that we will (we'll) only see hippos and camels in the zoo in the next century?
5. For two years our biology teacher has been telling us something about these problems every day, and that's why we have (we've) collected money for the poor animals of our planet in this time.

Das LERNSTOFF
Übungsbuch

Roland Zimmermann
Basiswissen Englisch
Band 1: Die Zeiten

LERNSTOFF
SKG-VERLAG

Roland Zimmermann unterrichtet seit mehr als 20 Jahren an bayerischen Gymnasien Schülerinnen und Schüler von der 5. Jahrgangsstufe bis zur Abiturklasse.
Daher weiß er ganz genau, wo Fehler gemacht werden, wann sich Wissenslücken bilden –
und warum. Basiswissen Englisch ermöglicht auf dieser Basis allen Englischlernenden, sich eine solide grammatikalische Grundlage zu erarbeiten.

Aus derselben Reihe von Roland Zimmermann sind erhältlich:
Basiswissen Englisch, Band 2: Die Verben   ISBN: 978-3-937270-01-2
Basiswissen Englisch, Band 3: Adjektiv, Adverb, Pronomen ...   ISBN: 978-3-937270-02-9

Die Deutsche Bibliothek – CIP-Einheitsaufnahme
Ein Titeldatensatz für diese Publikation ist bei der Deutschen Bibliothek erhältlich.

Der Inhalt des Buches ist mit größtmöglicher Sorgfalt erarbeitet und geprüft worden. Trotz aller Sorgfalt sind Fehler aber nicht immer ganz zu vermeiden. Wenn sich trotzdem ein Fehler eingeschlichen hat, sind Autor und Verlag dankbar für jede schriftliche Rückmeldung.

SKG-Verlag · Am Mühlberg 20 · 86441 Zusmarshausen
info@SKG-Verlag.de · www.SKG-Verlag.de

Copyright 2005 · SKG Verlag, Zusmarshausen
5. Auflage; Nachdruck 2021

Umschlaggestaltung, Layout und Satz: imprint, Zusmarshausen
Umschlagillustration: Evelyn Neuss, Hannover
Druck und Bindung: Druckerei Bayerlein GmbH, Neusäß
Printed in Germany

ISBN **978-3-937270-00-5**

Wozu dieses Buch?

Dieses Buch dient dazu, sich die englischen Zeiten zu erarbeiten. Wenn man es sorgfältig durcharbeitet, dann erlernt man damit die wichtigsten grammatikalischen Grundlagen der englischen Sprache.

Man kommt um diese Arbeit nicht herum, denn man wird von den Zeiten in jedem Text und in jeder Schulaufgabe „verfolgt", und es gibt sogar Abiturienten, die mit den englischen Zeiten immer noch auf Kriegsfuß stehen. Dieses Buch soll dazu beitragen, diese Schwierigkeiten zu verringern oder ganz zu beseitigen. Wer mit Basiswissen Englisch, Band 1, intensiv gearbeitet hat, für den sollten die Zeiten kein Problem mehr sein.

Welche Voraussetzungen sind nötig?

Wenn man den ersten Abschnitt genau gelesen hat, hat man sicherlich bemerkt, dass das Wort „Arbeit" erschreckend oft vorkommt. Und das aus gutem Grund: Ohne gründliche Arbeit nützt dieses Buch überhaupt nichts und die Beschäftigung damit wäre vergeudete Zeit. Der Wille, sich die Zeiten zu erarbeiten, ist die Voraussetzung, die man für dieses Buch mitbringen sollte.

Wie ist das Buch aufgebaut?

Das Buch ist „chronologisch" aufgebaut, das heißt, die Zeiten, die beim Spracherwerb am Anfang stehen, werden auch im Buch am Anfang behandelt. Ausnahmen sind die Zeiten des *going to-future* und des *will-future*, die wegen der besseren Übersichtlichkeit zusammen mit den anderen Formen des Futurs im letzten Teil des Buches durchgenommen werden.

Von wenigen Ausnahmen abgesehen, bauen die Kapitel über die einzelnen Zeiten aufeinander auf, was bedeutet, dass beispielsweise in den Übungen zum *present progressive* das *past perfect* nicht vorkommt.

Dies trifft auch auf den Wortschatz zu, der zu Beginn des Buches einfacher ist als am Ende.

Diese Vorgehensweise setzt sich bei den Übungen fort, bei denen sich der Schwierigkeitsgrad im Verlauf eines Kapitels steigert: So stehen relativ leichte Einsetzübungen am Anfang, während Übersetzungen normalerweise erst dann kommen, wenn man sich mithilfe der leichteren Übungen mit den Grundregeln der jeweiligen Zeit vertraut gemacht hat.

Am Ende des Buches gibt es noch Übungen, die den gesamten Stoff abprüfen. Anhand dieser Übungen lässt sich erkennen, ob man die englischen Zeiten wirklich beherrscht.

Wie geht man vor?

Die Vorgehensweise hängt stark davon ab, in welcher Klassenstufe man ist, ob man das Buch als Wiederholung einsetzt oder vielleicht als zusätzliches unterrichtsbegleitendes Material verwendet. Vor allem in höheren Klassen neigt man dazu, sich zu überschätzen, und Zeiten, die man am Anfang seines Englisch-Unterrichts gelernt hat, nicht mehr zu wiederholen. Es ist ratsam, sich in diesem Fall wenigstens eine der schwierigeren Übungen vorzunehmen (im Normalfall eine Übersetzung), um festzustellen, ob man die jeweilige Zeit wirklich beherrscht. Erst dann sollte man sich der nächsten Zeit zuwenden.

Was man tun sollte!

1. sorgfältiges Durcharbeiten der Grammatikregeln einer Zeit

2. eine Übung machen

3. diese Übung dann anhand des Lösungsheftes kontrollieren (was vielleicht eine zweite Person übernehmen könnte, das ist manchmal sicherer)

→ bei weniger als zehn Prozent Fehlern (z.B. 30 Sätze – 3 Fehler) kann man die nächste Übung angehen (wobei es bei Übersetzungen hauptsächlich auf die richtige Verwendung der entsprechenden Zeit ankommt, man darf also andere Fehler etwas großzügiger behandeln)

→ wenn man mehr als zehn Prozent falsch hat, sollte man unbedingt die Grammatikregeln noch einmal durcharbeiten, dann die gleiche Übung wieder machen, aber frühestens einen Tag später. Wenn dann wieder zu viele Fehler auftreten, muss man sich klar machen, dass man viel zu oberflächlich gearbeitet hat und noch einmal (aber wirklich genau) die Grammatikregeln durcharbeiten muss. Dann sollte es eigentlich klappen.

Was man auf keinen Fall tun sollte!

→ sich nur auf sein Sprachgefühl verlassen – dies ist meist nur eine Entschuldigung dafür, dass man die Regeln nicht lernen will. Außerdem wird man feststellen, dass es Regeln gibt, bei denen das Sprachgefühl überhaupt nichts nützt.

→ Fehler als sogenannte „Leichtsinnsfehler" bezeichnen. Es gibt sie kaum. Sie sind meist nur eine Entschuldigung oder Umschreibung dafür, dass man nicht gründlich genug gearbeitet oder dass man das Problem eben doch nicht so recht in den Griff bekommen hat. (Außerdem werden in Schulaufgaben leider auch „Leichtsinnsfehler" als ganz „normale" Fehler angestrichen.)

→ die Wörter, die man nicht mehr kann, nicht gleich mit lernen. Damit man keine unnötige Zeit mit dem Nachschlagen unbekannter Wörter vergeudet, stehen die wichtigsten Wörter am Rand der jeweiligen Übungen. Es ist aber trotzdem dringend erforderlich, die Wörter, die man nicht kann, aufzuschreiben und zu lernen.

→ die „Allgemeinen Regeln" am Anfang des Buches (Seite 7 und 8) übergehen. Das Verständnis dieser Regeln ist ungemein wichtig, weil sie kurz und übersichtlich die Grundstrukturen der englischen Zeiten zusammenfassen. Hat man diese Regeln wirklich verstanden, tut man sich später bei den jeweiligen Zeiten um vieles leichter.

Viel Vergnügen

… wünsche ich allen, die sich durch dieses Buch durcharbeiten. Wer sich an die oben genannten Regeln hält, wird schnell erkennen, dass es auch Spaß machen kann, sich mit englischer Grammatik auseinanderzusetzen.

In diesem Sinne
enjoy yourselves

Roland Zimmermann

The irregular verbs

be	was	been	sein		lie	lay	lain	liegen
beat	beat	beaten	schlagen, besiegen		lose	lost	lost	verlieren
become	became	become	werden		make	made	made	machen, herstellen
begin	began	begun	beginnen, anfangen		mean	meant	meant	bedeuten, meinen
blow	blew	blown	blasen, wehen		meet	met	met	treffen
break	broke	broken	kaputt machen, zerbrechen		overtake	overtook	overtaken	überholen
bring	brought	brought	(herbei)bringen		pay	paid	paid	(be)zahlen
build	built	built	bauen		put	put	put	legen, setzen, stellen
buy	bought	bought	kaufen		read	read	read	lesen
catch	caught	caught	fangen		ride	rode	ridden	fahren, reiten
choose	chose	chosen	wählen		ring	rang	rung	klingeln, läuten, anrufen
come	came	come	kommen		run	ran	run	rennen, laufen
cut	cut	cut	schneiden		say	said	said	sagen
do	did	done	tun, machen		see	saw	seen	sehen
draw	drew	drawn	zeichnen		sell	sold	sold	verkaufen
dream	dreamt dreamed	dreamt dreamed	träumen		send	sent	sent	schicken, senden
drink	drank	drunk	trinken		shake	shook	shaken	schütteln
drive	drove	driven	fahren		shine	shone	shone	scheinen
eat	ate	eaten	essen		show	showed	shown	zeigen
fall	fell	fallen	fallen		shut	shut	shut	schließen
feed	fed	fed	füttern		sing	sang	sung	singen
feel	felt	felt	fühlen		sink	sank	sunk	(ver)sinken, versenken
fight	fought	fought	(be)kämpfen		sit	sat	sat	sitzen
find	found	found	finden		sleep	slept	slept	schlafen
fly	flew	flown	fliegen		smell	smelt smelled	smelt smelled	riechen
forget	forgot	forgotten	vergessen		speak	spoke	spoken	sprechen
freeze	froze	frozen	(ge)frieren		spell	spelt	spelt	buchstabieren
get	got	got	bekommen		spend	spent	spent	verbringen, ausgeben
give	gave	given	geben		stand	stood	stood	stehen
go	went	gone	gehen		steal	stole	stolen	stehlen
grow	grew	grown	wachsen		swim	swam	swum	schwimmen
have	had	had	haben		take	took	taken	nehmen
hear	heard	heard	hören		teach	taught	taught	lehren, unterrichten
hide	hid	hidden	(sich) verstecken		tear	tore	torn	(zer)reißen
hit	hit	hit	treffen		tell	told	told	erzählen
hold	held	held	halten		think	thought	thought	denken
hurt	hurt	hurt	verletzen, weh tun		throw	threw	thrown	werfen
keep	kept	kept	halten		understand	understood	understood	verstehen
know	knew	known	wissen		wake up	woke	woken	aufwachen, (auf)wecken
lead	led	led	führen. leiten		wear	wore	worn	tragen (clothes)
leave	left	left	verlassen		weep	wept	wept	weinen
lend	lent	lent	(aus)leihen		win	won	won	gewinnen
let	let	let	lassen		write	wrote	written	schreiben

The tenses

Allgemeine Regeln

Die folgenden Regeln werden in den einzelnen Grammatikkapiteln zu den jeweiligen *tenses* (Zeiten) zum Teil noch einmal gesondert und ausführlich behandelt. Sie stellen hier nur einen allgemeinen Überblick dar, der es erleichtern soll, sich bestimmte grundlegende Prinzipien klar zu machen und einzuprägen.

1. Frage und Verneinung

Umschreibung mit *to do*

Im Englischen muss bei Frage und Verneinung immer ein Hilfsverb (also Formen von *to be*, *to have*, *to do*) verwendet werden. Dies hat folgende Konsequenzen:

Bei englischen *tenses*, die nur aus dem **Vollverb** gebildet werden und sich nicht aus Hilfsverb und Verb zusammensetzen, muss immer mit *to do* umschrieben werden. Es sind also nur zwei *tenses*, nämlich das *simple present* und das *simple past*, bei denen mit *to do* umschrieben werden muss:

He goes.	He **doesn't** go.	**Does** he go?	*(simple present)*
He went.	He **didn't** go.	**Did** he go?	*(simple past)*

Bei englischen *tenses*, die aus **Hilfsverb und Vollverb** gebildet werden, darf nicht mit *to do* umschrieben werden. Es sind dies alle *tenses* außer dem *simple present* und dem *simple past*. Hier eine Zusammenstellung der wichtigsten Zeiten:

He **is going**.	He **isn't going**.	**Is** he **going**?	*(present progressive)*
He **was going**.	He **wasn't going**.	**Was** he **going**.	*(past progressive)*
He **has gone**.	He **hasn't gone**.	**Has** he **gone**?	*(present perfect)*
He **has been going**.	He **hasn't been going**.	**Has** he **been going**?	*(present perfect progressive)*
He **had gone**.	He **hadn't gone**.	**Had** he **gone**?	*(past perfect)*
He **had been going**.	He **hadn't been going**.	**Had** he **been going**?	*(past perfect progressive)*
He **will go**.	He **won't go**.	**Will** he **go**?	*(will-future)*

Beim Gebrauch von **modalen Hilfsverben** (*must*, *can* etc.) darf ebenfalls nicht mit *to do* umschrieben werden, da hier ein Hilfsverb verwendet wird. Auch wenn das Hilfsverb in seiner Ersatzform verwendet wird, darf nicht mit *to do* umschrieben werden, da ein Bestandteil der Ersatzformen immer ein Hilfsverb ist:

He **can** go.	He **can't** go.	**Can** he go?	*(simple present)*
He **could** go.	He **couldn't** go.	**Could** he go?	*(simple past)*
He **has been** able to go.	He **hasn't been** able to go.	**Has** he **been** able to go?	*(present perfect)*

Da einige englische *tenses* mit den Hilfsverben *to be* oder *to have* gebildet werden, ist es ratsam, sich zuerst mit den entsprechenden Formen dieser beiden Hilfsverben vertraut zu machen (Vergleiche auch: Band 2 – Die Verben).

2. Satzstellung bei Fragen

Bei Fragen kommt im Englischen immer zuerst das **1. Hilfsverb**, dann das **Subjekt** und dann das **Vollverb** bzw. das **2. Hilfsverb** und dann das **Vollverb**:

Why	**is**	Mr Brown		working?	*(present progressive)*
What	**do**	you		do?	*(simple present)*
	Did	she		speak?	*(simple past)*
	Were	they		talking?	*(past progressive)*
What	**have**	they		done?	*(present perfect simple)*
What	**have**	they	**been**	writing?	*(present perfect progressive)*
	Had	Mary		learned?	*(past perfect)*
What	**had**	they	**been**	practising?	*(past perfect progressive)*
	Is	Mike	**going to**	sing?	*(going to-future)*
	Will	you		try?	*(will-future)*
Where	**will**	they	**be**	working?	*(future progressive)*
	Will	you	**have**	left?	*(future perfect)*

3. Satzstellung bei Verben mit Präpositionen

Bei Fragen, bei denen ein Fragepronomen (*what, where, who* etc.) und ein Verb, das mit einer Präposition verbunden ist (*to listen **to**, to talk **about*** etc.), verwendet wird, steht die Präposition hinter dem Verb (wie im Aussagesatz):

Who	does he listen	**to**	in the mornings?	*(simple present)*
Wem	hört er		am Morgen **zu**?	

(Aussagesatz: He **listens to** his teachers.)

What	are you talking	**about**	now?	*(present progressive)*
Worüber	sprichst du		gerade?	

(Aussagesatz: I'm **talking about** your problem.)

Kurzformen

Im Englischen gibt es bei einigen Verben sogenannte ***contracted forms*** (Kurzformen, zusammengezogene Formen). Hier einige Beispiele:

He is	at home.
He's	at home.

He has	been writing	a letter.
He's	been writing	a letter.

Diese Kurzformen verwendet man normalerweise in der Umgangssprache. In der förmlichen Schriftsprache werden keine Kurzformen gebraucht. Eine **Ausnahme** bildet mittlerweile die **Umschreibung mit *to do* bei verneinten Sätzen**. Sätze wie

He	**doesn't**	write	a book.	oder
We	**don't**	buy	a car every year.	

finden sich auch im Schriftenglischen wieder.

Die ausgeschriebene Form der Umschreibung mit *to do* dient häufig zur Verstärkung oder Betonung eines Sachverhalts:

Teachers	**do not**	discuss these things in our lessons.
Lehrer		reden über diese Dinge **(wirklich) nicht** im Unterricht.

The present progressive

Die Verlaufsform der Gegenwart

Beispiele

1. Aussagesätze

1.	I	**am**	**(I'm)**	stand**ing**	here	**now.**
2.	You	**are**	**(You're)**	finish**ing**	a letter	**at the moment.**
3.	He	**is**	**(He's)**	sing**ing**	a song	**today.**
	She	**is**	**(She's)**	wait**ing**	for the bus.	
	It	**is**	**(It's)**	sleep**ing**	in the cage.	
4.	We	**are**	**(We're)**	read**ing**	a text.	
5.	You	**are**	**(You're)**	walk**ing**	in the park.	
6.	They	**are**	**(They're)**	clean**ing**	their bikes.	

2. Verneinte Sätze

1.	I	**am**	**not**	**(I'm not)**	stand**ing**	here	**now.**
2.	You	**are**	**not**	**(You aren't/You're not)**	finish**ing**	a letter	**at the moment.**
3.	He	**is**	**not**	**(He isn't/He's not)**	sing**ing**	a song	**today.**
	She	**is**	**not**	**(She isn't/She's not)**	wait**ing**	for the bus.	
	It	**is**	**not**	**(It isn't/It's not)**	sleep**ing**	in the cage.	
4.	We	**are**	**not**	**(We aren't/We're not)**	read**ing**	a text.	
5.	You	**are**	**not**	**(You aren't/You're not)**	walk**ing**	in the park.	
6.	They	**are**	**not**	**(They aren't/They're not)**	clean**ing**	their bikes.	

3. Fragen

1.	Where	**am**	I	stand**ing**		**now?**
2.		**Are**	you	finish**ing**	a letter	**at the moment?**
3.	Why	**is**	he	sing**ing**	a song	**today?**
		Is	she	wait**ing**	for the bus?	
	Where	**is**	it	sleep**ing?**		
4.	What	**are**	we	read**ing?**		
5.		**Are**	you	walk**ing**	in the park?	
6.		**Are**	they	clean**ing**	their bikes?	

Bildung

1. Regelmäßige Bildung

Das *present progressive* (Verlaufsform des Präsens) wird gebildet aus der entsprechenden **Präsensform von *to be*** und dem **Infinitiv des Verbs (ohne *to*)**, an den *ing* angefügt wird:

Bildung		Präsensform von *to be*	Infinitiv des Verbs + *ing*	
to read:	I	am	read **ing**	a book now.
to listen:	He	is	listen **ing**	to a record at the moment.

Übersetzungs-Tipp

Bei der Übersetzung vom Englischen ins Deutsche wird die *ing*-Form nicht mitübersetzt. Die einzige Möglichkeit, bei der die *ing*-Form sichtbar wird, ist beim Einfügen von *gerade* oder *im Augenblick*, selbst wenn im englischen Satz keine Zeitangabe gegeben ist:

He	**is working**		in the garden.
Er	**arbeitet**	(gerade)	im Garten.

She	**is phoning**		her sister.
Sie	**telefoniert**	(im Augenblick)	mit ihrer Schwester.

2. Besonderheiten bei der Bildung der *ing*-Form

Konsonanten (*p, r, s, t* etc.) am Ende des Verbs werden nach einfachen, kurzen und betonten Vokalen (*a, e, i, o, u*) verdoppelt:

to si**t**:	He	is	si**tt**ing.	
to sto**p**:	We	are	sto**pp**ing	here.
to refe**r**:	I	am	refe**rr**ing	to your question.

Aber: Im *AE (American English)* wird das *l* am Ende des Verbs nicht verdoppelt:

to trave**l**:	We	are	trave**l**ing.
to cance**l**:	They	are	cance**l**ing.

Ein stummes *e* des Infinitivs wird weggelassen:

to com**e**:	I	am	co**m**ing.
to lov**e**:	She	is	lo**v**ing.

Aber:

to guarant**ee**:	He	is	guarant**ee**ing.
to fl**ee**:	They	are	fl**ee**ing.

---

ie am Ende des Infinitivs wird zu **y**:

to d**ie**:	They	are	d**y**ing.
to l**ie**:	It	is	l**y**ing.

3. Frage und Verneinung

Zur Satzstellung und zu Besonderheiten bei Verben mit Präpositionen siehe das Kapitel *Allgemeine Regeln*.

Bei Frage und Verneinung darf beim *present progressive* nicht mit *to do* umschrieben werden, da diese Zeit bereits mit einem **Hilfsverb** gebildet wird:

Are	you	working hard?
Arbeitest		du hart?

He	**is** not playing	tennis.
Er	spielt gerade kein	Tennis.

Verwendung

Das *present progressive* wird verwendet zur

➤ **Beschreibung einer im Augenblick stattfindenden Handlung oder einer Handlung, die noch nicht abgeschlossen ist:**

The bus	**is coming**	**now**.
Der Bus	**kommt**	**jetzt**.

He	**is washing**	the car **at the moment**.
Er	**wäscht**	**im Momen**t das Auto.

I	**am reading**	a good book **at the moment**.
Ich	**lese gerade**	ein gutes Buch.

Am letzten Beispiel wird deutlich, dass die Handlung nicht unbedingt im Moment des Sprechens stattfinden muss, sondern sich ganz allgemein in der Gegenwart abspielen kann.

Es muss nicht immer eine Zeitangabe wie *now* oder *at the moment* im Satz stehen, damit das *present progressive* verwendet werden kann. Es kann auch aus dem **Textzusammenhang** ersichtlich sein, dass eine Handlung im Augenblick stattfindet, oder aus satzeinleitenden Aufforderungen wie *Look, ...* oder *Listen, ...* deutlich werden:

Look,	Tom	**is playing**	with a cat.
Schau,	Tom	**spielt**	mit einer Katze.

Listen,	the band	**is** already **playing**.
Hör zu,	die Band	**spielt** schon.

Jack	**is sitting**	in his room **now**.	He	**is playing**	the guitar.
Jack	**sitzt**	**jetzt** in seinem Zimmer.	Er	**spielt**	Gitarre.

(Wenn Jack jetzt in seinem Zimmer sitzt, muss die nachfolgende Handlung des Gitarrespielens auch im Augenblick stattfinden.)

➤ **Beschreibung einer Ausnahme von gewohnheitsmäßigen Handlungen:**

He **usually**	goes to work by bus,	but	**today**	he is **walking**.
Normalerweise	fährt er mit dem Bus zur Arbeit,	aber	**heute**	**geht** er **zu Fuß**.

Ausnahmen & Besonderheiten

Wenn ***to be*** **als Vollverb** verwendet wird, wird das *present progressive* normalerweise nicht verwendet:

He	**is**	here now.
Er	**ist**	jetzt hier.

Bei **modalen Hilfsverben** wird das *present progressive* nicht verwendet. Es darf weder an das Hilfsverb noch an das Vollverb *-ing* angehängt werden:

I	**must go**	now.	
Ich	**muss**	jetzt	**gehen**.

He	**can drive**	now.	
Er	**kann**	jetzt	**fahren**.

Bei **Verben der Sinneswahrnehmung** darf das *present progressive* ebenfalls nicht verwendet werden. Hier muss man das *simple present* (siehe auch: Grammatikkapitel zum *simple present*) nehmen. Bei Verwendung des *present progressive* und auch aller anderen Verlaufsformen (*present perfect progressive, past progressive, past perfect progressive, future progressive*) haben diese Wörter eine **andere Bedeutung**. Diese andere Bedeutung kann jedoch auch in den einfachen Formen der Zeiten vorkommen:

Wichtig!	Verben der Sinneswahrnehmung	Bedeutung bei *Simple*-Formen	Bedeutung bei *Simple*- und *Progressive*-Formen
Die Bedeutung von Verben der Sinneswahrnehmung ändert sich entsprechend der verwendeten Zeit!	to taste	schmecken	probieren, kosten
	to hear	hören	verhandeln
	to feel	sich fühlen	etwas (be)fühlen, abtasten
	to smell	riechen, stinken	etwas riechen
	to see	sehen	treffen

The soup	**tastes**	excellent.
Die Suppe	**schmeckt**	hervorragend.
The cook	**is tasting**	the soup.
Der Koch	**probiert**	die Suppe.
The cook	**tastes**	the soup every day.
Der Koch	**probiert**	die Suppe jeden Tag.
The headmaster	**hears**	the pupils.
Der Direktor	**hört**	die Schüler.
The headmaster	**is hearing**	the case next week.
Der Direktor	**verhandelt**	die Sache nächste Woche.
I	**feel**	a pain in my leg.
Ich	**fühle**	einen Schmerz in meinem Fuß.
I	**am feeling**	fine.
Ich	**fühle mich**	wohl.
The meat	**smells**.	
Das Fleisch	**stinkt**.	
They	**are smelling**	the flowers.
Sie	**riechen**	die Blumen.
We	**see**	the cathedral over there now.
Wir	**sehen**	jetzt dort drüben die Kathedrale.

(Hier muss man jedoch betonen, dass ein Native Speaker normalerweise sagen würde: *We can see the cathedral over there*.)

He	**is seeing**	his boss at the weekend.
Er	**trifft**	seinen Chef am Wochenende.
He	**sees**	his boss every week.
Er	**trifft**	seinen Chef jede Woche.
Er	**sieht**	seinen Chef jede Woche.

Bei Verben, die einen **Besitz anzeigen** (*to belong to, to have, bzw. have got, to owe, to own, to possess* etc.), und bei Verben, die eine **Meinung ausdrücken** (*to believe, to guess, to think, to understand* etc.), muss das *simple present* stehen. Das *present progressive* darf hier nicht verwendet werden:

| They | **have got** | new bikes now. |
| Sie | **haben** | jetzt neue Fahrräder. |

| He | **thinks** | that you're wrong. |
| Er | **glaubt**, | dass du unrecht hast. |

Wenn *to have* nicht als Verb, das einen Besitz anzeigt, verwendet wird, sondern wenn es **im Zusammenhang mit einem Substantiv eine Handlung wiedergibt**, steht bei im Verlauf befindlichen Handlungen das *present progressive*:

| We | **are having a barbecue** | today. |
| Wir | **machen** | heute **eine Grillparty**. |

| They | **are having breakfast** | now. |
| Sie | **frühstücken** | gerade. |

Diese Zeit steht auch, wenn mit *to think* die Tätigkeit des Denkens und nicht *glauben* oder *meinen* ausgedrückt werden soll:

| Don't interrupt me! | I | **am thinking**. |
| Unterbrich mich nicht! | Ich | **denke gerade**. |

Zur Verwendung des *present progressive*, um zukünftiges Geschehen auszudrücken, vergleiche das Grammatikkapitel *The future with the simple present and the present progressive*.

Zeitangaben

Häufig beim *present progressive* verwendete Zeitangaben sind:

Wichtig!

➤ now
➤ at the moment
➤ today
➤ at present
➤ this week, this year, this century etc.

Exercise 1 – Fill in the correct forms of the present progressive.

1. My father _____ (to leave) the house now.

2. We _____ (to write) an essay at the moment.

3. You _____ (to do) a test today.

4. Jack _____ (to carry) a wardrobe downstairs.

5. Judy _____ (to sit) in the bath.

6. Many animals _____ (to die).

7. My parents _____ (to travel) abroad at the moment.

8. They _____ (to taste) the soup.

9. You _____ (to watch) a film now.

10. We _____ (not to run) down the street.

11. Michael _____ (to put) a book into the desk.

12. Our teachers _____ (not to come) across the hall.

13. Tom and Jerry _____ (to play) with a cat.

14. Jack's sister _____ (to make) a model plane today.

15. The mechanics _____ (to repair) the car now.

16. Jack _____ (not to clean) his bike today.

17. My brother _____ (to do) his homework at the moment.

18. The pupils _____ (not to listen) carefully.

19. We _____ (to have) a barbecue today.

20. _____ Judy _____ (to write) an essay?

21. She _____ (to wave) at him.

22. They _____ (to hide) behind the wardrobe.

23. Where _____ she _____ (to go)?

24. Mary _____ (to learn) her vocabulary today.

25. My father _____ (to read) his newspaper now.

26. The pupils _____ (to have) tea at the moment.

27. Look, Jimmy _____ (to work) in the garden.

28. We _____ (to wait) for our teachers today.

29. Listen, Sandy _____ (to sing) a song.

30. Peter _____ (to sleep) in the classroom now.

31. I _____ (to write) a sentence at the moment.

32. Mandy and Janet _____ (to play) the piano.

33. We _____ (to paint) the walls in our classroom.

34. Tom _____ (to carry) his bag.

35. We _____ (to look) at the pets.

---

essay – Aufsatz, Essay

wardrobe
    – Gardarobe(nschrank),
      Kleiderschrank
downstairs – hinunter
bath – Bad(ewanne)

to die – sterben

abroad – (ins/im) Ausland

to taste – (etwas Essbares)
      versuchen, probieren

hall – Aula, Gang

model plane – Modellflugzeug

mechanic – Mechaniker

carefully (adv.)
    – aufmerksam, sorgfältig

barbecue (BBQ) – Grillfest

to wave – winken

pupil – Schüler

sentence – Satz

pet – Haustier

Exercise 2 – Make sentences.

1. Jack/to do/in the classroom/now/his homework

2. my parents/to work/today/in the garden

3. the pupils/to see/the worksheets/at the moment/can't/on their desks
   worksheet – Arbeitsblatt

4. Judy/in her room/to be/now

5. where/our books/to be?

6. Jack's ruler/now/in his pencil-case/to be
   ruler – Lineal
   pencil case – Federmäppchen

7. at the moment/I/my parents' car/can't see

8. Tom/in the pool/to swim/now

9. an essay/the pupils/at the moment/in their classroom/to write

Excercise 3 – Here are some answers, find the questions.
Ask for the words in bold.

in bold – fett gedruckt

1. _____ ? – I'm playing **at home**.
2. _____ ? – **No,** Judy is a girl.
3. _____ ? – He is **in Hatfield** at the moment.   Hatfield – englische Stadt
4. _____ ? – **My mother** is repairing the car.
5. _____ ? – Jim is writing **a letter** today.
6. _____ ? – **It's nine o'clock**.
7. _____ ? – I'm **eleven**.
8. _____ ? – We are watching **a film** now.
9. _____ ? – Jack is painting **the door**.   to paint – (an)malen, streichen
10. _____ ? – We are playing **in the garden**.
11. _____ ? – We are cleaning **our bikes**.
12. _____ ? – The parents are sitting **in the room**.
13. _____ ? – I've got **five** pets.   pet – Haustier
14. _____ ? – **No,** I'm a bad pupil.   pupil – Schüler

Exercise 4 – Here are some answers, find the questions. Ask for the words in bold.

where – wohin, wo
where ... to – wohin

1. _____ ? – I'm going **to the zoo**.

2. _____ ? – He's lying **in his bed**.

3. _____ ? – He's doing **his homework**.

chess – Schach(spiel)
to play chess – Schach spielen

4. _____ ? – We're playing **chess**.

carefully *(adv.)*
    – sorgfältig, vorsichtig

5. _____ ? – They're working **carefully**.

6. _____ ? – **Jack** is singing terribly.

to pay attention
    – aufmerksam sein, zuhören

7. _____ ? – **No**, he isn't paying attention.

8. _____ ? – We're lying **on the beach**.

luggage – Gepäck

9. _____ ? – He's checking **the luggage**.

10. _____ ? – They're driving **now**.

11. _____ ? – I'm going **home**.

12. _____ ? – **Judy** is running.

13. _____ ? – He's watching **a film**.

14. _____ ? – They're driving **to London**.

to weigh – wiegen, abwiegen

15. _____ ? – He's weighing **the luggage**.

to cry – weinen, schreien

16. _____ ? – **Tom** is crying.

17. _____ ? – We're reading a **book**.

to spell – buchstabieren

18. _____ ? – **The pupil** is spelling the word.

towel – Handtuch

19. _____ ? – He's giving me **the towel**.

Exercise 5 – Translation.

Hamster – hamster
Trompete spielen
    – to play the trumpet
Ecke – corner

1. Davids Hamster spielt gerade an der Ecke unseres Gartens Trompete.

    _____

    _____

Regenschirm – umbrella

2. Weil es regnet, steht er unter einem Regenschirm.

    _____

Pinguin – penguin
holen – to fetch
kaputt – broken
(Koch)topf – pot
Schlagzeug – the drums

3. Davids Pinguine holen vier kaputte Kochtöpfe, weil sie kein Schlagzeug haben.

    _____

    _____

Lärm – noise
Angst haben – to be frightened

4. Es gibt einen schrecklichen Lärm, und seine Mutter hat Angst.

    _____

    _____

Haustier – pet
Käfig – cage

5. Jetzt ist die Musik vorbei, und die Haustiere gehen in ihre Käfige.

    _____

    _____

Exercise 6 – Fill in the correct forms of the verbs.

1. My brothers _____ (to read) good books at the moment.

2. It _____ (to be) a nice day today.

3. Jack _____ (to do) a dictation at the moment.   <small>to do a dictation
– ein Diktat schreiben</small>

4. I _____ (can't/to go) to school today.

5. Look, Janet _____ (to go) to school.

6. It _____ (to be) Saturday today.

   We _____ (not to be) at school.

7. The teacher _____ (to help) the pupils at the moment.

8. We _____ (to come) now.

9. She _____ (to try) everything at the moment.

10. Judy _____ (to carry) her schoolbag now.

11. My friends _____ (to wait) in the classroom at the moment.

12. The pupils _____ (to learn) English now.

13. What _____ you _____ (to do)?

Exercise 7 – Translation.

1. Mein Bruder und meine Mutter kaufen sich gerade einen CD-Spieler.   <small>CD-Spieler – CD player</small>

   _____

   _____

2. Schau, Jack arbeitet in seinem Zimmer.

   _____

3. Was machst du gerade? – Ich schreibe ein Diktat.   <small>ein Diktat schreiben
– to do a dictation</small>

   _____

   _____

4. Wie viele Schüler könnt ihr jetzt im Klassenzimmer sehen?

   _____

   _____

5. Wir können unsere Fahrräder nicht reparieren, weil wir jetzt Englisch haben.   <small>reparieren – to repair</small>

   _____

   _____

6. Meine Mutter sieht im Augenblick fern.   <small>fernsehen – to watch TV</small>

   _____

7. Wir sitzen gerade in unseren Zimmern und machen unsere Hausaufgaben.   <small>seine Hausaufgaben machen
– to do one's homework</small>

   _____

   _____

Exercise 8 – Translation.

1. Mein Sohn Peter, meine Tochter Mary und ihr Freund sind heute zu Hause und machen Musik.

(etwas) üben – to practise

2. Sie sind im Wohnzimmer und üben.

laut – noisy

3. Ich kann nicht lesen, weil sie so laut sind.

gegen – against

4. Aber das ist kein Problem, weil ich nichts gegen laute Musik habe.

Schlagzeug spielen
  – to play the drums

5. Peter spielt gerade mit seinem Bruder Schlagzeug.

Trompete spielen
  – to play the trumpet

6. Seine Schwester Betty singt, und ihr Freund spielt Trompete.

Topf – pot
aneinanderschlagen
  – to bang together

7. Peter schlägt zwei Töpfe aneinander.

Lärm – noise

8. Sie machen einen schrecklichen Lärm.

9. Das Schlagzeug steht vor der Tür des Zimmers seiner Eltern.

10. Sie können nicht hinausgehen, weil das Wetter schlecht ist.

11. Es regnet gerade.

12. Deshalb können wir nicht in den Garten gehen.

13. Wir können nicht mit unseren Fahrrädern fahren und wir können nicht mit unserem Hund Oliver spielen.

14. Weil unsere Eltern zu Hause sind, können wir keinen Lärm machen.

Exercise 9 – Fill in the correct forms of the verbs.

Eleven boys and sixteen girls (1) ⬚⬚⬚⬚⬚⬚⬚ (to sit)

in their classroom now. Their biros, rubbers and rulers (2) ⬚⬚⬚⬚⬚⬚⬚

(to be) in their pencil cases. They (3) ⬚⬚⬚⬚⬚⬚⬚ (to have)

English with Mr Jackson now. They (4) ⬚⬚⬚⬚⬚⬚⬚ (to wait) for their

teacher. He (5) ⬚⬚⬚⬚⬚ (to come) now and he (6) ⬚⬚⬚⬚⬚

⬚⬚⬚⬚⬚ (to carry) many books and papers. The teacher's school-bag (7) ⬚⬚⬚⬚⬚

⬚⬚⬚⬚⬚ (to be) brown.

It (8) ⬚⬚⬚⬚⬚ (to be) very old. The boys (9) ⬚⬚⬚⬚⬚

⬚⬚⬚⬚⬚ (to read) English texts now. Mark's English (10) ⬚⬚⬚⬚⬚

(not to be) very good. He (11) ⬚⬚⬚⬚⬚

(can't/to understand) his teacher. It (12) ⬚⬚⬚⬚⬚ (to be) terrible.

The girls (13) ⬚⬚⬚⬚⬚ (to be) in the garden. The sun (14) ⬚⬚⬚⬚⬚

⬚⬚⬚⬚⬚ (to shine) and they (15) ⬚⬚⬚⬚⬚ (to play) football.

Two girls (16) ⬚⬚⬚⬚⬚ (to sit) on the ground, four girls

(17) ⬚⬚⬚⬚⬚ (to watch) Mr Jackson, their teacher.

The teacher's car (18) ⬚⬚⬚⬚⬚ (to be) outside the school. Five pupils (19)

⬚⬚⬚⬚⬚ (to clean) it.

biro – Kugelschreiber
rubber – Radiergummi
ruler – Lineal
pencil case – Federmäppchen

terrible – schrecklich

ground – Boden

Exercise 10 – Translation.

1. Der Vater meines Freundes putzt gerade sein Auto.

2. Die Sonne scheint, und es regnet nicht.

3. Mein Bruder sitzt unten im Zimmer meiner Mutter und liest die Zeitung.

   unten (im unteren Stockwerk)
   – downstairs

4. Meine drei Schwestern sind im Garten und spielen Karten.

   Karte – card

5. Die Hunde meines Vaters spielen mit ihrem Fußball.

6. Mary öffnet jetzt das Fenster und schaut den Hunden zu.

7. Sie sitzen auf Stühlen und schauen Mary an.

8. Jetzt springen die Hunde auf einen Baum hinauf.

   auf ... hinauf – onto

Exercise 11 – Make sentences.

1. Mary/can't/English/to write

2. now/to read/father/the newspaper/my/in the garden

3. Jack/what/to do/at the moment?

4. David/with Mr Hill/in front of our house/tennis/now/to play

Exercise 12 – Translation.

1. „Hallo, Peter. Was machst du gerade?"

hinausschauen – to look out of

2. „Ich sitze in meinem Zimmer und schaue zum Fenster hinaus."

auf (... hinauf) – onto

3. „Ich kann gerade meine Schwester Betty sehen. Sie springt auf eine Mauer."

4. „Wo ist ihr Hund gerade?"

Korb – basket

5. „Er sitzt vor seinem Korb und hört den Vögeln zu."

6. „Kannst du die Vögel auch hören?"

7. „Nein. Das Fenster ist nicht offen."

8. „Springen Bettys Katzen auch auf die Mauer?"

9. „Sie können nicht auf die Mauer springen, weil sie zu hoch ist."

10. „Sitzt du im Bett?" – „Nein. Ich sitze nicht im Bett, weil ich auf dem Fenster stehe."

anrufen – to call

11. „Kannst du mich später anrufen?"

The simple present

Beispiele

1. Aussagesätze

1. I		**go**	to school	**every day.**
2. You		**work**	as a clerk	**on Fridays.**
3. He		**reads**	books	**sometimes.**
She		**looks**	in the mirror	**quite often.**
It	never	**builds**	a house	**in the winter.**
4. We	always	**do**	our homework	**at night.**
5. You		**get**	up before eight	**every morning.**
6. They		**ride**	motorbikes	**on weekends.**

2. Verneinte Sätze

1. I	**do not**	**(don't)**	**go**	to school	**every day.**
2. You	**do not**	**(don't)**	**work**	as a clerk	**on Fridays.**
3. He	**does not**	**(doesn't)**	**read**	books	**sometimes.**
She	**does not**	**(doesn't)**	**look**	in the mirror	**quite often.**
It	**does not**	**(doesn't)**	**build**	a house	**in the winter.**
4. We	**do not**	**(don't)**	**do**	our homework	**at night.**
5. You	**do not**	**(don't)**	**get**	up before eight	**every morning.**
6. They	**do not**	**(don't)**	**ride**	motorbikes	**on weekends.**

3. Fragen

1. When	**do**	I	**go**	to school	**in the winter?**
2.	**Do**	you	**like**	rock music?	
3.	**Does**	he	**work**		**in the summer?**
Where	**does**	she	**live?**		
When	**does**	it	**eat**		**on Sundays?**
4.	**Do**	we	**meet**	in the disco	**every day?**
5.	**Do**	you	**take**	maths?	
6. Why	**do**	they	**go**	home	**on Fridays?**

Bildung

1. Regelmäßige Bildung

Das *simple present* (einfaches Präsens) hat – **außer in der 3. Person Singular** *(he, she, it* bzw. deren Entsprechungen) – die gleiche Form wie der **Infinitiv des Verbs (ohne *to*):**

Bildung			
to **sleep**:	We	**sleep**	till 8 o'clock daily.
to **walk**:	They	**walk**	through the park every afternoon.

In der **dritten Person Singular** wird **ein *s* angefügt:**

to **swim**:	Peter	**swims**	every morning.
to **learn**:	She	**learns**	English on weekends.

2. Besonderheiten bei der Bildung der 3. Person Singular

Steht **am Ende eines Verbs** ein *y* nach einem **Konsonanten (*p, r, s, t* etc.),** wird das *y* durch *ies* ersetzt:

to **carry**:	He	carr**ies**	his bag alone.
to **try**:	She	tr**ies**	to find a friend.
to **fly**:	She	fl**ies**	to London once a month.

Steht das *y* nach einem **Vokal (*a, e, i, o, u*),** gilt die **regelmäßige Bildung** des *simple present:*

to pl**ay**:	Peter	pl**ays**	squash on Tuesday afternoons.
to s**ay**:	Mary	s**ays**	a lot of nonsense.

Endet das Verb mit einem **Zischlaut,** wird *es* angefügt:

to ca**tch**:	He	catch**es**	the ball.
to expre**ss**:	She	express**es**	her fears.

3. Ausnahmen bei der Bildung der 3. Person Singular

to **go**: he go**es**
to **do**: he do**es**

4. Umschreibung mit *to do* bei Frage und Verneinung:

Bei **Frage und Verneinung** muss beim *simple present* **mit *to do* umschrieben** werden (3. Person Singular: *does/does not/doesn't* + Infinitiv, alle anderen Personen: *do/do not/ don't* + Infinitiv):

He	**doesn't go**	to Spain.
Er	**geht nicht**	nach Spanien.

We	**don't play**	chess.
Wir	**spielen nicht**	Schach.

	Do you	like Latin?
	Magst	du Latein?

Where	**do** they **live**?	
Wo	**leben**	sie?

> **Wichtig!,**
>
> Die Form des Vollverbs bleibt in der Umschreibung bei Frage und Verneinung immer gleich, das heißt, zur entsprechenden Form von *to do* wird der Infinitiv des Verbs (ohne *to*) hinzugefügt:

Auch in der 3. Person Singular wird kein *s* an das Vollverb angefügt, weil das *s* schon im Umschreibungswort *does* bzw. *doesn't/does not* erscheint:

He	doe**s**n't **work**	on Saturdays.
Er	**arbeitet nicht**	an Samstagen.

	Doe**s** he **work**	on Saturdays?
	Arbeitet er	an Samstagen?

Das Adverb ***never*** (*nie, niemals*) hat zwar eine negative Bedeutung, darf aber nicht mit *to do* umschrieben werden:

We	**never get up**	early.
Wir	**stehen nie**	früh auf.

Das Hilfsverb ***do*** wird nicht ins Deutsche übersetzt:

	Do you **like**	English?
	Magst du	Englisch?

He	**does not like**	English.
Er	**mag**	Englisch nicht.

> **Wichtig!**
>
> Oft wird die Umschreibung mit *to do* vergessen, wenn *to do* das Vollverb in einem Satz ist. Auch in diesen Fällen muss mit *to do* umschrieben werden, selbst wenn dies zunächst eigenartig klingen mag:

He	**does**	his homework badly.	(***does*** = Vollverb)
Er	**macht**	seine Hausaufgaben schlecht.	

He	**doesn't do**	his homework badly.	(***do*** = Vollverb; ***doesn't*** = Umschreibung)
Er	**macht**	seine Hausaufgaben nicht schlecht.	

	Does he **do**	his homework badly?	(***do*** = Vollverb; ***does*** = Umschreibung)
	Macht	er seine Hausaufgaben schlecht?	

5. Besonderheiten bei Fragen

Ist das **Fragepronomen** Subjekt des Fragesatzes, wird **nicht mit *to do* umschrieben**:

Who	**lives**	in Brighton?
Wer	**lebt**	in Brighton?

(Frage nach dem Subjekt: **Wer oder was** lebt in Brighton?)

What	**goes**	on in your mind?
Was	**geht**	in deinem Kopf vor?

(Frage nach dem Subjekt: **Wer oder was** geht in deinem Kopf vor?)

Zur Satzstellung und zu Besonderheiten bei Verben mit Präpositionen siehe das Kapitel *Allgemeine Regeln*.

Verwendung

Das *simple present* wird verwendet,

➤ **um auszudrücken, was oft, regelmäßig, gewohnheitsmäßig, nie etc. geschieht:**

| Tom | **leaves** | the house at 6 o'clock **every morning**. |
| Tom | **verlässt** | **jeden Morgen** um 6 Uhr das Haus. |

| I | **never** | **watch** | football matches on TV. |
| Ich | | **sehe** | mir **nie** Fußballspiele im Fernsehen an. |

➤ **um Dauerzustände und allgemeingültige Feststellungen auszudrücken:**

| Jack's brother | **lives** | in Scotland. |
| Jacks Bruder | **lebt** | in Schottland. |

| The sun | **rises** | in the East. |
| Die Sonne | **geht** | im Osten **auf**. |

➤ **um Aussagen über einen Text, Film, ein Bühnenstück etc. zu machen:**

| The play | **deals** | with personal problems. |
| Das Stück | **handelt** | von persönlichen Problemen. |

| The book | **explains** | the problems of minorities. |
| Das Buch | **erläutert** | die Probleme von Minderheiten. |

➤ **um eine direkte Rede einzuleiten:**

| He | **says**: | "I don't like Mondays." |
| Er | **sagt**: | „Ich mag Montage nicht." |

| She | **asks**: | "Do you study in the afternoons?" |
| Sie | **fragt**: | „Lernt ihr am Nachmittag?" |

➤ **bei umgangssprachlicher Verwendung zusammen mit *here, there, down* etc.:**

Um Handlungen auszudrücken, die zwar im Augenblick stattfinden und für die normalerweise das *present progressive* (vergleiche das vorhergehende Grammatikkapitel zum *present progressive*) verwendet werden würde, die aber durch *here, there, down* etc. eingeleitet werden. Diese Verwendung benutzt man normalerweise in der gesprochenen Sprache:

| **Here** | **come** | the players. |
| **Hier** | **kommen** | die Spieler. |

| **There** | **goes** | your bus. |
| **Da** | **fährt** | dein Bus. |

Man beachte die veränderte Satzstellung: Die Subjekte (*the players* bzw. *your bus*) stehen hinter dem Verb, das heißt die übliche Satzstellung S – P – O (Subjekt – Prädikat – Objekt) darf hier nicht angewandt werden.

➤ **bei Verben der Sinneswahrnehmung:**

Bei Verben der Sinneswahrnehmung (*to feel – fühlen, to hear – hören, to smell – riechen, to taste – schmecken* etc.), selbst wenn damit verbundene Vorgänge von der Verwendung her im *present progressive* stehen müssten (zur Verwendung und Bedeutungsänderung dieser Verben im *present progressive*: vergleiche das vorhergehende Grammatikkapitel zum *present progressive*):

| The meat | **tastes** | awful now. |
| Das Fleisch | **schmeckt** | jetzt scheußlich. |

| The meat | **smells** | now. |
| Das Fleisch | **riecht** | jetzt. |

➤ **bei *to be* als Vollverb und bei modalen Hilfsverben:**

Wenn *to be* als Vollverb verwendet wird und bei modalen Hilfsverben nimmt man das *simple present* auch dann, wenn man eigentlich das *present progressive* erwarten würde (Vergleiche auch das Grammatikkapitel zum *present progressive*):

He **is** here now.
Er **ist** jetzt hier.

I **must** go now.
Ich **muss** jetzt gehen.

He **can** drive now.
Er **kann** jetzt fahren.

➤ **bei *to have* im Sinne von *besitzen* und bei *have got*:**

Wenn *to have* einen Besitz anzeigt und bei *have got* wird das *simple present* auch dann verwendet, wenn man eigentlich das *present progressive* erwarten würde. (Vergleiche auch das vorhergehende Grammatikkapitel zum *present progressive*.)

He **has** got a bike at the moment.
Er **hat** im Moment ein Fahrrad.

➤ **bei *to have* zur Beschreibung einer Handlung:**

Wenn *to have* nicht als Verb, das einen Besitz anzeigt, verwendet wird, sondern, wenn es im Zusammenhang mit einem Substantiv eine Handlung wiedergibt, kann das *present progressive* stehen, wenn es die Verwendung erfordert:

We **are having a barbecue** today.
Wir **machen** heute eine **Grillparty**.

They **are having breakfast** at the moment.
Sie **frühstücken** gerade.

➤ **bei zukünftigem Geschehen:**

Zur Verwendung des *simple present*, um zukünftiges Geschehen auszudrücken: Vergleiche das Grammatikkapitel *The future with the simple present and the present progressive.*

Zeitangaben

Häufig beim *simple present* verwendete Zeitangaben sind unter anderem:

Wichtig!

➤ always
➤ usually
➤ never
➤ sometimes
➤ rarely
➤ seldom
➤ often
➤ every day, every week, every month, every year etc.
➤ in the mornings, in the evenings, in the afternoons

Diese Zeitangaben können auch mit anderen Zeiten verwendet werden. Beziehen sie sich aber auf eine Handlung der Gegenwart, so steht mit diesen Zeitangaben immer das *simple present* und nicht das *present progressive*!

Exercise 1 – Fill in the correct forms of the simple present.

during – während

to do a test
      – einen Test schreiben

usually *(adv.)* – normalerweise

abroad – (ins/im) Ausland

to like being – gerne sein

to enjoy – genießen
theatre play – Theaterstück

to arrive – ankommen
on time – pünktlich, rechtzeitig

mouse, *pl.* mice – Maus

record – Schallplatte

to cry – weinen, schreien

to carry – tragen

1.   My father _____ (to go) to work at six o'clock during the week.

2.   We _____ (to do) a test every month.

3.   My parents usually _____ (to buy) food at the supermarket.

4.   Jack sometimes _____ (to carry) a bag for his mother.

5.   My dog often _____ (to catch) a ball easily.

6.   He _____ (to watch) TV every day.

7.   We _____ (to read) two books a week.

8.   Mr Jackson _____ (to fly) abroad once a year.

9.   He really _____ (to wish) you all the best.

10. The pupils _____ (not to learn) English, French and Latin.

11. Mark _____ (not to play) tennis every day.

12. I _____ (not to do) my homework in the afternoons.

13. Lessons in Germany _____ (to begin) at 8 o'clock.

14. Mr Miller _____ (to like) being a teacher.

15. My mother _____ (to do) the washing on Saturdays.

16. Our teacher always _____ (to finish) his lessons too late.

17. Tom _____ (to enjoy) every minute of theatre plays.

18. We _____ (not to study) at home in the afternoons.

19. You _____ (not to stay) up till 12 every day.

20. They _____ (to arrive) on time.

21. Tom and Jerry _____ (not to like) mice very much.

22. Mr Frankenstein _____ (to kill) many people.

23. Jill _____ (not to go) to parties during the week.

24. My brother _____ (to buy) two records every month.

25. Our parents _____ (to go) shopping on Saturdays.

26. Jack _____ (not to do) English in the afternoons.

27. My little sister often _____ (to cry) at night.

28. The pupils _____ (to play) football on Sundays.

29. Jack never _____ (to carry) anything heavy.

30. We _____ (not to go) out during the week.

31. Jill _____ (not to like) English.

32. Where _____ you normally _____
     (to spend) your holidays?

33. Mike often _____ (to meet) his girlfriend.

34. I never _____ (to go) to discos.

Exercise 2 – Make negative sentences first and then questions.
Ask for the words in bold.

Example: Jack leaves the house **in the morning**.
                Jack doesn't leave the house in the morning.
                When does Jack leave the house?

1. My father goes to work **at six o'clock in the morning**.

2. I do **my homework** in the afternoon.

3. The Jacksons are **at home** at the weekend.

4. **The pupils** have got to learn every day.

5. My father plays chess **in the evening**.   chess – Schach(spiel)

6. **Jack's sister** can speak Japanese.   Japanese – japanisch, Japaner(in)

7. My mother always does the washing up **after dinner**.   to do the washing up – abspülen

8. I've got to go to school **on weekdays**.

9. **Tom** works in the garden.

10. I like **English**.

Exercise 3 – Here are some answers, find the questions.
Ask for the words in bold.

1. _____ ? – I play tennis **in the morning**.

2. _____ ? – **Jack** cleans his room.

3. _____ ? – I do my homework **in the kitchen**.

4. _____ ? – We have tea **in the afternoon**.

5. _____ ? – School begins **at 8.10**.

break – Pause

6. _____ ? – Our first break is **after geography**.

assembly – Versammlung

7. _____ ? – **No,** there isn't an assembly here.

favourite subject – Lieblingsfach

8. _____ ? – My favourite subject is **Latin**.

9. _____ ? – He sees **Mary** quite often.

10. _____ ? – They go **to school**.

11. _____ ? – We like **sports**.

Exercise 4 – Translation.

am Morgen – in the morning

1. Wann geht ihr am Morgen in die Schule?

sondern – but

2. Ich treffe mich mit meiner Freundin nicht um halb acht, sondern um neun Uhr.

3 Wann habt ihr eure nächste Englischstunde?

4. Magst du Sport?

Religionslehrer
– religious education
teacher

5. Wie alt ist euer Religionslehrer?

Biologiestunde – biology lesson

6. Wir haben an Montagen keine Biologiestunde.

7. Wer spielt mit dir jeden Samstag Fußball?

8. Geht ihr jeden Freitag aus?

9. Jack spielt an Sonntagen nie Fußball.

10. Francis macht seine Hausaufgaben immer am Nachmittag.

Geschirr spülen, abwaschen
– to wash (do) the dishes

11. Wann wäscht deine Mutter das Geschirr ab?

Exercise 5 – Here are some answers, find the questions.
Ask for the words in bold.

1. _____ ? – Peter likes **pop music**.

2. _____ ? – I see a **slot-machine**.   slot-machine – Spielautomat

3. _____ ? – **Jack** goes to school at eight o'clock.

4. _____ ? – **No,** we don't have flowers in the garden.

5. _____ ? – Mike has got **a nice watch**.   watch – Armbanduhr

6. _____ ? – My pen-friend lives **in London**.   pen-friend – Brieffreund(in)

7. _____ ? – We watch TV **in the evenings**.

8. _____ ? – I'm **here**.

9. _____ ? – **We** don't play chess.   chess – Schach(spiel)

10. _____ ? – We go **to the disco**.

11. _____ ? – They have got **five** books.

12. _____ ? – They like **maths**.

13. _____ ? – He does his **homework**.

Exercise 6 – Make sentences.

1. Judy/to go/never/on Sundays/to school

   _____

2. Tom and Jerry/cats/for breakfast/not to like/in the mornings

   _____

3. not to do/Mike/in his room/his homework/after school

   _____

4. in a band/not to play/Norman/the guitar/often

   _____

5. teachers/sometimes/on Sundays/to work

   _____

6. Jill/never/in the garden/to sleep

   _____

7. not to go/out/we – when/it/to rain

   _____

8. Christmas songs/never/to sing/during the year/we   during – während

   _____

9. not to like/French songs/my friend

   _____

10. never/not to play/German music/the orchestra

   _____

Exercise 7 – Here are some answers, find the questions.
Ask for the words in bold.

1.   ? – We hate **English**.

2.   ? – We go out **in the evenings**.

3.   ? – **Jack** does the washing.

4.   ? – He does his homework **in the kitchen**.

5.   ? – She puts **the cups** into the cupboard.

6.   ? – They've got **many problems**.

7.   ? – The pupils are **at home**.

8.   ? – I would like to live **in London**.

9.   ? – **Tom** comes home every night.

10.   ? – The mechanics work **in the garage**.

11.   ? – Mary does **a dictation**.

12.   ? – We are **in the bathroom**.

cupboard – Schrank

Exercise 8 – Translation.

1. Mary: „Schalte bitte das Radio ein, Frank, die Nachrichten über das Fußballspiel zwischen England und Deutschland kommen um halb vier."

2. Frank: „Deine Uhr geht nach. Es ist schon acht nach dreiviertel vier – viel zu spät. Sie sind schon vorbei."

3. Mary: „Wie schade. Ich höre den Nachrichten gerne zu."

4. Frank: „Läuft heute Abend im Fernsehen ein Fußballspiel?"

5. Mary: „Ich will es nicht anschauen, weil Onkel George immer im Wohnzimmer mit Löffeln und Gabeln Schlagzeug spielt."

6. Frank: „Maul' nicht. Er spielt nach dem Abendessen nicht dort, sondern in seinem Zimmer."

7. Mary: „Aber man hört ihn immer. Es ist wirklich schrecklich."

8. Frank: „Tut mir leid, aber ich kann überhaupt nichts dagegen machen."

einschalten – to switch on
Nachrichten (über)
* – news (of) (Singular-Wort!)*

nachgehen – to be slow
vorbei – over

Schade! – What a pity!
etwas gerne tun
* – to like doing sth.*

laufen (im Fernsehen)
* – there is/are*

Löffel – spoon
Gabel – fork
Schlagzeug spielen
* – to play the drums*

maulen – to grumble
Abendessen – dinner
sondern – but

schrecklich – terrible

etwas dagegen tun
* – to do sth. about sth.*

Exercise 9 – Translation.

1. Peter und Mary sind im Herbst immer im Ausland im Urlaub.

   Herbst – autumn
   (ins/im) Ausland – abroad

2. Sie sind auf einem Campingplatz in Amerika.

   Campingplatz – caravan site

3. Sie verbringen ihren Urlaub gerne dort, weil die Strände sehr schön sind.

   etwas gerne tun
        – to like doing sth.
   Strand – beach

4. Manchmal fahren sie mit dem Auto in die Stadt und sehen sich die Sehenswürdigkeiten dort an.

   Sehenswürdigkeit – sight

5. Es gibt dort viele alte Schlösser und Kirchen.

   Schloss – castle
   Kirche – church

6. Manchmal mieten Peters Eltern ein fantastisches Appartement an der französischen Küste.

   mieten – to rent
   phantastisch – fantastic
   Küste – coast

7. Es hat schöne Möbel und einen großen Garten.

   Möbel – furniture

8. Dieses Jahr wollen die Kinder ohne ihre Eltern fahren und in einer lebhaften Jugendherberge an einem See in Schottland bleiben, weil sie das Monster dort sehen wollen.

   lebhaft – lively
   Jugendherberge – youth hostel
   bleiben – to stay
   See – lake

9. Sie wollen es fotografieren und die Fotos an eine Zeitschrift verkaufen.

   (etwas) fotografieren
        – to take photos (of sth.)
   Zeitschrift – magazine
   verkaufen – to sell

10. Sie reisen immer mit dem Zug nach England und fahren dann per Anhalter nach Schottland.

    mit dem Zug reisen
         – to travel (to go) by train
    per Anhalter fahren
         – to hitchhike

11. Sie übernachten oft in Jugendherbergen, weil es dort billiger als in Hotels ist.

    übernachten – to stay the night

12. Und in diesen Jugendherbergen ist es auch interessanter, weil man dort viele junge Leute treffen kann.

Vergleich:
Simple present – Present progressive

Simple present und *present progressive* gehören zu den *present tenses* (Zeiten der Gegenwart), das heißt, der Ausdruck *present tense* ist der Überbegriff für diese beiden Zeiten.

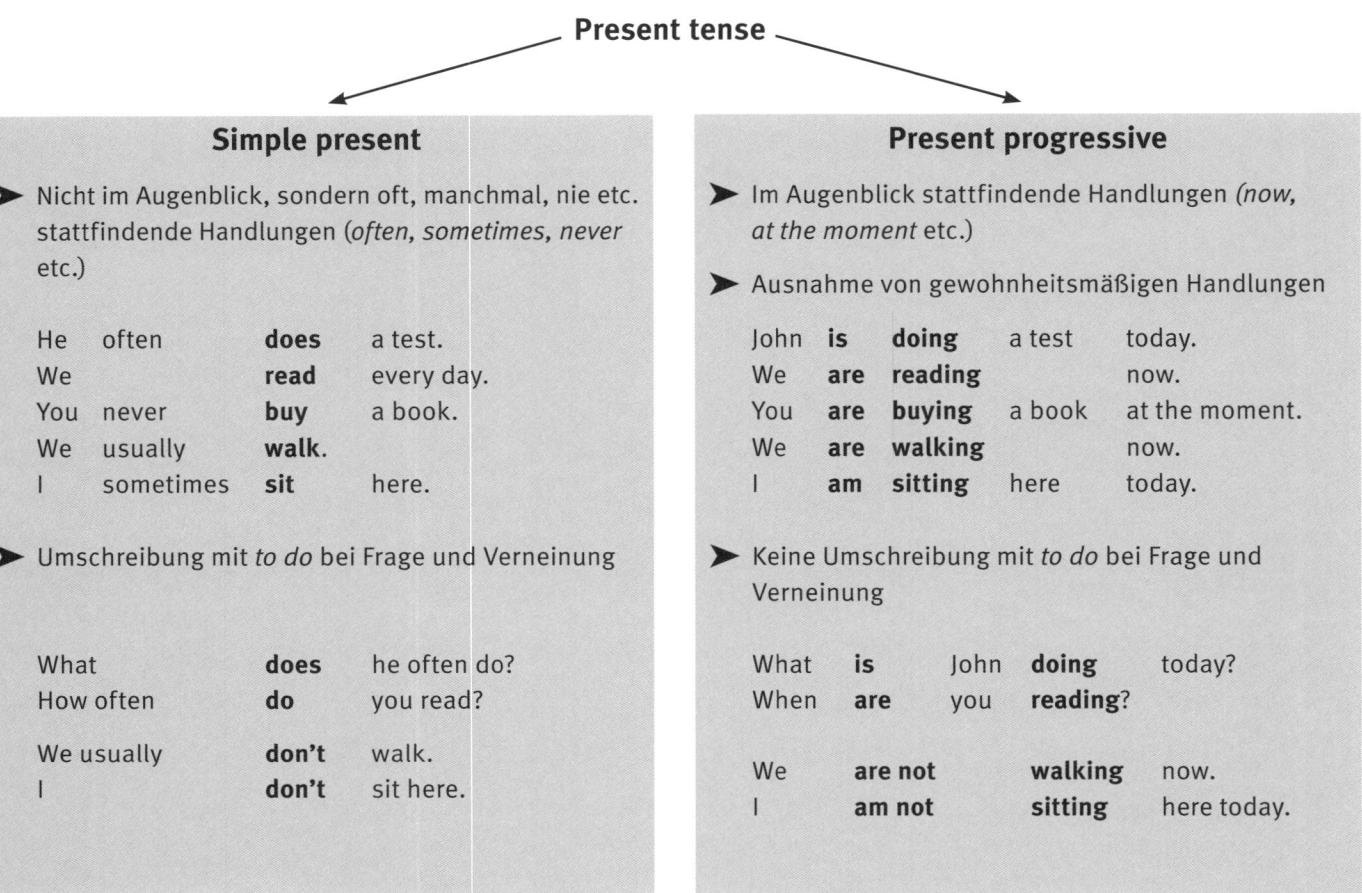

Present tense

Simple present

➤ Nicht im Augenblick, sondern oft, manchmal, nie etc. stattfindende Handlungen (*often, sometimes, never* etc.)

He	often	**does**	a test.
We		**read**	every day.
You	never	**buy**	a book.
We	usually	**walk**.	
I	sometimes	**sit**	here.

➤ Umschreibung mit *to do* bei Frage und Verneinung

| What | **does** | he often do? |
| How often | **do** | you read? |

| We usually | **don't** | walk. |
| I | **don't** | sit here. |

Present progressive

➤ Im Augenblick stattfindende Handlungen (*now, at the moment* etc.)

➤ Ausnahme von gewohnheitsmäßigen Handlungen

John	**is**	**doing**	a test	today.
We	**are**	**reading**		now.
You	**are**	**buying**	a book	at the moment.
We	**are**	**walking**		now.
I	**am**	**sitting**	here	today.

➤ Keine Umschreibung mit *to do* bei Frage und Verneinung

| What | **is** | John | **doing** | today? |
| When | **are** | you | **reading**? | |

| We | **are not** | **walking** | now. |
| I | **am not** | **sitting** | here today. |

Übersetzungs-Tipp Bei der Übersetzung vom Englischen ins Deutsche gibt es keinen Unterschied zwischen *present progressive* und *simple present*:

| He | **is working** | now. | *present progressive* |
| Er | **arbeitet** | jetzt. | |

| He | **works** | every day. | *simple present* |
| Er | **arbeitet** | jeden Tag. | |

Exercise 1 – Fill in the correct forms of the verbs.

Twelve boys and girls (1) _____ (to sit) in their classroom now.
Their teacher (2) _____ (to tell) them a nice story about English
towns and villages. The pupils (3) _____ (to listen) to him. Then he
(4) _____ (to test) Kevin. Kevin's vocabulary (5) _____
(to be) really terrible and he (6) _____ (can't/to pronounce)
the new English words right. And he (7) _____ (can't/to
read) them either. Mary (8) _____ (to get) up from her chair and
(9) _____ (to go) over to the window. She (10) _____
_____ (to open) it now. She (11) _____ (can/to
see) her teacher's dogs. They (12) _____ (to play) outside. The
boys (13) _____ (to read) English magazines. They (14) _____
_____ (to have got) newspapers, too, but they (15) _____
(to be) too difficult. So they (16) _____ (to play)
with their biros and pencil cases. Because Kevin (17) _____
(to make) a model plane, he (18) _____ (not to listen)
to his teacher. So the teacher (19) _____ (to be) very angry.
The teacher's books (20) _____ (to be) in his school-bag. They
(21) _____ (to be) brown. He (22) _____
(to carry) his books to his desk now. He (23) _____ (to put)
them into the desk.

to pronounce – aussprechen

not ... either – auch nicht

difficult – schwierig

biro – Kugelschreiber
pencil case – Federmäppchen

Exercise 2 – Translation.

1. Weil das Wetter schlecht ist, muss Kermit heute im Klassenzimmer bleiben.

bleiben – to stay

2. Er spielt jetzt mit seinen Beinen Schlagzeug und macht einen fürchterlichen Lärm.

Schlagzeug spielen
* – to play the drums*

Lärm – noise

3. Aber Kermit kann nicht singen, weil er Halsweh hat.

Halsweh haben
* – to have a sore throat*

4. Aber Kermit singt immer schlecht, auch wenn er kein Halsweh hat.

5. Jetzt singt er nicht, sondern hört einer Sendung im Radio zu.

eine Radio-Sendung
* – a programme on the radio*

Exercise 3 – Simple present or present progressive?
Fill in the correct forms of the verbs.

1. My mother never _____ (to go) shopping on Sundays.

2. Frank and Tom _____ (to take) a test today.

3. Jim never usually _____ (to get up) before eight, but today he _____ (to get up) already at six.

4. Judy _____ (have got) an English lesson every day.

5. Jim _____ (to be) at school at the moment.

6. The pupils _____ (to get) a lot of homework every day.

7. We _____ (have got to/to buy) some new blouses.

8. Sandy never _____ (to wear) a school uniform on Mondays, but today she _____ (to wear) a black blazer and a grey pair of trousers because they do an English test.

9. Jill usually _____ (to do) the washing in the mornings, but today she _____ (to do) it in the evening.

10. Peter _____ (cannot/to go) to school today, because he _____ (to be) ill.

11. Jim never _____ (to carry) his bag.

12. Peter never _____ (to watch) Knight Rider, but today he _____ (to sit) in front of the TV-set and _____ (to watch) it.

13. The pupils _____ (can't/to do) good tests today because they _____ (to be) too tired.

14. My friends sometimes _____ (to play) football, but today they _____ (to be) in the gym and _____ (to train) for the basketball final.

15. We _____ (to have got) an English lesson now. We _____ (to sit) in our classroom and _____ (to do) a dictation.

16. Mechanics normally _____ (not to work) on Sundays, but today they _____ (to be) in the garage and _____ (to prepare) the cars for the race.

17. What _____ you _____ (to do)?
    – I _____ (to wait) for my brother.

18. Look, my brother _____ (to watch) a movie although he never normally _____ (to watch) TV in the afternoon.

TV-set – Fernseher, Fernsehapparat

tired – müde

gym(nasium) – Turnhalle (nicht: Gymnasium!!)

to prepare – vorbereiten
race – Rennen

movie – Film

Exercise 4 – Simple present or present progressive?
Fill in the correct forms of the verbs.

1. Jack ░░░░░░░░░░░░░░░ (to do) his homework in the evenings.

2. My friend ░░░░░░░░░░░░░░░ (to carry) my luggage at the moment.　　　luggage – Gepäck

3. The Jacksons sometimes ░░░░░░░░░░░░ (to have) breakfast in the kitchen.

4. This afternoon Peter ░░░░░░░░░░░░ (to sit) in his room and

   ░░░░░░░░░░░░ (to watch) TV although he usually ░░░░░░░░░░░░　　　although – obwohl
   usually – normalerweise

   (to play) football on Sundays.

5. My mother usually ░░░░░░░░░░░░ (to cook) the dinner; sometimes

   I ░░░░░░░░░░░░ (to help) her.

6. Kevin never usually ░░░░░░░░░░░░ (to clean) his bike, but today he

   ░░░░░░░░░░░░ (to be) in the garden and ░░░░░░░░░░░░

   (to wash) everything.

7. You ░░░░░░░░░░░░ (can/to come) now.

8. My mother ░░░░░░░░░░░░ (to be) on holiday in Spain at the moment

   although she normally ░░░░░░░░░░░░ (to go) to Italy in the summer.

9. Sandra often ░░░░░░░░░░░░ (to watch) TV, but she ░░░░░░░░░░░░

   ░░░░░░░░░░░░ (to listen) to the radio at the moment.

10. Look, a new teacher ░░░░░░░░░░░░ (to come) into the room.

11. No, my brother ░░░░░░░░░░░░ (not to watch) TV at the moment.

12. My father usually ░░░░░░░░░░░░ (to go) to work by car, but today he

    ░░░░░░░░░░░░ (to go) by bus.

13. I can see my mother. She ░░░░░░░░░░░░ (to clean) the kitchen.

14. Where's Tom? – He ░░░░░░░░░░░░ (to help) his friend.

Exercise 5 – Translation.

1. Mein Hund Eugen ist gerade in seinem Zimmer und schreibt einen Brief an mich.

   ░░░░░░░░░░░░░░░░░░░░░░░░░░░░░░

2. Er muss ihn heute aufgeben, weil ich Geburtstag habe.　　　(einen Brief) aufgeben
   – to post (a letter)

   ░░░░░░░░░░░░░░░░░░░░░░░░░░░░░░

3. Meiner Meinung nach ist Eugen ziemlich dumm: Er klebt immer die falsche Briefmarke　　meiner Meinung nach
   auf den Umschlag und vergisst manchmal die Postleitzahl.　　　　　– in my opinion
   ziemlich – quite
   kleben – to stick
   ░░░░░░░░░░░░░░░░░░░░░░░░░░░░░░　　Briefmarke – stamp
   Postleitzahl – postcode
   ░░░░░░░░░░░░░░░░░░░░░░░░░░░░░░

   ░░░░░░░░░░░░░░░░░░░░░░░░░░░░░░

4. Aber er hilft mir oft und wäscht die Wäsche im Badezimmer unseres Reihenhauses.　　(die Wäsche) waschen
   – to do the washing
   Reihenhaus – terraced house
   ░░░░░░░░░░░░░░░░░░░░░░░░░░░░░░

   ░░░░░░░░░░░░░░░░░░░░░░░░░░░░░░

Exercise 6 – Simple present or present progressive?
Fill in the correct forms of the verbs.

1. Jack _____ (to play) in the garden at the moment.

2. Mary _____ (never/to watch) TV.

3. My parents _____ (not to go) shopping in the afternoons.

4. You _____ (cannot/to go) out now because it

    _____ (to rain).

5. We _____ (to be) in the garden at the moment.

6. My sister _____ (to get) up at seven every Sunday.

7. Listen, a band _____ (to play) in the park.

8. We _____ (to do) a dictation at the moment.

Exercise 7 – Translation.

1. Wir fangen die Englischstunden immer mit einem Diktat an.

    _____

2. Unser Lehrer gibt uns jeden Tag viele Hausaufgaben.

    _____

Reifenpanne – puncture, flat tyre

3. Ich fahre jeden Tag mit dem Auto in die Schule, aber heute laufe ich, weil ich eine Reifenpanne habe.

    _____

    _____

Gitarre spielen
  – to play the guitar
üben – to practise

4. Am Nachmittag spiele ich Gitarre oder übe Klavier.

    _____

sammeln – to collect

5. Mein Bruder sammelt Briefmarken und Pinguine.

    _____

normalerweise – usually

6. Ich sehe normalerweise nie am Abend fern, aber heute sitze ich in meinem Zimmer und sehe mir Tom und Jerry an.

    _____

    _____

7. Ich gehe heute nach der Schule nicht nach Hause, weil wir am Nachmittag Unterricht haben.

    _____

    _____

8. Ich gehe nicht vor halb zehn ins Bett.

    _____

9. Meine Eltern trinken am Morgen nicht Kaffee, sondern Tee.

10. Tragt ihr in der Schule Uniformen?

    _____

Exercise 8 – Simple present or present progressive?
Fill in the correct forms of the verbs.

1. Mary _____ (to sit) in her room now and _____ (to play) the guitar.

2. She _____ (must/to practise) every day because she _____ (not to be) very good.

to practise – üben

3. It's Wednesday afternoon. Her father _____ (to be) in his bedroom and _____ (to listen) to Mary.

4. He usually _____ (to go) to work on Wednesdays, but he _____ (to be) on holiday today.

usually – normalerweise

5. Her mother _____ (to leave) the house at the moment.

6. She _____ (to go) shopping every day in the afternoon.

7. She sometimes _____ (to buy) food at the supermarket near their house, but today she _____ (to stand) in the little shop in Croydon.

8. From Monday till Wednesday Mary's mother _____ (to work) at a shop in London.

9. She _____ (to arrive) there at eight o'clock every day.

Exercise 9 – Translation.

1. An vielen Schulen in Großbritannien tragen Schüler eine Schuluniform.

2. Sie müssen von halb neun bis dreiviertel vier in der Schule bleiben.

bleiben – to stay

3. Aber heute können sie schon um ein Uhr nach Hause gehen, weil die Queen Geburtstag hat.

4. Tom sitzt jetzt in seinem Zimmer und macht seine Hausaufgaben.

5. Er fängt immer mit Deutsch an, aber heute macht er Englisch.

6. Weil seine Schwester Susanna heute nicht in der Schule ist, sitzt sie in ihrem Zimmer und isst eine Pizza.

7. Susanna hat viele Hobbys: Sie sammelt Pinguine und Krokodile und spielt Gitarre und Klavier.

Krokodil – crocodile
Gitarre/Klavier spielen – to play the guitar/piano

Exercise 10 – Fill in the correct forms of the following verbs.

to do – to do – to do – to be – to be – to see – to live – not to do – to forget – to have got – to have got – to give – to tell

1. My brother _____ in London.

2. He _____ a teacher and _____ many nice pupils.

3. He _____ them every day.

4. Today he _____ them a dictation.

5. They _____ it now.

6. They _____ some problems with it.

7. They never _____ good tests because they _____ too lazy.

8. They sometimes _____ a lot of work at school, but today they _____ anything.

9. Unfortunately they often _____ their homework, although their teacher always _____ them not to forget anything.

lazy – faul

unfortunately – leider

Exercise 11 – Translation.

1. Es gibt heute keine schönen Kleider in der Abteilung für Mädchenkleidung.

2. Mary steht gerade vor den Regalen und schaut sich einige teure Pullover an.

3. Aber sie kauft sich° nichts, weil sie kein Geld hat.

4. Sie mag immer die teuren Sachen, aber ihre Eltern haben nicht genügend Geld, und so sieht sie sich oft nur billige Kleidung an.

5. Deshalb findet sie sehr oft überhaupt nichts.

6. Sie ist dann immer sehr enttäuscht und läuft in der ganzen Stadt herum, um etwas Passendes zu finden.

Kleid – dress
Abteilung für Mädchenkleidung – girls' department

Regal – shelf (pl. shelves)
teuer – expensive

nichts – not anything, nothing

genügend – enough
billig – cheap
Kleidung – clothes

deshalb – that's why
überhaupt nichts – nothing at all

enttäuscht – disappointed
in der ganzen Stadt – all over town
etwas Passendes – something suitable

° nicht übersetzen

Exercise 12 – Simple present or present progressive?
Fill in the correct forms of the verbs.

1. We _____ (to have got) our first English lesson today.

2. We _____ (to sit) in our classroom and _____
   (to wait) for our teacher.

3. He _____ (to be) a tall man.   tall – groß

4. He _____ (to come) to school at seven o'clock every morning.

5. There _____ (to be) 30 pupils in our class.

6. They sometimes _____ (to do) their homework at school,
   sometimes they _____ (to study) at home.

7. Our teacher _____ (to stand) in front of the board now and   board – Tafel
   _____ (to ask) questions.

8. He often _____ (to set) tests, but they _____   to set a test – einen Test machen
   (to be) very easy.

9. He _____ (to like) us very much because we _____
   (to be) very nice pupils.

10. That's why he always _____ (to go) on trips to London with us
    when the weather _____ (to be) fine.

Exercise 13 – Translation.

1. Toms Familie hat einen großen Garten hinter ihrem Haus.

   _____

2. Es gibt auch einen Balkon mit vielen Blumen.   Balkon – balcony

   _____

3. Tom frühstückt mit seinen Eltern und seinen Schwestern jeden Sonntag im Esszimmer.   Esszimmer – dining-room

   _____

   _____

4. Dann liest Vater immer die Zeitung.

   _____

5. Aber heute sieht er fern, weil es ein interessantes Fußballspiel gibt.

   _____

6. Tom sitzt in seinem Zimmer und liest eine Zeitschrift.

   _____

7. Er hört auch Musik.

   _____

8. An Sonntagnachmittagen geht er manchmal in die Diskothek, weil er laute Musik mag.

   _____

   _____

Exercise 14 – Make sentences.

1. usually/Tom/in the morning/at five o'clock/to get up

2. in my room/to work/I/can't/at the moment

3. never/to carry/my mother/anything/for my father/in the supermarket/on weekends

4. Jack/to do/what/at the moment?

5. sometimes/on Sunday/my father/to work

6. to run/Judy/now/down the hill

shelf (*pl.* shelves) – Regal

7. onto/my brother/to put/the shelf/the books/at the moment

to prepare – vorbereiten

8. never/the teacher/to prepare/any lessons

Exercise 15 – Translation.

abtrocknen – to dry up

1. Jane ist gerade in der Küche und trocknet ab.

sich anziehen – to get dressed

2. Mein Bruder steht im Augenblick im Bad und zieht sich an, weil er um halb acht in die Schule gehen muss.

normalerweise – usually
die Wäsche waschen
    – to do the washing

3. Normalerweise kaufe ich ein, aber heute wasche ich die Wäsche.

4. Ich stehe gerade im Badezimmer und sehe mein Gesicht an.

5. Manchmal stehe ich morgens um halb acht, aber manchmal schon um halb sieben auf.

6. Ich kann dir jetzt nicht helfen, weil ich abtrocknen muss.

Exercise 16 – Translation.

1. Janet und Peter müssen heute sehr früh aufstehen, weil sie nicht mit ihrem Vater in die Schule fahren können.

2. Er hat starke Kopfschmerzen und kann nicht in die Arbeit gehen.

   starke Kopfschmerzen – bad headache

3. Er arbeitet normalerweise als Verkäufer in einem Supermarkt.

   normalerweise – usually
   Verkäufer – shop assistant

4. Er verkauft Eier, Limonade und Orangensaft.

   Orangensaft – orange juice

5. Abends ist seine Arbeit immer um halb sieben zu Ende, und dann fährt er nach Hause.

6. Er trinkt zum Abendessen immer Kaffee und isst Schinkenspeck mit Spiegeleiern.

   Abendessen – supper
   Schinkenspeck mit Spiegeleier – ham and eggs

7. Aber heute isst er nur Milch und Cornflakes.

8. Nach dem Abendessen räumt seine Frau das Geschirr weg und wäscht ab.

   Geschirr abräumen – to clear the table
   abwaschen – to do the washing up

9. Janet und Peter helfen ihr: Peter trocknet ab und Janet stellt das Geschirr in den Schrank.

   abtrocknen – to dry up
   Geschirr – dishes

10. Manchmal lesen sie am Abend oder machen Spiele zusammen.

    zusammen – together

11. Aber heute sitzen sie alle vor dem Fernseher und sehen sich einen langweiligen Film über Enten und Katzen an.

    langweilig – boring
    Ente – duck

12. Er handelt von Donald Duck und seiner Entenfamilie.

13. Donald Duck hat immer Probleme mit seinem reichen Onkel und seinen kleinen Neffen.

    rich – reich
    Neffe – nephew

14. Sie gehen ihm sehr oft auf die Nerven, weil sie nicht das tun, was er will.

    jemandem auf die Nerven gehen – get on one's nerves

Exercise 17 – Translation.

beliebt – popular

1. Tom und Jerry sind in einer beliebten Schule in London.

CD-Spieler – CD player

2. Ihre Klassenzimmer sind sehr modern mit CD-Spieler, und so können sie immer CDs anhören.

Heizkörper – radiator

3. Es gibt dort viele schöne Bilder, Lampen und Heizkörper.

schrecklich – terrible
(etwas) satt haben
    – to be tired (of), to be fed
    up (with) sth.

4. Aber heute haben Tom und Jerry die schreckliche Schule satt.

eine Fahrradtour machen
    – to go on a bike trip
blöd – stupid
to do a test
    – eine Schulaufgabe
    schreiben

5. Sie können keine Fahrradtour machen, weil sie eine blöde Englischschulaufgabe schreiben.

6. Das ist nicht komisch!

Exercise 18 – Simple present or present progressive? Fill in the correct forms of the verbs.

1. My brother never _____ (to do) his homework in the evening, but he _____

(al)though – obwohl

_____ (to learn) English now, although it _____

(to be) already nine o'clock.

2. I _____ (to have got to/to go) now because my mother _____

_____ (to wait) for me.

3. Can't you be quiet? I _____ (to write) a letter.

4. Look, Jacky _____ (to sit) in the swimming pool.

Exercise 19 – Translation.

ausschauen wie – to look like

1. Einer unserer Lehrer schaut aus wie ein Pinguin, aber er ist ganz nett.

überhaupt nicht – not at all
langweilig – boring

2. Er mag unsere Klasse überhaupt nicht, weil wir oft in seinen langweiligen Unterrichtsstunden reden und weil wir manchmal unsere Hausaufgaben nicht machen.

korrigieren – to correct
an (etwas) interessiert sein
    – to be interested in (sth.)

3. Er braucht immer lange, um unsere Schulaufgaben zu korrigieren, und manchmal macht er es überhaupt nicht, weil er nicht an ihnen interessiert ist.

Exercise 20 – Here are some answers, find the questions. Ask for the words in bold.

1. _____ ? – I repair my bike **every day**.

2. _____ ? – They're buying **a car** now.

3. _____ ? – Jill watches TV **at night**.

4. _____ ? – I'm listening to **a pop song**.

5. _____ ? – **Jack** sleeps in the evening.

6. _____ ? – She buys **a magazine**.

7. _____ ? – **Tom** answers questions.

8. _____ ? – I do my homework **at home**.

9. _____ ? – **Peter** speaks French.

Exercise 21 – Translation.

1. Mein Freund Tom spielt jeden Tag Fußball, weil er einmal in der ersten englischen Liga spielen will.

   _____

   _____

   erste englische (Fußball-)Liga – the Premier League
   einmal – some time

2. Heute steht er auf dem Platz und übt die ganze Zeit Freistöße.

   _____

   _____

   Platz – field
   üben – to practise
   Freistoß – free-kick

3. Er ist sehr enttäuscht, weil er nie ein Tor schießt.

   _____

   _____

   enttäuscht – disappointed
   ein Tor schießen – to score

4. Obgleich ihm das auf die Nerven geht, weiß er, dass er das tun muss, wenn er besser werden will.

   _____

   _____

   obgleich – although
   auf die Nerven gehen – to get on one's nerves

5. Er spielt jeden Samstag mit seinen Freunden gegen ein Team der Schüler seiner Klasse.

   _____

   _____

6. Meistens gewinnen sie, weil sie viel besser spielen können.

   _____

   _____

7. Dann träumt Tom immer davon, der Mittelstürmer von Bayern München zu sein.

   _____

   _____

   Mittelstürmer – centre forward

Exercise 22 – Fill in the correct forms of the verbs.

We (1) _____ (to be) in London now. We (2) _____ (to visit) some interesting sights. My brother Tom (3) _____ (not to be) here because he (4) _____ (to see) his boss at the moment. Tom (5) _____ (must/to be) there today because his boss (6) _____ (to have) important business there.

My mother is at home at the moment. She (7) _____ (to cook) the dinner. She (8) _____ (to taste) the meal and (9) _____ (to see) that it (10) _____ (to taste) excellent. She (11) _____ (to smell) something funny because some of the vegetables (12) _____ (to smell) a little bit strange, but that (13) _____ (not to matter).

My parents (14) _____ (to have got) a nice dining-room. They (15) _____ (to have) dinner there now. Sometimes they (16) _____ (to have) breakfast there in the morning, but they often (17) _____ (to have) tea in the kitchen, too.

My sister Mary (18) _____ (to sit) in her room at the moment and (19) _____ (to read) a book. It (20) _____ (to deal) with environmental problems of the earth. She (21) _____ (to stop) reading now because there (22) _____ (to be) a film on TV which (23) _____ (to explain) these problems.

Exercise 23 – Translation.

1. Mein Großvater ist ziemlich gut situiert. Er hat fünf Einfamilienhäuser, einige Hunde, 14 Sekretärinnen und eine Ehefrau.

   _____

   _____

2. Donnerstags geht er oft ins Kino, obwohl er die Filme dort meist hasst.

   _____

3. Aber heute sitzt er im Wohnzimmer und klebt Briefmarken auf die Briefe an seine Freundinnen.

   _____

   _____

4. Er kann die Adressen nicht finden. Dann zieht er sich an und verlässt das Haus.

   _____

   _____

5. Er geht in ein Restaurant und isst einen schönen großen Cheeseburger.

   _____

(Randglossar linke Spalte:)

important – wichtig

to taste – probieren, schmecken

vegetables – Gemüse

strange – eigenartig

to deal with – handeln von
environmental problem – Umweltproblem
earth – Erde

gut situiert sein – to be well off
ziemlich – quite, rather
Einfamilienhaus – detached house
Sekretärin – secretary

obwohl – although
meist – mostly
hassen – to hate

kleben – to stick

anziehen – to get dressed

The simple past

Beispiele

1. Aussagesätze

1. I	**helped**	my mother	**yesterday.**
2. You	**worked**	here	**last Sunday.**
3. He	**visited**	me	**three days ago.**
She	**cleaned**	her bike	**last month.**
It	**needed**	a new cage	**last year.**
4. We	**watched**	television	**yesterday.**
5. You	**played**	football	**last Monday.**
6. They	**parked**	in High Street	**last week.**

2. Verneinte Sätze

1. I	**did not (didn't)**	**help**	my mother	**yesterday.**
2. You	**did not (didn't)**	**work**	here	**last Sunday.**
He	**did not (didn't)**	**visit**	me	**three days ago.**
She	**did not (didn't)**	**clean**	her bike	**last month.**
It	**did not (didn't)**	**need**	a new cage	**last year.**
4. We	**did not (didn't)**	**watch**	television	**yesterday.**
5. You	**did not (didn't)**	**play**	football	**last Monday.**
6. They	**did not (didn't)**	**park**	in High Street	**last week.**

3. Fragen

1. When	**did**	I	**help**	your mother?	
2.	**Did**	you	**work**	here	**last Sunday?**
3. When	**did**	he	**visit**	me?	
	Did	she	**clean**	her bike	**last month?**
What	**did**	it	**need**		**last year?**
4.	**Did**	you	**watch**	television	**yesterday?**
5. When	**did**	you	**play**	football?	
6. Where	**did**	they	**park**		**last week?**

Bildung

1. Regelmäßige Bildung

Das *simple past* (einfache Vergangenheit) wird bei **allen Personen** dadurch gebildet, dass man **ed an den Infinitiv des Verbs** (ohne *to*) **anfügt**:

Bildung		Infinitiv des Verbs + *ed*	
to work:	He	work**ed**	last Sunday.
to play:	We	play**ed**	football yesterday.

In der **3. Person Singular** wird beim *simple past* **kein s** angefügt:
He **cleaned** his bike yesterday.
She **washed** the car two days ago.

2. Besonderheiten der Bildung

➤ Steht **am Ende eines Verbs ein y nach einem Konsonanten** (*p, t, s* etc.), wird das **y durch ied** ersetzt:

to ca**rry:**	We	carr**ied**	the bag a day ago.
to t**ry:**	He	tr**ied**	to cheat him.

Aber: Steht das **y nach einem Vokal** (*a, e, i, o, u*) wird das *simple past* **regelmäßig** gebildet:

to pl**ay:**	We	pl**ayed**	football.
to st**ay:**	He	st**ayed**	at home.

➤ Steht am Ende des Verbs *ee* oder ein stummes *e*, wird nur *d* angehängt:

to hat**e:**	They	hat**ed**	her.
to agr**ee:**	We	agr**eed**	with his plans.

➤ Steht ein **Konsonant** (*l, p, s, t* etc.) **am Ende eines Verbs nach einem kurz gesprochenen Vokal** (*a, e, i o, u*), dann wird der **Konsonant verdoppelt**:

to st**op:**	I	sto**pp**ed	him.
to comm**it:**	He	commi**tt**ed	a crime.

Im amerikanischen Englisch wird ein *l* nach einem Vokal nicht verdoppelt:

to trav**el:**	We	trave**l**ed	to Canada last year.

➤ Die **unregelmäßigen Verben** haben **eigene Formen**, z. B.:

to **come:**	I	**came**	yesterday.
to **go:**	She	**went**	away last month.

Eine Liste der unregelmäßigen Verben befindet sich auf Seite 6.

3. Frage und Verneinung

Bei Frage und Verneinung wird mit der Form des *simple past* von *to do* (*did, didn't, did not*) umschrieben. Das Verb bleibt immer im Infinitiv (ohne *to*):

Where	**did**	you	**go**	yesterday?
Wohin	**bist**	du		gestern **gegangen**?
	Did	you	**buy**	a book last week?
	Hast	du		letzte Woche ein Buch **gekauft**?

| I | **didn't** | **like** | English last year. |
| Ich | **mochte** | | Englisch letztes Jahr **nicht**. |

| She | **did not** | **go** | to school the day before yesterday. |
| Sie | **ging** | | vorgestern **nicht** in die Schule. |

Das Hilfsverb *did* wird **nicht ins Deutsche übersetzt**:

| They | **did not go** | | to school last week. |
| Sie | **gingen** | | letzte Woche **nicht** in die Schule. |

	Did you buy	a book yesterday?
	Kauftest du	gestern ein Buch?
	Hast du	gestern ein Buch **gekauft**?

4. Besonderheiten bei Fragen

Ist das Fragepronomen Subjekt eines Fragesatzes, wird nicht mit *to do* umschrieben:

| **Who** | **worked** here yesterday? |
| **Wer** | **hat** gestern hier **gearbeitet**? |

(Frage nach dem Subjekt: Wer oder was hat gestern hier gearbeitet?)

| What | **happened** to him? |
| Was | **ist** ihm **passiert**? |

(Frage nach dem Subjekt: Wer oder was ist ihm passiert?)

Zur Satzstellung und zu Besonderheiten bei Verben mit Präpositionen siehe das Kapitel Allgemeine Regeln.

Verwendung

Man verwendet das *simple past*

➤ **zur Beschreibung wiederholter (a), einmaliger (b) oder aufeinanderfolgender (c) Handlungen, die in der Vergangenheit begannen und beendet wurden:**

| a) | When he | **was** | at school, he | **had** | a test every day. |
| | Als er in der Schule | **war,** | | **schrieb** | er jeden Tag einen Test. |

| b) | They | **went** | away yesterday. |
| | Sie | **gingen** | gestern fort. |

| c) | First he | **cleaned** his teeth, then he | **left** | the house. |
| | Zuerst | **putzte** er sich die Zähne, dann | **verließ** | er das Haus. |

➤ **bei historischen Ereignissen:**

| Columbus | **discovered** | America in 1492. |
| Kolumbus | **entdeckte** | Amerika 1492. |

➤ **bei Handlungen, die zu einem früheren Zeitpunkt abgeschlossen waren:**

Handlungen, die zwar **in einem noch nicht abgeschlossenen Zeitraum stattgefunden haben** (z.B. *this year, this month, today, this morning*) und für die man normalerweise das *present perfect* erwartet, bei denen man jedoch darauf hinweisen will, dass die **Handlungen** bereits **zu einem früheren Zeitpunkt** des jeweiligen Zeitabschnitts **abgeschlossen waren:**

| We | **had** | a test | **today.** |
| Wir | **haben heute** | eine Schulaufgabe | **geschrieben**. |

(Man macht diese Aussage nach der Schule oder abends, wenn die Schulaufgabe schon vorbei ist.)

| **Übersetzungs-Tipp** | Das englische *simple past* kann im **Deutschen** mit dem **Perfekt** wiedergegeben werden: |

I   **worked** hard last week.
Ich **habe**   letzte Woche hart **gearbeitet**.

| **Vorsicht!** | Bei der Übersetzung vom Englischen ins Deutsche stellt dies normalerweise kein Problem dar. Vorsicht ist bei der **Übersetzung vom Deutschen ins Englische** geboten: |

Ausnahmen: Vergleiche das Grammatikkapitel zum *present perfect*.

Ist die Handlung in der **Vergangenheit abgeschlossen**, steht **immer**, auch **wenn im Deutschen das Perfekt** steht, **im Englischen** das *simple past*:

Ich **bin gestern** zu Hause **gewesen**.   (bin gewesen = **Perfekt**)
I   **was** at home **yesterday**.   (was = **simple past**)

Er **hat**   **vor zwei Wochen** seinen Führerschein **bestanden**.   (hat bestanden = **Perfekt**)
He **passed** his driving-test two weeks ago.   (passed = **simple past**)

Zeitangaben

| **Wichtig!** | Häufig beim *simple past* verwendete Zeitangaben sind: |

➤ yesterday
➤ the day before yesterday
➤ two days ago
➤ last week, last month, last year, last century
➤ in 1957

| **Übersetzungs-Tipp** | Das **deutsche** zeitlich gebrauchte *vor* (vor zwei Wochen, Monaten, Jahren etc.) wird immer mit *ago* übersetzt und **verlangt normalerweise das *simple past***: |

Two days **ago**   they **went** to the zoo.
Vor zwei Tagen   **gingen** sie in den Zoo.

Three years **ago**   there **were** many tourists.
Vor drei Jahren   **gab** es viele Touristen.

| **Übersetzungs-Tipp** | Das englische *for* + Zeitangabe (*for two days/weeks/months* etc.) **drückt einen Zeitraum aus** und wird normalerweise mit dem *present perfect* bzw. dem *present perfect progressive* gebraucht (vergleiche zur genaueren Verwendung das Kapitel zu *since and for*). Es wird im Deutschen mit *seit* wiedergegeben: |

He **has been** here **for two days**
Er   **ist**   **seit zwei Tagen** hier.

Exercise 1 – Fill in the forms of the simple past.

1. The day before yesterday the weather _____ (to be) really nice.

2. Tom and Jerry _____ (to be) in the fields.   field – Feld

3. They _____ (to want) to have a race.   race – Rennen

4. But they _____ (not to want) to ride in the mud.   mud – Schlamm

5. Suddenly it _____ (to begin) to rain.   suddenly – plötzlich

6. Jerry _____ (to go) round a bend.   bend – Kurve

7. There _____ (to be) a lot of mud.

8. Jerry _____ (to brake), but he _____ (to be) too fast.   to brake – bremsen

9. So he _____ (to fall) off his bike.

10. He _____ (to fly) into the mud.

11. He _____ (to cut) his finger.

12. The wheels of the bike _____ (to break).   wheel – Rad
    to break – (sich) brechen (broke, broken)

13. He _____ (not to like) it.

14. When he _____ (to get) home, his mother _____ (to be) very angry.

15. Tom _____ (to drink) some milk, but he _____ (not to eat) anything.

16. He _____ (not to be) in bed before nine o'clock.

17. He _____ (to fall) asleep at once.   to fall asleep – einschlafen (fell, fallen)

18. He _____ (to dream) about a film.

19. When he _____ (to wake) up the next morning, he _____ (to feel) sick.   to feel sick (felt, felt) – schlecht sein, übel sein

20. He _____ (not to get) up and _____ (to stay) in bed all day.

21. In the evening he _____ (to decide) to go to London, but he _____ (not to know) where the station was.   to decide – sich entschließen, entscheiden

22. So he _____ (to take) a taxi.

23. He _____ (to get) on the wrong train and _____ (to arrive) in Manchester five hours later.

24. He _____ (to fly) back home even though he _____ (not to have) any money.   even though – obwohl

25. He _____ (to be) really happy, when he _____ (to be) home again.

26. He _____ (to go) to bed at once and _____ (to fall) asleep immediately.   immediately *(adv.)* – sofort

27. He _____ (not to wake up) before twelve o'clock yesterday.

Exercise 2 – Fill in the forms of the simple past.

1. There _____ (to be) a race at Selhurst School two days ago.

2. Many pupils _____ (to be) at a race track near Croydon.

3. The weather _____ (to be) nice.

4. Some of them _____ (not to ride) BMX bikes.

5. They only _____ (to have got) ordinary bikes.

6. They _____ (not to have) good brakes.

7. The race _____ (to start) at two o'clock in the afternoon.

8. Boys and girls _____ (to take) part in the same race.

9. Judy _____ (to try) to overtake Mary because Mary _____ _____ (to be) so slow.

10. Suddenly there _____ (to be) a bend in front of them.

11. Judy _____ (to brake), but she _____ (to be) too fast.

12. So there _____ (to be) an accident.

13. She _____ (to crash) into Mary.

14. The girls _____ (to fall) off their bikes and _____ (to break) their legs.

15. Mary _____ (to start) to cry.

16. An ambulance _____ (to take) them to hospital.

17. The race track _____ (to be) really dangerous.

18. Some other pupils _____ (to have) an accident, too.

19. They _____ (to crash) into a tree.

20. The starter _____ (to help) the pupils.

21. The pupils _____ (not to want) to go on any more.

22. They _____ (not to like) the track.

23. At home they _____ (to clean) their bikes.

24. The fathers _____ (to repair) their children's bikes.

25. The boys _____ (to be) really tired and _____ (to go) to bed at once.

26. When they _____ (to get) up the next day, they _____ (to feel) awful.

27. They _____ (to have) problems getting out of their beds in the morning after the race.

28. But they _____ (to recover) quickly and _____ (to go) back to the race track in the afternoon.

29. And then all the problems _____ (to begin) again.

Margin vocabulary:
- race track – Rennstrecke
- ordinary – normal, gewöhnlich
- brake – Bremse
- to take part – teilnehmen (took, taken)
- to overtake – überholen (overtook, overtaken)
- bend – Kurve
- to brake – bremsen (broke, broken)
- to break – (sich) brechen
- ambulance – Krankenwagen
- dangerous – gefährlich
- awful – schrecklich
- to recover – sich erholen, gesunden

Exercise 3 – Fill in the forms of the simple past.

1. I ⬚⬚⬚⬚⬚ (to drive) to London yesterday.

2. My father ⬚⬚⬚⬚⬚ (not to watch) TV last night.

3. A bad accident ⬚⬚⬚⬚⬚ (to happen) two weeks ago.   to happen – passieren

4. We ⬚⬚⬚⬚⬚ (not to have) breakfast in America last year.

5. Tom ⬚⬚⬚⬚⬚ (to find) his book the day before yesterday.

6. The Jacksons ⬚⬚⬚⬚⬚ (to see) the Tower two weeks ago.

7. My brother ⬚⬚⬚⬚⬚ (to take) me to the station last night.

8. We ⬚⬚⬚⬚⬚ (not to learn) Latin last year.

9. The teachers ⬚⬚⬚⬚⬚ (not to give) back the tests.

Exercise 4 – Here are some answers, find the questions.
Ask for the words in bold.

1. ⬚⬚⬚⬚⬚ ? – I saw **an exciting film**.   exciting – aufregend

2. ⬚⬚⬚⬚⬚ ? – We played **in the fields**.

3. ⬚⬚⬚⬚⬚ ? – He went to bed **at seven o'clock**.

4. ⬚⬚⬚⬚⬚ ? – She bought a book **yesterday**.

5. ⬚⬚⬚⬚⬚ ? – **Tom** cleaned his bike.

6. ⬚⬚⬚⬚⬚ ? – Jim saw **Sandy**.

7. ⬚⬚⬚⬚⬚ ? – **Mr Jackson** taught English.

8. ⬚⬚⬚⬚⬚ ? – Judy crossed **the street**.

9. ⬚⬚⬚⬚⬚ ? – He swam **in the lake**.   lake – See

Exercise 5 – Translation.

1. Gestern bekam ich ein neues BMX-Rad von meinem Vater.   bekommen – to get (got, got)

2. Ich war in einer Kurve und musste plötzlich bremsen.   Kurve – bend
plötzlich – suddenly
bremsen – to brake

3. Ich raste in einen Baum hinein und fiel vom Rad herunter.   hinein rasen – to crash into
herunterfallen – to fall off
(fell, fallen)

4. Die Sanitäter brachten mich sofort ins Krankenhaus.   Sanitäter – ambulance man
(weg)bringen – hier: to take (took,
taken)

5. Dort war ich den ganzen Tag im Bett.   den ganzen Tag (lang)
– all day long

6. Das war keine sehr schöne Erfahrung.   experience – Erfahrung

Exercise 6 – Here are some answers, find the questions.
Ask for the words in bold.

1. ▨▨▨▨▨▨▨▨▨▨▨▨▨▨▨▨▨▨ ? – I saw Jimmy **at school**.

2. ▨▨▨▨▨▨▨▨▨▨▨▨▨▨▨▨▨▨ ? – Tim bought **the book** two days ago.

3. ▨▨▨▨▨▨▨▨▨▨▨▨▨▨▨▨▨▨ ? – I wrote a letter **because it was my brother's birthday**.

to feed (fed, fed) – füttern

4. ▨▨▨▨▨▨▨▨▨▨▨▨▨▨▨▨▨▨ ? – We fed the **cows**.

5. ▨▨▨▨▨▨▨▨▨▨▨▨▨▨▨▨▨▨ ? – **Tom** got a new car.

6. ▨▨▨▨▨▨▨▨▨▨▨▨▨▨▨▨▨▨ ? – In Africa school began **at one o'clock**.

7. ▨▨▨▨▨▨▨▨▨▨▨▨▨▨▨▨▨▨ ? – I was **at home**.

8. ▨▨▨▨▨▨▨▨▨▨▨▨▨▨▨▨▨▨ ? – **No**, I didn't do my homework.

9. ▨▨▨▨▨▨▨▨▨▨▨▨▨▨▨▨▨▨ ? – He ate **five** sandwiches.

soldier – Soldat
to fight – kämpfen
(fought, fought)

10. ▨▨▨▨▨▨▨▨▨▨▨▨▨▨▨▨▨▨ ? – **The soldier** fought against the king.

11. ▨▨▨▨▨▨▨▨▨▨▨▨▨▨▨▨▨▨ ? – They really felt **bad**.

12. ▨▨▨▨▨▨▨▨▨▨▨▨▨▨▨▨▨▨ ? – He had **a red BMW**.

station – Bahnhof

13. ▨▨▨▨▨▨▨▨▨▨▨▨▨▨▨▨▨▨ ? – We were **at the station**.

14. ▨▨▨▨▨▨▨▨▨▨▨▨▨▨▨▨▨▨ ? – Jack didn't find **his bag**.

15. ▨▨▨▨▨▨▨▨▨▨▨▨▨▨▨▨▨▨ ? – We left the bags **in the bus**.

16. ▨▨▨▨▨▨▨▨▨▨▨▨▨▨▨▨▨▨ ? – They had **five** sandwiches.

17. ▨▨▨▨▨▨▨▨▨▨▨▨▨▨▨▨▨▨ ? – **Jack** went to London.

18. ▨▨▨▨▨▨▨▨▨▨▨▨▨▨▨▨▨▨ ? – My parents saw Tom **yesterday**.

to forget – vergessen
(forgot, forgotten)

19. ▨▨▨▨▨▨▨▨▨▨▨▨▨▨▨▨▨▨ ? – Kate forgot **her homework**.

match – Spiel, Wettkampf

20. ▨▨▨▨▨▨▨▨▨▨▨▨▨▨▨▨▨▨ ? – The pupils watched **the match**.

21. ▨▨▨▨▨▨▨▨▨▨▨▨▨▨▨▨▨▨ ? – They were interested **in books**.

Exercise 7 – Translation.

1. Vor drei Monaten waren wir in England, weil wir Englisch lernen wollten.

Ferien verbringen
– to be on holidays

2. Wir haben unsere Ferien letztes Jahr in London verbracht.

obwohl – although
schlechter als – worse than

3. Es war sehr schön, obwohl das Wetter dort oft schlechter als in Deutschland ist.

deshalb
– so, therefore, that's why
Jugendherberge – youth hostel

4. Die Hotels waren teuer, deshalb schliefen wir in Jugendherbergen.

5. Wir aßen nicht in Restaurants, sondern kauften uns Hamburger im McDonald's.

Exercise 8 – Make sentences.

1. school/yesterday/to leave/at five o'clock/Janet

2. to meet/him/in London/last year/we

3. she/a letter/not to write/last week

4. always/to go/to the cinema/on Sundays/they/two years ago

5. at the party/to play/the band/yesterday/a pop song

Exercise 9 – Here are some answers, find the questions.
Ask for the words in bold.

1. _____ ? – I bought **this car yesterday**.

2. _____ ? – Tom read **a book**.

3. _____ ? – **Jane** wore **a dress** a week ago.   dress – Kleid

4. _____ ? – **Yes**, I got a good grade in English.   a good grade – eine gute Note

5. _____ ? – **The cat** fell into the water.

Exercise 10 – Translation.

1. Gestern war ein seltsamer Tag, weil uns unser Lehrer keine Arbeitsblätter gab.

   seltsam – strange
   Arbeitsblatt – worksheet

2. Er beschloss, uns etwas Interessantes über englische Badezimmer zu zeigen.

   beschließen – to decide
   über – about

3. Die Duschen in England sind viel kleiner als in Deutschland.

   Dusche – shower

4. Wir haben auch etwas über das Land aufgeschrieben.

   aufschreiben – to write down
   (wrote, written)

5. Du kannst dort Fisch und Pommes Frites oder herrlichen Rinderbraten mit frischen Bohnen essen, aber du bekommst keine deutschen Würste.

   (gebackener, panierter) Fisch und Pommes – fish and chips
   Rinderbraten – roastbeef
   Bohne – bean
   Wurst – sausage

6. Bevor die Stunde vorbei war, war unser Lehrer sehr böse auf uns, weil wir ihm einen Streich spielten und viel Spaß hatten.

   vorbei sein – to be over
   böse sein (auf) – to be angry (with)
   jemandem einen Streich spielen – to play a trick on sb.
   Spaß haben – to have fun

Exercise 11 – Put the following sentences into the simple past.

1. I often work in the garden.

2. It is Monday today.

wardrobe – (Kleider-)Schrank
downstairs
    – (die Treppen nach) unten

3. He carries the wardrobe downstairs.

dining-room – Esszimmer

4. I do my homework in the dining-room.

5. Does he go to school every day?

dress – Kleid

6. She has got a new dress.

to recognize – (wieder)erkennen

7. They recognize him at once.

to feel tired (felt, felt)
    – müde sein

8. They feel tired.

fluently *(adv.)*
    – fließend (Sprache)

9. He speaks English fluently.

10. They don't like biology.

Exercise 12 – Translation.

gefährlich – dangerous
Abenteuer – adventure

1. Letzten Sommer hatte Mr. Smith ein gefährliches Abenteuer.

ein Taxi nehmen – to take a taxi
                    (took, taken)

2. Er nahm ein Taxi nach London.

plötzlich – suddenly

3. Plötzlich waren fünf Pinguine auf der Straße.

sofort – at once

4. Der Fahrer hielt sofort an und Mr. Smith fiel aus dem Taxi heraus.

Krankenwagen – ambulance
(weg)bringen – to take

5. Der Krankenwagen brachte ihn ins Krankenhaus.

überhaupt nicht – not at all
gerne dort sein
    – to like being there

6   Mr. Smith war überhaupt nicht gerne dort.

nicht mehr – not anymore

7. Jetzt mag er keine Pinguine mehr.

Exercise 13 – Here are some answers, find the questions.
Ask for the words in bold.

1. _____ ? – The race started **at two o'clock**.   race – Rennen

2. _____ ? – **Judy** fell off the bike.

3. _____ ? – The fathers cleaned **the bikes**.

4. _____ ? – The starter helped **the pupils**.

5. _____ ? – **No**, the pupils didn't like the track.   track – Strecke

6. _____ ? – **Judy and Mary** had an accident.

7. _____ ? – The track was **near Croydon**.   Croydon – englische Stadt

8. _____ ? – **The race** took place in the woods.

9. _____ ? – The teachers watched **the race**.

10. _____ ? – The mothers were afraid of **accidents**.

11. _____ ? – They didn't like **the dangerous track**.   dangerous – gefährlich

12. _____ ? – They went home **after the race**.

13. _____ ? – They took **their children** with them.

14. _____ ? – They reparied **the bikes**.

Exercise 14 – Translation.

1. Frankenstein junior lebte vor 212 Jahren in einem keltischen Museum.   keltisch – Celtic

   _____

2. Er versteckte sich immer hinter einigen ägyptischen Mumien und las langweilige Bücher.   sich verstecken – to hide (hid, hidden)
   hinter – behind
   ägyptisch – Egyptian
   Mumie – mummy
   langweilig – boring

   _____

   _____

3. Er spielte sehr gerne Fußball mit den Köpfen der Mumien und stellte sich vor, ein berühmter Fußballspieler zu werden, aber er war schlechter als David Beckham.   etwas gerne tun – to like doing something
   sich (gedanklich) vorstellen – to imagine

   _____

   _____

   _____

4. Als die Besucher ihn sahen und wegrannten, hörte Frankenstein auf, spazierenzugehen.   aufhören etw. zu tun – to stop doing sth.
   spazieren gehen – to walk around

   _____

   _____

5. Er kaufte sich ein noch viel fantastischeres Gebäude, die Überbleibsel einer alten Burg in der Hauptstadt von Schottland, und schreibt gerade Bücher über seine Vergangenheit.   fantastisch – fantastic
   Überbleibsel – ruins
   Burg – castle
   Hauptstadt – capital
   Vergangenheit – past

   _____

   _____

   _____

Exercise 15 – Fill in the forms of the simple past.

to smash – zerbrechen

1. Yesterday Peter _____ (to throw) a rock through a window

    and _____ (to smash) it.

in deep troube
    – in echten Schwierigkeiten

2. The window _____ (to break) into thousands of pieces and

    so he _____ (to be) in deep trouble.

owner – Eigentümer
flat – Wohnung

fortunately *(adv.)*
    – glücklicherweise

successful – erfolgreich

3. A man, the owner of the flat, _____ (to come) out at

    once and _____ (to try) to hit Peter, but fortunately he

    _____ (not to be) successful.

neighbour – Nachbar
to notice – bemerken

4. The man's neighbour _____ (to notice) everything and

    _____ (to try) to help.

although – obwohl

5. Although Peter _____ (to run) away quickly, they _____

    _____ (to follow) him and _____ (to catch) him after half a mile.

6. They _____ (to make) a phone call to the police.

7. But Peter _____ (to get) away again and _____

cave – Höhle
mine – Mine

    (to hide) in a cave of an old mine where he _____ (to be) safe again.

8. When it _____ (to get) dark he _____ (to run) home

immediately *(adv.)* – sofort

    and _____ (to go) to bed immediately. What a nice day!

Exercise 16 – Translation.

Kinderlähmung – polio
deshalb
    – that's why, so, therefore
Rollstuhl – wheelchair

1. Als Judy elf war, hatte sie Kinderlähmung und muss deshalb immer im Rollstuhl sitzen.

    _____

    _____

gerne Sport treiben
    – to like doing sports
fast wie – almost as

2. Sie treibt gerne Sport und ist mit dem Rollstuhl fast genauso schnell wie die anderen Kinder.

    _____

    _____

an einem Rennen teilnehmen
    – to take part in a race
      (took, taken)
erfolgreich – successfull
die Erste sein – to be first
schaffen – to do (did, done)

3. Letztes Jahr verlor sie zwei Rennen, aber vorgestern nahm sie erfolgreich an einem Rennen teil und war die Erste, weil sie 100 Meter in 22 Sekunden schaffte.

    _____

    _____

trainieren – to train
regelmäßig – regular

4. Sie trainiert regelmäßig sehr hart in der Schule.

    _____

lernen – to learn
sorgfältig – carefully

5. Sie lernt aber auch sorgfältig für die wichtigsten Fächer, weil sie besser sein will als ihre Freundinnen.

    _____

    _____

Exercise 17 – Make sentences.

1. in the zoo/two days ago/the pupils/to be

2. the farmers/the cows/to feed/every day/last year   to feed (fed, fed) – füttern

3. Judy/to lose/yesterday/her bag

4. five/to drink/bottles of coke/the day before yesterday/we

5. to read/many books/last year/the pupils/in the lessons

6. my parents/to get up/before eight o'clock/never/three years ago

7. the car/in the garage/the mechanics/to leave/last night

8. John/his homework/to forget/last week/twice   twice – zweimal

9. not to understand/we/last year/the grammar rules   grammar rule – Grammatikregel

Exercise 18 – Translation.

1. Tom und Jerry veranstalteten am letzten Samstag ein Rennen.   veranstalten – to organize

2. Jerry ritt auf einer Katze, Tom fuhr auf seinem BMX-Rad.

3. Weil es um ihre Häuser herum zu langweilig war, nahmen sie den gefährlicheren Weg durch den Wald mit seinen hohen Hügeln und Kurven.

    um ... herum – round ...
    gefährlich – dangerous
    Weg – path
    Wald – woods
    Hügel – hill
    Kurve – bend

4. Tom war viel schneller als Jerry, aber plötzlich gab es einen Unfall: Toms Pedal brach, und er fuhr in einen Baum hinein.

    plötzlich – suddenly
    Unfall – accident
    Pedal – pedal
    brechen
       – to break (broke, broken)

5. Weil er keinen Helm trug, fiel sein Kopf in den Schlamm.   Helm – helmet
                                                                              Schlamm – mud

6. Jetzt ist er im Krankenhaus und wartet auf einen neuen Kopf.

Exercise 19 – Fill in the correct forms of the following verbs.

to explain – to have – to be – to be – to get – not to have – to pay

We really (1) _____ excellent teachers last year. They (2) _____ everything very carefully to us. The tests (3) _____ quite difficult, but as we (4) _____ attention in the lessons, we (5) _____ any problems. At the end of the year we (6) _____ good reports, and so our parents (7) _____ happy.

Exercise 20 – Translation.

careful – sorgfältig, genau

report – hier: Zeugnis

1. Peter musste vor vier Wochen seine Fahrprüfung ablegen.

Fahrprüfung ablegen – to take a driving-test

2. Er bekam seinen Führerschein und durfte am Nachmittag mit seinem neuen Auto fahren.

Führerschein – driving-licence
bekommen – to get (got, got)

3. Kein erfahrener Fahrer musste mit ihm fahren.

erfahren – experienced

4. Aber schon nach einigen Metern hatte er einen Unfall.

5. Er musste bremsen, weil fünf blöde Enten über die Straße liefen und ihre Eier verloren.

bremsen – to brake (broke, broken)
blöd – stupid
Ente – duck

6. Wegen der Eier war die Straße nass, und Peter rutschte geradeaus in eine Verkehrsampel.

nass – wet
rutschen – to slip, to skid
Verkehrsampel – traffic lights

7. Aber er hatte Glück, weil er angeschnallt war.

Glück haben – to be lucky
angeschnallt sein – to wear a seatbelt (wore, worn)

8. Auch sein Auto war in Ordnung – es war nur ein klein wenig gelb, und so musste er es am Nachmittag waschen.

in Ordnung sein – to be o.k.
ein klein wenig – a bit

9. Die nächsten zwei Wochen durfte er nicht mehr mit seinem Wagen fahren und musste deshalb mit seinem alten Motorroller in die Schule fahren.

Motorroller – scooter

10. Und die Moral von der Geschicht': Fahr' über Enteneier nicht!

Moral – moral

The past progressive

Beispiele

1. Aussagesätze

1. I	was	doing	my homework	all morning.
2. You	were	writing	letters	all afternoon.
3. He	was	cleaning	his bike	all Sunday.
She	was	riding	her horse	the whole day.
It	was	making	a nest	for two hours.
4. We	were	eating	a cake	during the match.
5. You	were	reading	a book	when she came in.
6. They	were	sleeping		when the phone rang.

2. Verneinte Sätze

1. I	was	not	(wasn't)	doing	my homework	all morning.
2. You	were	not	(weren't)	writing	letters	all afternoon.
3. He	was	not	(wasn't)	cleaning	his bike	all afternoon.
She	was	not	(wasn't)	riding	her horse	the whole day.
It	was	not	(wasn't)	making	a nest	for two hours.
4. We	were	not	(weren't)	eating	a cake	during the match.
5. You	were	not	(weren't)	reading	a book	when she came in.
6. They	were	not	(weren't)	sleeping		when the phone rang.

3. Fragen

1.	Was	I	doing	my homework	all morning?
2.	Were	you	writing	a letter	all afternoon?
3. When	was	he	cleaning		his bike?
	Was	she	riding	her horse	the whole day?
What	was	it	making		for two hours?
4. When	were	we	eating		a cake?
5. When	were	you	reading		a book?
6.	Were	they	sleeping		when the phone rang?

Bildung

Das *past progressive* (Verlaufsform des Imperfekts/der 1. Vergangenheit) wird gebildet aus der entsprechenden **past tense**-Form von **to be** (*was* in der 1. und 3. Person Singular, bei allen anderen Personen *were*) und der *ing*-Form des Verbs:

Bildung		past tense von *to be*	ing-Form des Verbs	
to **go**:	I	was	go**ing**	to the supermarket.
to **fish**:	They	were	fish**ing**	in the pool.

Zu Besonderheiten bei der Bildung der *ing*-Form: Vergleiche das Grammatikkapitel zum *present progressive*.

Übersetzungs-Tipp   Bei der Übersetzung vom Englischen ins Deutsche wird die *ing*-Form nicht mitübersetzt. Die einzige Möglichkeit, bei der die *ing*-Form sichtbar werden kann, ist beim Einfügen von *gerade*:

I	**was reading**	a book when the phone rang.
Ich	**las (gerade)**	ein Buch, als das Telefon klingelte.

He	**was overtaking**	a car when a lorry appeared at the end of the bend.
Er	**überholte (gerade)**	ein Auto, als ein Lkw am Ende der Kurve auftauchte.

Frage und Verneinung

Zur Satzstellung und zu Besonderheiten bei Verben mit Präpositionen siehe das Kapitel *Allgemeine Regeln*.

Da das *past progressive* bereits mit einem **Hilfsverb** gebildet wird, darf man bei Frage und Verneinung nicht mit *to do* umschreiben:

Were	you writing	a letter?
Hast	du	einen Brief geschrieben?

He	**was** not singing	in the lesson.
Er	sang nicht	in den Stunden.

Verwendung

Das *past progressive* wird verwendet

➤ **bei Handlungen, die sich in der Vergangenheit über einen längeren Zeitraum erstreckten:**

I	**was doing**	my homework the **whole afternoon** yesterday.
Gestern	**habe**	ich **den ganzen Nachmittag** meine Hausaufgaben **gemacht**.

He	**was repairing**	the car	**from six till eight**.
Er	**reparierte**	das Auto	**von sechs bis acht**.

Hier wird die Dauer des Vorgangs betont – nicht die Tatsache, dass das Auto repariert wurde.

Will man nur die Tatsache der Reparatur (nicht den Vorgang) hervorheben, steht das *simple past*:

He	**repaired**	the car from six till eight yesterday.	We can pick it up now.
Er	**reparierte**	gestern das Auto von sechs bis acht.	Wir können es jetzt bekommen.

Hier ist nicht wichtig, wie lange er gebraucht hat, sondern dass das Auto fertig ist.

He	**was repairing**	a car from six till eight yesterday.	So he didn't repair ours afterwards.
Er	**reparierte**	gestern ein Auto von sechs bis acht.	Deshalb machte er unseres danach nicht mehr.

Hier ist die Tatsache wichtig, dass er **zwei Stunden lang** ein Auto reparierte und danach keine Lust mehr hatte, weiterzumachen.

➤ **bei Handlungen, die zu einem bestimmten Zeitpunkt in der Vergangenheit im Verlauf waren:**

Diese Handlungen werden oft von einer anderen Handlung unterbrochen:

I	**was sitting**	in my room	when suddenly the phone rang.
Ich	**saß**	in meinem Zimmer,	als plötzlich das Telefon klingelte.
We	**were waiting**	for the bus	when it began to rain.
Wir	**warteten gerade**	auf den Bus,	als es zu regnen anfing.

Ausnahmen

> **Zustandsverben und Verben der Sinneswahrnehmung stehen nicht in der Verlaufsform:**
> (z. B. *to matter, to contain, to look, to see*)   **Wichtig!**

I	**didn't see**	him yesterday,	but it	**didn't matter**.
Ich	**sah**	ihn gestern nicht,	aber es	**machte nichts aus**.
The dustbin constantly	**contained**	a lot of valuable things.		
Der Mülleimer	**enthielt**	immer viele wertvolle Dinge.		

Aufzählung von Handlungen zu Informationszwecken:

Bei Aufzählungen, deren Handlungen sich zwar über einen längeren Zeitraum in der Vergangenheit erstrecken, bei denen es aber nicht auf den Verlauf dieser Handlungen sondern auf die bloße Information ankommt, wird nicht das *past progressive*, sondern das *simple past* verwendet.

We **watched** a film first, then we **had** dinner, and then we **waited** for him to come home.
Zuerst **sahen** wir uns einen Film **an**, dann **aßen** wir zu Mittag und dann **warteten** wir darauf, dass er heimkam.

In the morning we **had** breakfast from nine till eleven, then we **swam** in the afternoon, and then we **danced** from eight till midnight.
Am Morgen **frühstückten** wir von neun bis elf, dann **schwammen** wir nachmittags und dann **tanzten** wir von acht bis Mitternacht.

Zeitangaben

> Häufig beim *past progressive* verwendete Zeitangaben sind: **Wichtig!**
> ➤ all morning, all afternoon, all day
> ➤ two hours, three days, four weeks long etc.
> ➤ during (the match, the lesson, etc.)
> ➤ all day long, all night long, all morning etc.
> ➤ while

Exercise 1 – Fill in the correct forms of the past progressive.

1. Yesterday I _____ (to sleep) all morning.

2. We _____ (to have) dinner for two hours last night.

essay – Aufsatz

3. They _____ (to write) an essay all morning.

4. Jill _____ (to wait) for the bus for more than three hours.

5. My parents _____ (to watch) TV all morning.

6. After lunch Tom and Jerry _____ (to clean) their bikes till the evening.

7. He _____ (to make) model planes all morning two days ago.

bath(tub) – Badewanne

8. She _____ (to sit) in the bath the whole day.

9. Who _____ you _____ (to talk) to yesterday morning?

10. The pupils _____ (to run) down the street.

to overtake – überholen (overtook, overtaken)
lorry – Lastwagen

11. The taxi-driver _____ (not to overtake) the lorry.

12. _____ you really _____ (to listen) to the teacher?

13. Jack _____ (to do) his homework all afternoon.

14. My parents _____ (to paint) the kitchen all morning.

jigsaw – Puzzle

15. They _____ (to put) together the pieces of the jigsaw for most of the day.

16. The pupils _____ (not to listen) to their teacher during the lesson.

to pay attention – aufpassen (paid, paid)

17. _____ you really _____ (to pay) attention at school?

18. I _____ (to watch) TV all night long.

19. The mechanics _____ (to clean) the car for more than five hours.

quite – ziemlich

20. She _____ (to look) at him for quite a long time.

21. The soldiers _____ (to drive) across the river.

witness – Zeuge

22. The policemen _____ (to interview) the witnesses.

23. The sun _____ (to shine) all morning.

24. He _____ (not to come) down the hall.

25. Where _____ you _____ (to wait) for us?

thouroughly *(adv.)* – sorgfältig, ausführlich

26. The politicians _____ (to discuss) everything thoroughly.

to feed (fed, fed) – füttern

27. The farmers _____ (to feed) the cows.

sentence – Satz

28. The pupils _____ (to translate) English sentences all morning.

29. Why _____ they _____ (not to listen)?

30. The cats _____ (to play) in the garden all day long.

31. I _____ (to watch) TV for some time.

32. They _____ (to run) across the street.

square – (Markt-)Platz

33. She _____ (to cross) the square.

34. The parents _____ (to discuss) the problem.

35. Mike _____ (to study) all morning.

Exercise 2 – Here are some answers, find the questions. Ask for the words in bold.

1. _____? – He was watching **Robin Hood**.
2. _____? – **Jack** was running across the field.
3. _____? – Sandy was sitting **in the classroom**.
4. _____? – **No,** I wasn't paying attention.
5. _____? – **Tom** was driving the car.
6. _____? – We were doing **maths**.
7. _____? – My father was cleaning **my bike**.
8. _____? – He was explaining **the tenses**.
9. _____? – They were learning **English**.
10. _____? – **Susan** was carrying the luggage.
11. _____? – They were discussing **the problem**.
12. _____? – He was looking for **his friend**.
13. _____? – She was taking care of the **babies**.

to pay attention – aufpassen (paid, paid)

luggage – Gepäck

Exercise 3 – Make sentences.

1. all morning/my brother/to read/his newspaper/two weeks ago

   _____

   _____

2. I/the irregular verbs/to learn/all yesterday morning

   _____

3. last week/every day/to write/essays/we/during the lessons

   essay – Aufsatz

   _____

   _____

4. the whole day/two days ago/to watch/the children/TV

   _____

Exercise 4 – Translation.

1. Vor zwei Tagen haben wir zwei Stunden lang gefrühstückt.

   frühstücken – to have breakfast

   _____

2. Gestern hat uns unser Lehrer drei Stunden lang das Past progressive erklärt.

   erklären (jemandem) – to explain (to sb.)

   _____

3. Ich habe vorgestern mehr als 30 Minuten auf meinen Bus gewartet.

   _____

4. Mein Bruder hat gestern den ganzen Abend ferngesehen.

   _____

Vergleich:
Simple past – Past progressive

Simple past und *past progressive* gehören zu den *past tenses* (Zeiten der Vergangenheit),
das heißt, *past tense* ist der Überbegriff für diese beiden Zeiten.

Past tense

Simple past

➤ Wiederholte, einmalige oder aufeinanderfolgende
in der Vergangenheit stattfindende und auch abge-
schlossene Handlungen

➤ Historische Ereignisse
(*yesterday, two days ago, last year, last century* etc.)

He	**did**	a test	two years ago.
We	**read**	two books	every day.
You	**bought**	a book	last week.
We	**walked**		yesterday.
I	**sat**	here	last night.

➤ Umschreibung mit *to do* bei Frage und Verneinung

I **didn't**	**sit**	here	last night.
Did you	**sit**	here	last night?

Past progressive

➤ In der Vergangenheit sich über einen längeren
Zeitraum erstreckende Handlungen

➤ Handlungen, die zu einem bestimmten Zeitpunkt in
der Vergangenheit im Verlauf waren und oft durch
ein anderes, plötzlich eintretendes Ereignis unterbrochen werden (*two hours long, all morning, while* etc.)

John	**was**	**doing**	a test	all morning.
We	**were**	**reading**		all day long.
You	**were**	**watching**	TV	for two hours.
We	**were**	**walking**		all afternoon.
I	**was**	**sitting**	here	all night long.

➤ keine Umschreibung mit *to do* bei Frage und
Verneinung

I	**wasn't**	**sitting**	here	all night long.
Were you		**sitting**	here	all night long?

Übersetzungs-Tipp   Bei der Übersetzung vom Englischen ins Deutsche gibt es keinen Unterschied zwischen
past progressive und *simple past*:

He	**was working**	all day yesterday.
Er	**arbeitete**	gestern den ganzen Tag.

He	**worked**	yesterday.
Er	**arbeitete**	gestern.

Exercise 1 – Simple past or past progressive? Fill in the correct forms.

1. While I _____ (to do) my homework, my father _____ _____ (to phone) me.

2. Last Sunday the Smiths _____ (to sit) in their garden when it suddenly _____ (to begin) to rain.

3. What _____ you _____ (to do) when I _____ (to see) you at school?

4. Mr Jackson _____ (to drive) down the road when a lorry _____ (to crash) into him.

5. My last holidays _____ (to be) really boring. First we _____ (to go) to Italy, then we _____ (to go) to Spain, and then we _____ (to stay) in Portugal.

6. Sandy and Marc _____ (to talk) during the English lesson until the teacher _____ (to tell) them to be quiet.

7. When the killer _____ (to come) into the room, the police _____ (to wait/already) for him.

8. Yesterday we _____ (to decide) to go to the cinema. When the film _____ (to begin), we _____ (to sit) down. The other people _____ (to sit/already) there.

9. John _____ (to wait) for his girlfriend until ten o'clock. Then he _____ (to leave) the bus stop.

10. We _____ (not to play) tennis yesterday because it _____ (to rain) the whole afternoon.

11. Terry _____ (to overtake) a lorry when a car _____ (to appear) in front of him.

suddenly – plötzlich

lorry – Lastwagen

boring – langweilig

until – bis

to decide – sich entscheiden

to appear – auftauchen, erscheinen

Exercise 2 – Translation.

1. Gestern sind wir nach Schottland geflogen.

   _____

2. Wir saßen den ganzen Vormittag im Flugzeug – es war wirklich schrecklich.

   _____

   _____

3. Bevor wir ausstiegen, gab es einige alte Kartoffeln und ein paar seltsame Würste.

   _____

   _____

Vormittag – morning

aussteigen – to get out (got, got)
ein paar – some
seltsam – strange

Execrcise 3 – Simple past or past progressive? Fill in the correct forms.

suddenly – plötzlich

The day before yesterday I (1) .... (to read) a book. Suddenly the phone (2) .... (to ring). It (3) .... (to be) my mother. She (4) .... (to talk) to me for more than three hours. After the phone call I (5) .... (to go) to bed. I (6) .... (to sleep) for more than 15 hours. Then I (7) .... (to get) up. At school we (8) .... (to wait) for our teacher all day long, but he (9) .... (not to come) because he (10) .... (to be) ill. So we (11) .... (to sit) there and (12) .... (not to know) what to do. Some pupils (13) .... (to learn) their new vocabulary, some (14) .... (to play) cards. We (15) ....

noisy – laut
headmaster – Direktor

(to be) really noisy. Suddenly our headmaster (16) .... (to come) in and (17) .... (to tell) us to be quiet.

at once – sofort

So everybody (18) .... (to start) to work at once. But we (19) .... (only/to work) until the headmaster (20) .... (to leave) the room again.

Exercise 4 – Translation.

1. Tom: „Was hast du gestern den ganzen Nachmittag gemacht, Judy?"

fliegende Untertasse
      – flying saucer
Männchen – little man
vom Mars – from Mars

2. Judy: „Ich habe mir etwas Komisches angesehen, etwas über fliegende Untertassen und grüne Männchen vom Mars."

Anzeige – ad(vertisment)
entscheiden
      – to decide to do something
lernen – *hier:* to study

3. Tom: „In der Zeitung habe ich eine Anzeige darüber gelesen, aber ich entschied, den Film nicht anzuschauen, weil ich lernen wollte."

ziemlich – rather
jemanden einen Streich spielen
      – to play a trick on sb.

4. Judy: „Er war ziemlich langweilig. Die ganze Zeit spielten die Leute vom Mars anderen Leuten irgendwelche blöden Streiche."

Pech – bad luck

5. Tom: „Wirklich° Pech. Willst du mich noch° besuchen?"

6. Judy: „Ich weiß noch nicht. Vielleicht später. Bis bald."

° = nicht übersetzen

The present perfect (simple)

Das *present perfect (simple)* (einfaches Perfekt, 2. Vergangenheit) stellt für den Lernenden mitunter ein Problem dar, weil es mit drei deutschen Zeiten wiedergegeben werden kann, nämlich mit dem Präsens, dem Imperfekt und dem Perfekt.

Im Englischen wird das *present perfect* – anders als im Deutschen, wo es sowohl in Bezug auf die Vergangenheit als auch in Bezug auf die Gegenwart gebraucht werden kann – immer als eine **Zeit der Gegenwart** verwendet.

Im weiteren Verlauf wird das einfache Perfekt mit der Bezeichnung *present perfect* und nicht mit der Bezeichnung *present perfect simple* verwendet.

Beispiele

1. Aussagesätze

1.	I	**have**	**lived**	here	**for some time.**
2.	You	**have**	**worked**		**since 1982.**
3.	He	**has**	**driven**	a car	**for nine years.**
	She	**has**	**come**		**into the room.**
	It	**has**	**built**	a nest	**for three weeks.**
4.	We	**have**	**taken**	tests	**for many years.**
5.	You	**have**	**been**	to England	**before.**
6.	They	**have**	**come**	to see us.	

2. Verneinte Sätze

1.	I	**have**	**not**	**(haven't)**	**lived**	here	**for some time.**
2.	You	**have**	**not**	**(haven't)**	**worked**		**since 1982.**
3.	He	**has**	**not**	**(hasn't)**	**driven**	a car	**for nine years.**
	She	**has**	**not**	**(hasn't)**	**come**		**into the room.**
	It	**has**	**not**	**(hasn't)**	**built**	a nest	**for three weeks.**
4.	We	**have**	**not**	**(haven't)**	**taken**	tests	**for many years.**
5.	You	**have**	**not**	**(haven't)**	**been**	to England	**before.**
6.	They	**have**	**not**	**(haven't)**	**come**	to see us.	

Fragen

1.		**Have**	you	**lived**	here	**for some time?**
2.	Since when	**have**	you	**worked**	here?	
3.	Who	**has**		**driven**	a car	**for nine years?**
	Who	**has**		**come**		**into the room?**
	What	**has**	it	**built?**		
4.	What	**have**	you	**written**		**since last year?**
5.		**Have**	you	**been**	to England	**before?**
6.	Who	**has**		**come**	to see us?	

Bildung

Das *present perfect* wird aus der **simple present Form von *to have* und dem past participle** (3. Form) **des Verbs gebildet**. In der 3. Person Singular steht *has* bzw. *hasn't/has not*, bei allen anderen Personen *have* bzw. *haven't/have not*. Die *past participle*-Form des Verbs bleibt immer unverändert:

Bildung			*simple present* *von to have*	**+**	*past participle* *des Verbs*	
to **walk**:	We		**have**		**walked**.	
to **go**:	He		**has**		**gone**.	
to **see**:	I		**have**		**seen**	him.
to **be**:	She		**has**		**been**	here.

Eine Liste der unregelmäßigen Formen für das *past participle* befindet sich auf Seite 6.

Frage und Verneinung

Zur Satzstellung und zu Besonderheiten bei Verben mit Präpositionen siehe das Kapitel *Allgemeine Regeln*.

Da ein **Hilfsverb** bereits Bestandteil des *present perfect* ist, darf bei Frage und Verneinung nicht mit *to do* umschrieben werden:

Have	you	seen	him?
Hast	du	ihn	gesehen?

I	**have** not met	him.
Ich	habe	ihn nicht getroffen.

Verwendung

Zustandsverben sind z. B.:
– *to be*
– *to believe*
– *to have*
– *to know etc.*

Das *present perfect* wird verwendet

> ➤ **bei Handlungen, die (in Verbindung mit Zustandsverben) in der Vergangenheit begonnen haben und immer noch andauern:**

He	**has known**	her	**since September**.
Er	**kennt**	sie	**seit September**.

(Er hat sie im September kennen gelernt und kennt sie immer noch.)

We	**have been**	on holiday **for ten days**.
Wir	**sind**	**seit zehn Tagen** im Urlaub.

(Der Urlaub hat vor zehn Tagen begonnen und dauert immer noch an.)

> ➤ **bei Handlungen, die in einem noch andauernden oder kurz vor dem Zeitpunkt des Sprechens beendeten Zeitraum einmal, mehrmals, manchmal oder nie stattgefunden haben:**

In this century	scientists **have made many** inventions.
In diesem Jahrhundert	**haben** Wissenschaftler viele Erfindungen **gemacht**.

(Der Zeitabschnitt *dieses Jahrhundert* dauert immer noch an.)

They	**have taken** two tests **this year**.
Sie	**haben in diesem Jahr** zwei Arbeiten **geschrieben**.

(Der Zeitabschnitt *dieses Jahr* dauert immer noch an.)

Aber:

Tom	**had**	a lousy breakfast today.
Tom	**hatte**	heute ein miserables Frühstück.

(Diese Aussage wird am Abend gemacht.)

Dagegen:

She	**hasn't eaten**	anything today.
Sie	**hat**	heute noch nichts **gegessen**.

(Diese Aussage bezieht sich auf die Zeit vom Morgen bis zum Abend.)

➤ **bei Handlungen, die in der Vergangenheit stattgefunden und Auswirkungen auf die Gegenwart haben:**

I	**have broken**	my arm,	**so I can't write today.**
Ich	**habe**	mir den Arm **gebrochen,**	**deshalb kann ich heute nicht schreiben**.

(Der Vorgang des Unglücks, der in der Vergangenheit stattgefunden hat und auch beendet wurde, dauert nicht mehr an, aber die Auswirkungen sind vorhanden.)

I'm not allowed to go out tonight because **I have taken** a bad test.
Ich darf heute nicht ausgehen, weil ich eine schlechte Schulaufgabe **geschrieben habe**.
(Die Schulaufgabe wurde zwar in der Vergangenheit geschrieben, aber das Ergebnis wirkt sich auf die Gegenwart aus.)

Sobald eine Zeitangabe der Vergangenheit (*yesterday, last year, two weeks ago* etc.) im Satz erscheint, muss das *simple past* stehen. Es spielt dann keine Rolle, ob diese Handlungen Auswirkungen auf die Gegenwart haben:	**Vorsicht!**

Yesterday I **broke** my arm.	That's why I can't play football today.	Vergleiche:
Gestern **habe** ich mir den Arm **gebrochen**.	Ich kann deshalb heute nicht Fußball spielen.	Grammatikkapitel zum *simple past*

I	**got**	a bad report **last week,**	so I must learn more now.
Ich	**bekam**	**letzte Woche** ein schlechtes Zeugnis,	deshalb muss ich jetzt mehr lernen.

Die Auswirkung einer in der Vergangenheit abgeschlossenen Handlung auf die Gegenwart muss direkt im Anschluss an diese Handlung erscheinen, wenn man das *present perfect* verwenden will. Da fast alle vergangenen Handlungen in irgendeiner Weise Auswirkungen auf die Gegenwart haben, könnte man sonst immer das *present perfect* verwenden:	**Vorsicht!**

Tom **learned** English at school.   At university he studied Spanish.
Tom **hat** in der Schule Englisch **gelernt**.   An der Universität studierte er Spanisch.
(Natürlich hat das Erlernen der englischen Sprache Auswirkungen auf die Gegenwart, da Tom jetzt etwas über diese Sprache weiß. Aber hier ist kein direkter Bezug zur Gegenwart vorhanden.)

Aber:

Because Tom **has learned** English, he can apply for a job in Dover now.
Weil Tom Englisch **gelernt hat**, kann er sich jetzt um eine Stelle in Dover bewerben.
(Hier ist der direkte Bezug der vergangenen Handlung zur Gegenwart hergestellt.)

➤ **bei Handlungen, die erst kurz vorher passiert sind (in Verbindung mit *just*):**

My mother	**has**	**just**	**come**	into the room.
Meine Mutter	**ist**	**gerade**		ins Zimmer	**gekommen.**

I	**have**	**just**	**seen**	him disappear.
Ich	**habe** ihn	**gerade**		verschwinden	**sehen**.

| **Wichtig:** | **Sobald jedoch eine Zeitangabe mit *ago* vorkommt, muss man das *simple past* verwenden, auch wenn die Handlung erst kurz vorher beendet wurde:** |

	He	**arrived**	a minute	**ago.**
	Er	**kam**	**vor** einer Minute	**an.**
	I	**told**	him a second	**ago.**
	Ich	**habe**	es ihm	**gerade erst gesagt.**

| **Übersetzungs-Tipp** | Bei der Übersetzung vom Deutschen ins Englische muss Folgendes beachtet werden: |

➤ **Ein deutsches Präsens (a) oder Imperfekt (b) muss im Englischen oft mit dem *present perfect* wiedergegeben werden. Es kommt darauf an, ob eine der oben angegebenen Bedingungen zutrifft:**

a) Ich **bin** seit zwei Stunden hier. (bin = **Präsens**)
   I **have been** here for two hours. (have been = **present perfect**)
   (Der Vorgang begann in der Vergangenheit und dauert immer noch an.)

b) Wir **hatten** dieses Jahr nette Lehrer. (hatten = **Imperfekt**)
   We **have had** nice teachers this year. (have had = **present perfect**)
   (Der Vorgang findet in einem noch nicht abgeschlossenen Zeitraum statt: *this year.*)

➤ **Das englische Hilfsverb *have/has* kann ins Deutsche sowohl mit einer Form von *haben* (a) wie auch mit einer Form von *sein* (b) übersetzt werden:**

a) He **has worked** hard.
   Er **hat** hart gearbeitet.

b) We **have gone** to the club.
   Wir **sind** in den Club gegangen.

➤ **Muss ein deutsches Präsens (in Verbindung mit *schon*) im Englischen mit dem *present perfect* wiedergegeben werden, wird im Englischen *already* (*schon*) normalerweise weggelassen:**

Er **ist schon** seit drei Stunden hier. (ist = **Präsens**)
He **has been** here for three hours. (has been = **present perfect**)

Zeitangaben

Häufig beim *present perfect* verwendete Zeitangaben sind:

| **Wichtig!** | ➤ since/for
➤ this week/month/century etc.
➤ so far, until now, up to now |

| **Übersetzungs-Tipp** | Das deutsche, zeitlich gebrauchte *vor* (vor zwei Wochen, Monaten, Jahren etc.) wird immer mit *ago* übersetzt und verlangt normalerweise das *simple past* (siehe dort): |

Two days ago they **went** to the zoo.
Vor zwei Tagen gingen sie in den Zoo.

Three years ago there **were** many tourists.
Vor drei Jahren gab es viele Touristen.

Zur Übersetzung des englischen *for* siehe das nächste Grammatikkapitel.

Since – for

Da *since* und *for* häufig in Verbindung mit dem *present perfect* oder dem *present perfect progressive* (vgl. nächstes Grammatikkapitel) stehen, wird dieses Grammatikkapitel hier eingefügt.

... beim present perfect (progressive)

since und *for* werden als Präposition beim *present perfect* und beim *present perfect progressive* immer mit *seit* übersetzt:

He has been here	**for**	hours.	
Er ist schon	**seit**	Stunden	hier.

He has been working	**since**	four o'clock.	
Er arbeitet schon	**seit**	vier Uhr.	

Since wird immer mit einem **Zeitpunkt**, von dem ab etwas geschehen ist, verwendet: **since – Zeitpunkt**

He's been here	**since**	**five o'clock.**	
Er ist	**seit**	**fünf Uhr**	hier.

We've been sleeping	**since**	**yesterday.**	
Wir haben	**seit**	**gestern**	geschlafen.

They've been playing	**since**	**Monday.**	
Sie haben	**seit**	**Montag**	gespielt.

For wird immer mit einem **Zeitraum**, in dem etwas geschehen ist, verwendet: **for – Zeitraum**

He's been here	**for**	**two hours.**	
Er ist	**seit**	**zwei Stunden**	hier.

We've been sleeping	**for**	**two days.**	
Wir haben	**seit**	**zwei Tagen**	geschlafen.

They've been playing	**for**	**weeks.**	
Sie haben	**seit**	**Wochen**	gespielt.

Inhaltlich beziehen sich sowohl Sätze mit *since* wie auch mit *for* auf einen Zeitraum, in dem etwas geschehen ist bzw. immer noch geschieht. Nur ist bei *since* der Beginn dieses Zeitraums konkret festgelegt, während sich *for* auf den ganzen Zeitraum bezieht.   **since – for Unterscheidung**

Eine Hilfe für die Verwendung von *for* bietet das Anfügen von *-lang* an den jeweiligen Zeitraum:

He has been writing	**for**	**hours.**
Er schreibt schon	**seit**	**Stunden.**
(Er schreibt schon		**stundenlang.**)

He's been learning	**for**	**six days.**
Er lernt schon	**seit**	**sechs Tagen.**
(Er lernt schon		**sechs Tage lang**.)

Die Anfügung von *-lang* wäre bei *since* nicht möglich:

He's been doing his homework	**since**	**five o'clock.**
Er macht seine Hausaufgaben schon	**seit**	**fünf Uhr.**

(Fünf Uhr lang ist logischerweise hier nicht möglich.)

Weitere Verwendungen

1. *Since* als Konjunktion mit der Bedeutung seit

seit

Since als Konjunktion mit der Bedeutung *seit* kann mit folgenden Zeiten verwendet werden:

➤ **mit dem *simple past*:**

Es wird im Nebensatz, das heißt in dem mit *since* eingeleiteten Satzteil, eine Handlung beschrieben, die in der Vergangenheit stattfand. Im Hauptsatz muss das *present perfect* oder *present perfect progressive* stehen:

He	**has been** ill	**since**	he	**was born**.
Er	**ist** krank,	**seit**	er	**geboren wurde**.

We	**have been working**	**since**	we	**came** home.
Wir	**haben gearbeitet,**	**seit**	wir	nach Hause **gekommen sind**.

➤ **mit dem *present perfect*:**

Es wird eine Handlung beschrieben, die in der Vergangenheit begann und immer noch andauert:

Nothing has happened	**since**	he	**has been**	here.
Nichts ist passiert,	**seit**	er	hier **ist**.	

➤ **mit dem *present perfect progressive*:**

Es wird im Nebensatz, das heißt in dem mit *since* eingeleiteten Satzteil, eine Handlung beschrieben, die in der Vergangenheit stattfand. Im Hauptsatz muss das *present perfect* oder *present perfect progressive* stehen:

Since	he	**has been working**	harder,	his marks have become better.
Seit	er härter	**arbeitet,**		sind seine Noten besser geworden.

➤ **mit dem *past perfect* (a) bzw. *past perfect progressive* (b):**

Es drückt dann eine Handlung aus, die in der Vergangenheit begonnen hatte und auch in der Vergangenheit beendet wurde:

Vergleiche die entsprechenden Grammatikkapitel zu den jeweiligen Zeiten.

(a)	**Since** 1982 he	**had worked**	in Leeds,	then he went to Manchester.
	Seit 1982	**hatte**	er in Leeds **gearbeitet,**	dann ging er nach Manchester.

(b)	**Since** 9 o'clock he	**had been doing** his work	when suddenly his mother came in.
	Seit 9 Uhr	**hatte** er seine Arbeit **gemacht,**	als plötzlich seine Mutter herein kam.

2. *Since* als Adverb

seither
seit dieser Zeit

Since als Adverb in der Bedeutung *seither* oder *seit dieser Zeit* kann mit dem *present perfect* (a) bzw. dem *present perfect progressive* (b) verwendet werden. Es steht am Ende eines Satzes:

a)	He	**has been**	here	**since**.
	Er	**ist**	**seither**	hier **gewesen**.

b)	He	**has been working**	**since**.
	Er	**hat**	**seit dieser Zeit/seither** **gearbeitet**.

3. *Since als* Konjunktion mit der Bedeutung *da* oder *weil*

Since als Konjunktion mit der Bedeutung *da* oder *weil* kann mit allen Zeiten verwendet werden: **da/weil**

Since he **is** here now anyway,   you can talk to him at once.
Da   er nun schon mal hier **ist**,   kannst du gleich mit ihm sprechen.

Since he **had been** in England for ten years,   his English was perfect.
Weil   er zehn Jahre in England **gewesen war**,   war sein Englisch perfekt.

4. *For* als Präposition

For kann als Präposition **in der Bedeutung *lang*** mit dem simple past verwendet werden. Das Wort *lang* kann dabei auch weggelassen werden: **... lang**

In 1972   he **studied**   English **for five months**.
1972   **studierte** er   **fünf Monate (lang)** Englisch.

He   **worked**   as a secretary **for two years**.
Er   **arbeitete**   **zwei Jahre (lang)** als Sekretär.

5. *For* als Konjunktion

For kann als Konjunktion mit der Bedeutung *denn* mit allen Zeiten verwendet werden: **denn**

You shouldn't punish him   **for**   he is a good boy.
Du solltest ihn nicht bestrafen,   **denn**   er ist ein guter Junge.

We can't do the work   **for**   the problem hasn't been solved yet.
Wir können die Arbeit nicht machen,   **da**   das Problem noch nicht gelöst ist.

Exercise 1 – Fill in *for* or *since*.

to beat – schlagen

1. Munich has beaten Bremen _____ ten years.

2. We have drunk milk _____ two days.

3. Jack has had a bike _____ October.

4. I've had English _____ I was ten.

5. I've worn jeans _____ my fifth birthday.

6. They've had maths _____ last year.

7. The pupils have been on holiday _____ three months.

driving licence – Führerschein

8. Have you had your driving licence _____ last July?

9. I haven't seen him _____ August.

10. He has sent me letters _____ I left London.

11. The workers have thought about the problem _____ years.

several – einige

12. They have shown the same film _____ several months.

13. We haven't heard anything from him _____ last year.

14. Have they said anything _____ yesterday?

to happen – passieren

15. _____ ten days nothing interesting has happened here.

rubbish – Müll

16. They have sold rubbish _____ twenty years.

17. Have you seen him _____ the day before yesterday?

18. Sandy has been the best pupil of her class _____ three years.

19. Judy has been a girl _____ she was born.

20. I've made machines _____ many years.

21. The boys in class 8a have been worse than the girls _____ some time.

22. Have you heard anything from him _____ the last three years?

23. Sally has lain in hospital _____ May.

24. We have been in Spain _____ years.

25. I've had a bike _____ two months.

26. He's been away _____ the day before yesterday.

27. She's had English _____ some months.

28. He's been stupid _____ I first saw him.

29. We haven't had any problems _____ we left school.

30. Has he had any tests _____ last week?

31. Jack hasn't learned anything _____ some days.

32. They've been here _____ the last two hours.

33. I haven't heard anything from him _____ his birthday.

34. She hasn't been here _____ July.

Exercise 2 – Put the following verbs into the present perfect.

1. We _____ (to learn) English for three years.

2. Jill _____ just _____ (to come) back from a trip to Wales.

3. I _____ never _____ (to visit) my granddad.

4. Tom _____ (to collect) stamps.   to collect – sammeln
                                                                             stamp – Briefmarke

5. Jack _____ (to try) to do well in his exams this year.

6. Nothing funny _____ (to happen) today.   to happen – passieren

7. _____ you _____ (to guess) my answer?

8. My brother _____ (to teach) me all my life.

9. Our teachers _____ (to shout) a lot this year.   to shout – schreien

10. My father _____ (to cut) down some trees.

11. We _____ (to jump) over fences.   fence – Zaun

12. My sister _____ (not to brush) her teeth for two days.

13. We _____ (not to decide) where to go.

14. They _____ (to need) English all their lives.

15. For a long time Jill _____ (to want) to become a teacher.

16. Jill and Judy _____ (to play) in a football club.

17. We _____ (to try) everything.

18. _____ you _____ (to forget) your homework?

19. You _____ (not to clean) the blackboard.   blackboard – Tafel

Exercise 3 – Translation.

1. Dieses Jahr haben wir viel im Englischunterricht gelernt.

    _____

2. Hast du jemals Pinguine gesammelt?   sammeln – to collect

    _____

3. Unser Lehrer hat gerade das Zimmer betreten.   betreten – to enter

    _____

4. In dieser Woche haben wir im Sportunterricht oft Fußball gespielt.   Sportunterricht
                                                                              – physical education
    _____

5. Seit zwei Monaten lernen wir einmal in der Woche unregelmäßige Verben.

    _____

    _____

6. Sie hat sich ein neues Kleid gekauft.   Kleid – dress

    _____

Vergleich:
Present perfect – Simple past

Present perfect	Simple past
➤ Handlungen, die in der Vergangenheit beginnen und immer noch andauern	➤ In der Vergangenheit abgeschlossene Handlungen
➤ Handlungen, die erst kurz zuvor beendet wurden	
➤ Handlungen mit Auswirkungen auf die Gegenwart	
➤ Handlungen in einem nicht abgeschlossenen Zeitraum	

Present perfect			Simple past			
I	**have learned**	English since 1982.	I	**learned**	English	yesterday.
He	**has eaten**	ham this year.	Jack	**ate**	cornflakes	two days ago.
Mac	**has broken**	his arm, so he can't write now.	Jill	**broke**	her arm	yesterday.
Jack	**has caught**	penguins for two weeks.	Jack	**caught**	a penguin	last week.
We	**have been**	here for ten days.	We	**were**	here	last month.
Jack	**has** just **entered** the room.		Jack	**entered**	the room	two minutes ago.

Present perfect	Simple past
➤ keine Umschreibung mit *to do* bei Frage und Verneinung	➤ Umschreibung mit *to do* bei Frage und Verneinung

Present perfect			Simple past			
Jack	**hasn't eaten**	his dinner.	We	**didn't enter**	the room	two minutes ago.
	Has Jack **eaten**	his dinner?		**Did** you **enter**	the room	two minutes ago?

Present perfect	Simple past
➤ häufig verwendete Zeitangaben: since, for, this week/month etc, so far, until now, up to now	➤ häufig verwendete Zeitangaben: yesterday, the day before yesterday, two days ago, last week, last month, last year, last century, in 1957

Exercise 1 – Present perfect or simple past?

We (1) _____ (to be) at school in Eton for almost two years now. During this time we (2) _____ (to learn) a lot. We (3) _____ (to have) all the important subjects like English, German, maths or geography. Subjects like arts or physical education (4) _____ (to be) rather easy in the beginning, but (5) _____ (to become) more and more difficult over the last few months. We (6) _____ (to have) very good teachers so far. Last year we (7) _____ (to have) the same teachers as this year. But our tests (8) _____ (to be) better then than now. Since the beginning of this year we (9) _____ (to be) quite lazy. We (10) _____ (not to do) our homework carefully and we (11) _____ (not to be) quiet in the lessons either. So we (12) _____ (not to do) well in tests this year. Last week we (13) _____ (to have) a test in English and the result (14) _____ (to be) a catastrophe. Our dear Mr Brown (15) _____ (to be) very angry. Since that day he (16) _____ (to give) us a lot of homework and we (17) _____ (to work) a lot. This (18) _____ (to be) the worst time at Eton. In the first year we (19) _____ (to find) everything very easy, but since September it (20) _____ (to be) quite hard. We (21) _____ (to do) all the difficult grammar problems in English and German, and maths (22) _____ (to become) difficult, too. But since the beginning of the year we (23) _____ (to be) in a fantastic classroom. One year ago our headmaster (24) _____ (to decide) to give us the room in the basement. So for five months we (25) _____ (to be) downstairs.

almost – fast
in Eton – in (der Stadt) Eton

important – wichtig

physical education
*   – Sport(unterricht)*
rather – ziemlich

lazy – faul

careful – sorgfältig

homework – Hausaufgabe/n

at Eton – in (dem College) Eton

quite – ziemlich

downstairs – unten

Exercise 2 – Translation.

1. Seit fünf Jahren hat unsere Regierung eine Energiekrise.

   _____

   Regierung – government
   Energiekrise – energy crisis

2. Seit dieser Zeit konnten wir nicht mehr ins Ausland fahren, weil das° Benzin zu teuer war.

   _____

   (ins/im) Ausland – abroad
   Benzin – petrol (AE: gasoline)
   teuer – expensive

3. Letztes Jahr wollten wir eine Reise ins sonnige Spanien machen, aber wir mussten unseren Urlaub zu Hause verbringen, weil wir nicht genug Taschengeld hatten.

   _____

   _____

   Reise – journey
   Urlaub – holidays
   Taschengeld – pocket money

4. Wir haben seither unsere Ferien in unserem Garten verbracht.

   _____

° = nicht übersetzen

Exercise 3 – Make sentences.

1. to Munich/last Easter/John and Mary/to fly

2. since his accident/my father/in hospital/to be

3. to be/ever/to London/Jack ?

4. to sing/Michael Jackson/pop songs/at his last concert

Exercise 4 – Here are some answers, find the questions.
Ask for the words in bold.

1. _____ ? – I've been here **since yesterday**.

2. _____ ? – Tom drank **milk** last night.

3. _____ ? – **No**, we haven't unloaded the van yet.

4. _____ ? – **Nothing** has happened to Jim.

5. _____ ? – I was worried about **maths**.

6. _____ ? – They've pulled down **our school**.

7. _____ ? – My parents bought **a car**.

8. _____ ? – **Mary** got the worst test result.

to unload – ent-, abladen
van – Lastwagen

to happen – passieren

to worry – sich Sorgen machen

to pull down – abreißen

to buy – kaufen
 (bought, bought)

Exercise 5 – Translation.

1. Vor zwei Tagen hatten die Schüler der 6 d Angst vor der Schule, weil sie eine Schulaufgabe über das Present Progressive schrieben.

Angst haben vor etwas –
 to be frightened of
eine Schulaufgabe schreiben
 – to have a test

2. Sie saßen die ganze Stunde da und dachten über die schwierigen Sätze nach.

Schulstunde – lesson
da sitzen – to sit there
 (sat, sat)

3. Seither machen sie sich Sorgen um ihre Noten.

sich Sorgen machen (um) –
 to be worried (about)
(Schul-)Note – mark

4. Sie haben die Schulaufgabe noch nicht zurückbekommen, weil der Lehrer sie noch nicht korrigiert hat.

korrigieren – to correct

5. Sie haben schon oft schwierige Übungen gemacht, und auch die anderen Lehrer haben ihnen seltsame Arbeitsblätter gegeben.

seltsam – strange
Arbeitsblatt – worksheet

Exercise 6 – Fill in the correct forms of the verbs.

We (1) _____ (to be) in a holiday camp since September. We (2) _____   holiday camp – Ferienlager

(to have) a brilliant time. The people (3) _____ (to be) nice, and the food

(4) _____ (to taste) excellent. The camp last year in Spain (5) _____

(to be) not as good as this one. They (6) _____ (not to have) a swimming

pool and the rooms (7) _____ (to be) rather small. Since I (8) _____   rather – ziemlich

(to be) ten, I (9) _____ (to go) to a lot of places abroad. I (10) _____

(not to fly) by plane so far because I (11) _____ (to think) that it

(12) _____ (to be) too dangerous. So mostly I (13) _____ (to   dangerous – gefährlich

go) by bus or train so far. Only last year I (14) _____ (to ride) by bike,

but (15) _____ (not to enjoy) it.

Exercise 7 – Translation.

1. „Wo bist du gestern gewesen, Tom?" – „Ich war in der Stadt und habe Hefte für die   Heft – exercise-book
   Schule gekauft."

   _____

   _____

2. „Hast du jemals etwas für Englisch gelernt?" – „Bisher noch nicht, aber das war auch   jemals – ever
   nicht nötig, weil ich so gescheit bin."   bisher – so far
   gescheit – clever

   _____

   _____

3. „Mach die Türe auf, Tom, jemand hat gerade geklopft."   klopfen – to knock

   _____

   _____

4. „Leider habe ich meine Hausaufgaben nicht gemacht. Muss ich jetzt eine Extraüber-   leider – I'm afraid/unfortunately
   setzung schreiben?"   schreiben – hier: to do

   _____

   _____

5. „Wo bist du gewesen?" – „Ich war nirgends."   nirgends – not anywhere

   _____

6. „Hast du Sandy schon zu deiner Party eingeladen?" – „Ja, das habe ich gestern   einladen – to invite
   gemacht."

   _____

7. „Vor zwei Tagen habe ich fünf sehr teure Bücher gekauft. Deshalb habe ich heute kein   teuer – expensive
   Taschengeld mehr."   Taschengeld – pocket money

   _____

   _____

Exercise 8 – Simple past or present perfect? Fill in the correct forms.

to wear – tragen
   (wore, worn)

ugly – hässlich
dress – Kleid

Sarah (1) _____ (to wear) nice clothes all her life, but

three days ago she (2) _____ (to buy) an ugly dress. In the

evening she (3) _____ (to go) to the best disco in town

and everybody (4) _____ (to say): "What a horrible dress."

Since that day she (5) _____ (not to go) out again and she

(6) _____ (to spend) the evenings in her room. Yesterday she

shop assistant – Verkäufer(in)

(7) _____ (to take) the dress back to the shop, but the shop assistant

(8) _____ (not to want) to take it back. We (9) _____

_____ (not to see) her since then. I (10) _____

_____ (to try) to phone herlast night, but she (11) _____

_____ (not to answer). Poor girl.

Exercise 9 – Translation.

etwas bezahlen
   – to pay for something
   (paid, paid)

1. Gestern hat Judy ein schönes Kleid gekauft, aber sie hat es noch nicht bezahlt, weil sie
    kein Geld hatte.

    _____

    _____

Taschengeld – pocket money
sparen – to save

2. Sie bekommt seit drei Jahren £10 Taschengeld, aber sie hat bisher nichts gespart.

    _____

    _____

sich Sorgen machen – to worry
fett – fat

3. Seit einiger Zeit macht sie sich Sorgen, weil sie immer fetter wird.

    _____

    _____

eng – tight
Bluse – blouse
stehen/kleiden – to suit
wegwerfen – to throw away
   (threw, thrown)

4. Ihre Hosen sind jetzt zu eng und ihre Blusen stehen ihr nicht mehr; deshalb muss sie
    verschiedene Sachen wegwerfen.

    _____

    _____

hübsch – pretty

    _____

5. Obwohl sie seit letzten Mittwoch weniger isst, sieht sie immer noch nicht hübscher
    aus.

    _____

    _____

6. Aber dieses Problem hat sie schon ihr ganzes Leben. Arme Judy.

    _____

    _____

Exercise 10 – Make sentences.

1. not to see/Mary/John/since October

   _____

2. Peter/to leave/school/five years ago

   _____

   to leave – verlassen (left, left)

3. Friedhelm/to ride/since Monday/a motorbike

   _____

4. Susan/yesterday/to wear/a nice dress

   _____

   dress – Kleid

Exercise 11 – Fill in the correct form of the verbs.

Three months ago our teacher (1) _____ (to tell) us to learn more.

Since then we (2) _____ (to have) a hard time with a lot of work,

and so our results (3) _____ (to be) better. Last week, however, we

(4) _____ (to have) a difficult test. It (5) _____

(to be) about the present progressive. Till now our teacher (6) _____ (not

to have) the time to correct it because he (7) _____ (to give)

us a lot of new worksheets. On Wednesday we (8) _____ (to get)

worksheet – Arbeitsblatt

a translation, on Thursday he (9) _____ (to give) us a dictation.

We (10) _____ (to have) difficult things last year, too, but this year

everything (11) _____ (to become) even more difficult.

Exercise 12 – Fill in the correct forms of the verbs.

Peter (1) _____ (to get) worked up two weeks ago. Johnny, his little

to get worked up – sich aufregen (got, got)

penguin, (2) _____ (to have) an accident. He (3) _____

(to cross) the street when suddenly a big car (4) _____ (to appear) and

suddenly – plötzlich
to appear – erscheinen

(5) _____ (to crash) into some traffic lights. Because of the noise, Johnny

traffic lights – Verkehrsampel

(6) _____ (to be) so shocked that he (7) _____ (to fall)

on his little, nice nose. They (8) _____ (to take) him to hospital at once,

and he (9) _____ (not to be) out of bed since. He (10) _____

_____ (even/not to eat) any ice-cream, and only two days ago Peter

(11) _____ (to have to/to bring) him something to eat. Poor

Johnny!

Exercise 13 – Translation.

ankommen – to arrive
verbringen – to spend
                (spent, spent)

1. Wir sind vor drei Wochen in Schottland angekommen, um dort unsere Ferien zu verbringen.

Sehenswürdigkeit – sight

2. Seither waren wir in einigen Museen und haben viele andere Sehenswürdigkeiten gesehen.

am Anfang (von etwas)
   – at the beginning (of sth.)
schrecklich, fürchterlich
   – terrible

3. Am Anfang der Ferien war das Essen im Hotel sehr gut, aber seit einer Woche bekommen wir nur noch schreckliche Sachen.

4. Deshalb sind wir in dieser Woche nur zu McDonald's gegangen.

5. Als wir letztes Jahr in Italien waren, war das Essen viel besser.

6. Wir haben dort so viele Spaghetti und Pizzas bekommen, dass wir seit dieser Zeit solche Dinge nicht mehr essen wollen.

etwas satt haben –
   to be tired of sth.

7. Aber jetzt sind wir in Schottland und hätten gerne wieder Pizzas und Spaghetti, obwohl wir sie letztes Jahr so satt hatten.

froh sein – to be happy (that)

8. Deshalb sind wir froh, dass wir morgen wieder° nach Hause fahren können.

Exercise 14 – since or for? Fill in the correct words.

Two years ago we began to learn English. (1) _____ that time we

quite – ziemlich

have done a lot. It was quite easy in the beginning, but (2) _____ the

last two months we have had to work a lot. (3) _____ last week we

have often talked about the present progressive and (4) _____ the day

before yesterday we have only done translations. We haven't learned anything difficult like

that (5) _____ we started school.

° = nicht übersetzen

Exercise 15 – Here are some answers, find the questions.
Ask for the words in bold.

1. _____ ? – I have hated **French**.

2. _____ ? – They bought the book **yesterday**.

3. _____ ? – The Romans founded **London**.   to found – gründen

4. _____ ? – **Sarah** taught French last year.

5. _____ ? – We have been to **the zoo**.

6. _____ ? – I bought the book **yesterday**.

7. _____ ? – She's just finished **her homework**.

8. _____ ? – **No**, I couldn't go to the disco yesterday.

9. _____ ? – I didn't hear him **because I was sleeping**.

10. _____ ? – He found his bag **yesterday**.

11. _____ ? – We've seen him **twice**.   twice – zweimal

12. _____ ? – He's gone to **London**.

13. _____ ? – They have translated **everything**.

14. _____ ? – Judy ate **some oranges**.

15. _____ ? – My brother has gone to **New York**.

Exercise 16 – Translation.

1. Vor zwei Wochen habe ich mich aufgeregt, weil ich einen Unfall hatte.   sich aufregen – to get worked up (got, got)

_____

_____

2. Ein Schweizer Hubschrauber mit fünf verletzten Enten konnte in einer Kurve nicht mehr bremsen und krachte in mein altes, dreckiges Motorrad.   Schweizer – Swiss / Hubschrauber – helicopter / verletzt – injured / Ente – duck / Kurve – bend / krachen – to crash

_____

_____

_____

3. Ich fiel von meinem Motorrad herunter und darf seit dieser Zeit nicht mehr aufstehen.   herunterfallen – to fall down (fell, fallen) / aufstehen – to get up (got, got)

_____

_____

4. Gestern sah ich den ganzen Tag fern. Plötzlich kam (gab es) Donald Duck. Weil ich seit meinem Unfall Enten hasse, verließ ich das Krankenhaus sofort und bin seither zu Hause.   den ganzen Tag – all day long / verlassen – to leave (left, left) / sofort – at once

_____

_____

_____

Exercise 17 – Fill in *since* or *for*.

1. Mr John has been a teacher ▭▭▭▭ many years.

grammar school – Gymnasium

2. ▭▭▭▭ 1978 he has taught at a grammar school in Croydon.

3. He has had the 7a ▭▭▭▭ last September.

4. ▭▭▭▭ that time he has had a difficult time.

5. He has done the present perfect ▭▭▭▭ the last ten days.

Exercise 18 – Here are some answers, find the questions.
Ask for the words in bold.

1. ▭▭▭▭▭▭▭▭▭▭▭? – I did my homework **yesterday**.

2. ▭▭▭▭▭▭▭▭▭▭▭? – Jack has lived **in London** for two years.

3. ▭▭▭▭▭▭▭▭▭▭▭? – Jill has been **at home**.

dress – Kleid

4. ▭▭▭▭▭▭▭▭▭▭▭? – **Susan** bought a dress two days ago.

5. ▭▭▭▭▭▭▭▭▭▭▭? – Mr Jack taught children **last year**.

Exercise 19 – Present perfect or past tense? Fill in the correct tenses.

Two days ago my dog Fritz (1) ▭▭▭▭▭▭▭ (to sleep) all day. When he

(2) ▭▭▭▭▭ (to get) up, he (3) ▭▭▭▭▭▭▭ (to look) out

of the window and (4) ▭▭▭▭▭▭ (to see) that it (5) ▭▭▭▭▭

(to rain). Since then he (6) ▭▭▭▭▭ (not to eat) anything. He (7) ▭▭▭▭▭

▭▭▭▭▭ (to be) a stupid dog all his life, and so I (8) ▭▭▭▭▭

to be worried
 – sich Sorgen machen
to behave – sich verhalten

▭▭ (not to be worried) when I noticed that he (9) ▭▭▭▭▭▭▭ (to behave)

stupidly that day, too.

Exercise 20 – Fill in *since* or *for*.

1. He's played in a pop group ▭▭▭▭ five years.

2. We've lived in London ▭▭▭▭ 1952.

3. I've been here ▭▭▭▭ yesterday.

4. They haven't seen him ▭▭▭▭ years.

5. He's had his job ▭▭▭▭ Monday.

6. He's had his job ▭▭▭▭ last week.

7. Tom has gone to school ▭▭▭▭ three days.

8. I have had this problem ▭▭▭▭ two weeks.

9. We have seen him twice ▭▭▭▭ Friday.

10. She's been a secretary ▭▭▭▭ 1992.

11. Where has Tom been ▭▭▭▭ last year?

Exercise 21 – Make sentences.

1. pictures/to draw/my brother/never/any

2. not to feed/last year/the Jacksons/the animals/in the cowshed/in the mornings

   to feed (fed, fed) – füttern
   cowshed – Kuhstall

3. yet/to do/homework/John/his ?

4. in the cupboard/Jill's dog/last week/not to hide

   cupboard – Schrank

5. into the water/yesterday/Kate/to fall

Exercise 22 – Translation.

1. Ich mache mir seit einiger Zeit Sorgen um die Klasse 8a.

   sich Sorgen (um) machen
   – to be worried (about)

2. Seit zwei Wochen passen viele Schüler nicht auf und lernen nichts.

   aufpassen – to pay attention
   (paid, paid)

3. Vorgestern mussten sie ein wirklich leichtes Diktat über Krankenwagen und Tankstellen schreiben, aber niemand bekam eine Top-Note.

   Krankenwagen – ambulance
   Tankstelle – petrol station
   Top-Note – top grade

4. Deshalb habe ich mich entschlossen, heute einen Test zu schreiben.

   (sich) entscheiden – to decide
   schreiben – hier: to have

5. Aber davon geht die Welt für meine Schüler nicht unter.

   Welt ... nicht untergehen
   – not to be the end of the
   world

Exercise 23 – Fill in the correct forms of the verbs.

For years we (1) _____ (to go) on holiday to Scotland. Two years ago we (2) _____ (to fly) to Edinburgh, last year we (3) _____ (to spend) two weeks in Glasgow. Since that time our English (4) _____ (to become) better although we (5) _____ (not to have) many lessons at school. So we (6) _____ (to do) well in our tests this year. Only the dictations (7) _____ (not to be) very good. Last week my brother and I (8) _____ (to get) very bad marks. Never mind!

Exercise 24 – Here are some answers, find the questions.
Ask for the words in bold.

1.   ? – Tom has collected **crocodiles**.

2.   ? – We chose maths **yesterday**.

3.   ? – **Jim** had five tests last year.

4.   ? – They left **the books** in the bus.

5.   ? – Tom caught a penguin **yesterday**.

6.   ? – Judy has lived **in London**.

7.   ? – **The Jacksons** sold their house.

to collect – sammeln

Exercise 25 – Translation.

1. Gestern hat mich mein Freund zu einer Party eingeladen, obwohl ich ihn seit Wochen nicht mehr getroffen habe.

einladen – to invite
treffen – hier: to see (saw, seen)

2. Seit drei Jahren sind wir schon in derselben Schule, aber bis jetzt hatten wir kein Glück: wir waren immer in verschiedenen Klassen.

Glück haben – to be lucky
verschieden – different

3. Leider kann ich nicht zu seiner Party gehen, weil ich meinen Großvater zum Bahnhof bringen muss.

Großvater – grandpa
Bahnhof – station

4. Er wohnt südlich von London und muss mit dem Zug fahren, weil er seit Jahren kein eigenes Auto hat.

südlich von – south of

5. Vor fünf Jahren hatte er eines, ein schönes grünes, aber die Leute in seiner Straße haben es kaputt gemacht, weil es viel zu laut war.

etwas kaputt machen
*   – to break something*
*   (broke, broken)*

Exercise 26 – Simple past or present perfect? Fill in the correct forms.

1. I   (to see) him yesterday.

2. We   (not to see) him for years.

3. He   (to have) the piano since September.

4. Tom   (to steal) a motor bike last night.

5. We   (to have) excellent teachers this year.

6. I   (to do) my homework already.

Exercise 27 – Translation.

1. Wir sind schon seit drei Wochen in England.

2. Gestern war zum ersten Mal schönes Wetter.

   zum ersten Mal – for the first time

3. Wir machten einen Ausflug an die Küste.

   einen Ausflug machen
   – to go on a trip (went, gone)
   Küste – coast

4. Seit vielen Jahren gibt es an der Südküste Englands viele Touristen.

   Tourist – tourist

5. Aber seit einiger Zeit kommen nicht mehr so viele Besucher aus dem Ausland.

   Besucher – visitor
   (im/ins) Ausland – abroad

6. Vor 14 Tagen haben wir das Museum in Colchester besucht.

7. Wir brauchten nichts dafür zu bezahlen, weil der Onkel unseres Lehrers der Manager des Museums ist.

8. Er ist schon seit 35 Jahren in diesem Museum und sieht fast wie ein alter Ägypter aus.

   alt (historisch) – ancient
   Ägypter – Egyptian

9. Aber er ist ziemlich verrückt und fährt seit drei Jahren Motorrad.

   ziemlich verrückt – *hier:* a bit mad
   Motorrad fahren
   – to ride a motorbike (rode, ridden)

10. Gestern hatte er einen Unfall, weil er nicht auf den Verkehr aufpasste, sondern an eine römische Statue dachte.

    aufpassen – to pay attention (paid, paid)
    römisch – Roman
    Statue – statue

Exercise 28 – Fill in *since* or *for*.

1. The Smiths have lived in London   ten years.

2. My brother has been a teacher   yesterday.

3. We have learned English   last year.

4. I've had a boy-friend   ten days.

5. Bob has been in hospital   last week.

6. My father has been in the garden   three hours.

7. Ulli has been at school   she was eleven.

Exercise 29 – Translation.

beunruhigt sein – to be worried
Note – mark

1. Judy ist seit einigen Wochen beunruhigt, weil sie in Englisch keine guten Noten mehr hat.

Angst haben vor
    – to be frightened of

2. Sie hat Angst vor ihrem Lehrer, weil er ihr in diesem Jahr nur schlechte Noten gegeben hat.

hinaus werfen – to throw out
              (threw,
              thrown)
unordentlich – untidy

3. Vorgestern hat er sie aus dem Klassenzimmer geworfen, weil sie während des Unterrichts wieder einmal sehr unordentlich war.

4. Seither war sie nicht mehr in der Schule, sondern ist den ganzen Tag zu Hause geblieben.

leider – I'm afraid, unfortunately

5. Leider hilft ihr das überhaupt nicht: Sie kann ihrem Lehrer nicht zuhören und lernt deshalb nur wenig.

Exercise 30 – Fill in the correct forms of the verbs.

We (1) _____ (to be) on holiday in England for two weeks. The weather (2) _____ (to be) really excellent. Two years ago, when we (3) _____ (to go) to Italy, we (4) _____ (to spend) the nights in terrible hotels and only (5) _____ (to have) terrible food. The spaghettis (6) _____ (to taste) terrible there and the drinks (7) _____ (to look) horrible, too. We (8) _____ (not to eat) Italian food since then. So we (9) _____ (to eat) Chinese food at the moment. My brother (10) _____ (to want) to go to Spain next year. I (11) _____ (never/to travel) there, but my sister Mary (12) _____ (to drive) there with her car once and she (13) _____ (to like) it very much. She (14) _____ (not to be)

abroad – im/ins Ausland

abroad very often, so she (15) _____ (not to know) a lot about foreign countries.

She sometimes (16) _____ (to tell) us nice stories about her holidays although they (17) _____ (not to be) very interesting so far.

Exercise 31 – Make sentences.

1. she/to go/to school/two days ago

2. here/to be/for ten hours/we

3. to live/since last year/in Manchester/the Bells

4. in 1978/Tom/his driving test/to pass

    to pass – bestehen

5. Jim/to go/to the dentist/yesterday

    dentist – Zahnarzt

Exercise 32 – Translation.

1. Vor kurzem besuchte ich mit meinen Eltern zum ersten Mal einen Safari-Park.

    vor kurzem – not long ago

2. Ich habe schon immer Angst vor wilden Tieren gehabt, und deshalb war ich nicht sehr glücklich, als ein Löwe von einem Felsen auf unser Auto heruntersprang.

    Angst haben vor
    – to be afraid of sth.
    Löwe – lion
    Felsen – rock

3. Aber er war ziemlich jung – wahrscheinlich erst ein Jahr alt, und so machte ich mir keine Sorgen.

    ziemlich – rather, quite
    wahrscheinlich – probably
    sich Sorgen machen
    – to be worried

4. Wir fragten den Wärter der Tiere: „Ist das ihrer?" – „Nein, das ist nicht meiner, das ist ein Löwe aus einem anderen Zoo. Meine sind in ihren Höhlen."

    (Tier)Höhle – den

Exercise 33 – Here are some answers, find the questions.
Ask for the words in bold.

1.   ? – We've been **in the garden**.

2.   ? – Tom was in London **yesterday**.

3.   ? – He's had his job **for six years**.

4.   ? – He's lived in Leeds **since 1968**.

5.   ? – She bought **a book** two days ago.

6.   ? – **John** has just come into the room.

Exercise 34 – Translation.

1. Ich habe vor drei Wochen ein BMX-Rad bekommen.

ein Rennen veranstalten
– to have a race

2. Seit dieser Zeit wollen alle meine Freunde ein Rennen mit mir veranstalten.

Reifen – tyre
Bremse – brake
Lenkstange – handlebar

3. Wir können in den Wäldern fahren, weil wir spezielle Reifen, hervorragende Bremsen und sehr gute Lenkstangen haben.

Helm – helmet
schützen – to protect
Verletzung – injury

4. Wenn wir vom Rad fallen, schützen uns unsere Helme vor schlimmen Verletzungen am Kopf.

Lieblingsstrecke – favourite track
tief – deep
Schlamm – mud

5. Unsere Lieblingsrennstrecke hat eine Menge Kurven und nach Regen sogar einige Teile mit tiefem Schlamm.

Unfall – accident

6. Am letzten Samstag gab es einen schrecklichen Unfall.

bremsen – to brake
plötzlich – suddenly
Bremse – brake

7. Ich fuhr auf eine Kurve zu und wollte bremsen, als plötzlich meine Bremse entzweibrach.

zusammenstoßen, hineinrasen,
krachen – to crash

8. Dave fuhr gerade vor mir und ich raste in ihn hinein.

Helm – helmet

9. Er fiel von seinem Rad herunter und verlor seinen Helm.

gebrochen – broken
schmerzen – to hurt (hurt, hurt)

10. Sein Gesicht war voller Schlamm, sein Fuß war gebrochen und seine beiden Arme schmerzten fürchterlich.

Krankenwagen – ambulance
Krankenhaus – hospital

11. Der Krankenwagen brachte Dave ins Krankenhaus und seither ist er dort.

The present perfect progressive

Beispiele

1. Aussagesätze

1.	I	have	(I've)	been	working		for six hours.
2.	You	have	(You've)	been	watching	the film	since one o'clock.
3.	He	has	(He's)	been	living	here	for ten weeks.
	She	has	(She's)	been	driving		for two weeks.
	It	has	(It's)	been	building	a nest	all morning.
4.	We	have	(We've)	been	learning		for a long time.
5.	You	have	(You've)	been	doing	the test	for some time.
6.	They	have	(They've)	been	swimming	in the pool	all afternoon.

2. Verneinte Sätze

1.	I	have not	(I haven't)	been	working		for six hours.
2.	You	have not	(You haven't)	been	watching	the film	since one o'clock.
3.	He	has not	(He hasn't)	been	living	here	for ten weeks.
	She	has not	(She hasn't)	been	driving		for two weeks.
	It	has not	(It hasn't)	been	building	a nest	all morning.
4.	We	have not	(We haven't)	been	learning		for a long time.
5.	You	have not	(You haven't)	been	doing	the test	for some time.
6.	They	have not	(They haven't)	been	swimming	in the pool	all afternoon.

3. Fragen

1.		Have	I	been	working	for six hours?
2.	Have		you	been	watching	the film	since one o'clock?
3.	Where	has	he	been	living	for ten weeks?
	Why	has	she	been	driving	for two weeks?
	Has		it	been	building	a nest	all morning?
4.	What	have	we	been	learning	for a long time?
5.	Have		you	been	doing	the test	for some time?
6.	Where	have	they	been	swimming	all afternoon?

Bildung

Das *present perfect progressive* (Verlaufsform des Perfekt/der 2. Vergangenheit) wird aus der *present perfect*-Form von **to be** (*has been* in der 3. Person Singular, *have been* bei allen anderen Personen) und der ***ing*-Form des Verbs** gebildet:

Bildung			*present perfect*-Form von *to be*	*ing*-Form des Verbs	
to **work**:	I		**have been**	work**ing**	since 5 o'clock.
to **run**:	He		**has been**	runn**ing**	for ten minutes.

Zu Besonderheiten der Bildung der *ing*-Form vergleiche das Grammatikkapitel zum *present progressive*.

Übersetzungs-Tipp

Bei der Übersetzung vom Englischen ins Deutsche wird die *ing*-Form nicht mitübersetzt. Die einzige Möglichkeit, bei der die *ing*-Form *sichtbar* werden kann, ist bei der Verwendung des Präsens im Deutschen und/oder durch das Wort *schon*:

He	**has been living**	here for years.	(has been living – *present perfect progressive*)
Er	**lebt schon**	jahrelang hier.	(lebt – Präsens)

They	**have been working**	since five o'clock.	
Sie	**haben schon**	seit fünf Uhr	**gearbeitet**.

Muss ein deutsches Präsens (in Verbindung mit *schon*) im Englischen mit dem *present perfect progressive* wiedergegeben werden, wird im Englischen *already* (*schon*) normalerweise weggelassen:

Er	**schreibt schon**	seit drei Stunden.	(schreibt – Präsens)
He	**has been writing**	for three hours.	(has been writing – *present perfect progressive*)

Frage und Verneinung

Bei Frage und Verneinung darf beim *present perfect progressive* nicht mit *to do* umschrieben werden, da diese Zeit bereits mit **Hilfsverben** gebildet wird:

Have	you	**been** working	hard?
Hast	du hart	gearbeitet?	

He	**has**	not	**been** playing	tennis.
Er	hat	kein	Tennis	gespielt.

Zur Satzstellung und zu Besonderheiten bei Verben mit Präpositionen siehe das Kapitel *Allgemeine Regeln*.

Verwendung

Das *present perfect progressive* wird verwendet

➤ **bei Handlungen, die in der Vergangenheit begonnen haben und immer noch andauern:**

Im Deutschen steht normalerweise das Präsens mit *schon*. Im Gegensatz zum *present perfect simple* soll hier der Verlauf der Handlung betont werden:

He **has been doing** his homework for three hours and hasn't finished it yet.
Er **macht** seine Hausaufgaben (**schon**) seit drei Stunden und ist immer noch nicht fertig.

I **have been living** here for ten years and still don't know this town.
Ich **lebe** (**schon**) seit zehn Jahren hier und kenne diese Stadt immer noch nicht.

➤ **bei Handlungen, die in einem Zeitraum, der noch andauert, wiederholt geschehen sind:**

As she **has been teaching** the same subject since 1985, she knows the subject matter well.
Da sie das gleiche Fach seit 1985 **gelehrt hat,** kennt sie den Lehrstoff gut.

Though she **has been working** hard for years, she is a bad pupil.
Obwohl sie seit Jahren hart **gearbeitet hat,** ist sie eine schlechte Schülerin.

➤ **bei Handlungen, die relativ kurze Zeit vor dem Sprechen beendet wurden:**
Auch hier liegt, anders als beim *present perfect*, die Betonung auf dem Verlauf der Handlung. Im Deutschen kann man *gerade* oder *vorhin* einfügen:

He **has just been watching** TV.
Er **hat gerade ferngesehen.**

We **have been talking** about the class trip.
Wir **haben uns gerade** (**vorhin**) über die Klassenfahrt unterhalten.

Zeitangaben

Häufig beim *present perfect progressive* verwendete Zeitangaben sind:
➤ for hours, for weeks, for years etc.
➤ since yesterday, since last year, since last month etc.
➤ Since when ... ?
➤ How long ... ?

Wichtig!

Zur Verwendung von *since* und *for*: Vergleiche das entsprechende Grammatikkapitel.

Exercise 1 – Fill in the forms of the present perfect progressive.

mechanic – Mechaniker

1. The mechanics _____ (to work) all morning.

2. She _____ (not to learn) for two hours.

3. I _____ (to repair) my bike since nine o'clock.

4. They _____ (to think) about it all the time.

to unload – ab-, entladen

5. The workers _____ (to unload) the plane since yesterday.

6. My mother _____ (not to cook) the whole morning.

7. Jimmy _____ (to do) his homework for more than three hours.

8. My parents _____ (to live) in London for ten years.

to practise – üben

9. Tom and Jerry _____ (to practise) since last week.

10. The Jacksons _____ (to play) together since eight o'clock.

to do tricks
    – Kunststücke machen
    (did, done)

11. My hamsters _____ (not to do) tricks all day long.

12. I _____ (to wait) for the bus for 30 minutes.

13. The pupils _____ (to sit) in the classroom all morning.

to do high jump (did, done)
    – Hochsprung machen

14. We _____ (to do) high jump for 45 minutes.

15. The teacher _____ (not to talk) about the problem again and again.

16. Johnny's sisters _____ (to sing) for two hours.

17. The band _____ (to practise) for a long time.

intensively
    – ausführlich, intensiv

18. We _____ (to discuss) the problem intensively.

to organize – organisieren

19. They _____ (to organize) everything for a long time.

20. You _____ (not to learn) too long.

21. She _____ (to go) on and on about it.

22. The teacher _____ (to explain) everything for hours.

23. We _____ (not to discuss) the problems.

24. He _____ (to sit) here for some time.

25. My parents _____ (to clean) the kitchen all morning.

to redecorate – renovieren

26. The members of the youth club _____ (to redecorate) the room.

27. My sister _____ (to listen) to her new CD all day long.

28. Jack's friends _____ (to carry) boxes downstairs all the time.

29. What _____ you _____ (to do) all morning?

to practise – üben

30. They _____ (to practise) the alphabet for two hours.

31. Why _____ they _____ (to wait) for another five minutes?

32. I _____ (to look) at you.

33. She _____ (to help) him all morning.

Vergleich: Present perfect progressive Present perfect (simple)

Die Unterscheidung zwischen *present perfect* und *present perfect progressive* ist nicht ganz einfach, weil **bei bestimmten Fällen beide Zeiten anwendbar** sind. Im Zweifelsfall neigen *Native Speaker* dazu, die Verlaufsform zu verwenden.

1. Verwendung beider Zeiten möglich

So ist es z.B. im folgenden Fall möglich, sowohl das *present perfect* wie auch das *present perfect progressive* zu verwenden, ohne dass es einen Bedeutungsunterschied gibt:

We	**have lived**	here for ten years.
We	**have been living**	here for ten years.
Wir	**leben** (schon)	seit zehn Jahren hier.

2. Bedeutungsunterschiede je nach Verwendung

Bei anderen Fällen gibt es jedoch einen **Unterschied**:

He	**has read**	the book.
Er	**hat**	das Buch **gelesen.**

(Er hat das Buch irgendwann **in der Vergangenheit beendet.**)

He	**has been reading**	the book.
Er	**hat**	das Buch **gelesen**.

(Er hat irgendwann in der Vergangenheit begonnen, das Buch zu lesen, hat es aber **noch nicht beendet.**)

He	**has been reading**	the book since two o'clock.
Er	**liest** (schon)	seit zwei Uhr das Buch.

(Er ist seit zwei Stunden dabei, das Buch zu lesen.)

The pupils	**have learned**	the present progressive since last year.
Die Schüler	**haben**	das Present Progressive seit letztem Jahr **gelernt**.

(Sie haben den Vorgang des Lernens irgendwann **in der Vergangenheit abgeschlossen** und können jetzt das *present progressive*.)

The pupils	**have been learning**	the present progressive.
Die Schüler	**haben**	das Present Progressive **gelernt**.

(Sie sind **immer noch dabei**, das *present progressive* zu lernen, sie können es noch nicht.)

Wichtig!

Man verwendet also das *present perfect progressive* hauptsächlich dann, wenn – übrigens wie bei den *progressive*-Formen aller anderen Zeiten auch – der Schwerpunkt auf dem Verlauf der Handlung liegt, während beim einfachen *present perfect* das Ergebnis einer Handlung im Vordergrund steht.

Diese Beispiele zeigen übrigens auch, dass bei *since* und *for* nicht immer das *present perfect progressive* verwendet werden muss.

3. Verwendung des *present perfect*

Bei Zustandsverben, Verben der Sinneswahrnehmung, bei Verben, die eine Meinung ausdrücken, und bei Verben, die einen Besitz anzeigen (siehe Grammatikkapitel zum *present
progressive*), muss das einfache *present perfect* verwendet werden. Man darf hier nicht das
present perfect progressive verwenden.

I	**have** always	**thought**	that he's a clever boy.
Ich	**habe** schon immer	**geglaubt**,	dass er ein intelligenter Junge ist.
He	**has owned**		a car for three years.
Er	**besitzt**		schon seit drei Jahren ein Auto.
He	**has seen**		me twice this week.
Er	**hat**		mich in dieser Woche zwei mal **getroffen**.
I	**have** not **heard**		of him again.
Ich	**habe** nie wieder		etwas von ihm **gehört**.

── **Unterscheidung** ──

Present perfect simple

➤ Handlungen, die in der Vergangenheit begonnen
haben und immer noch andauern (vor allem bei
Zustandsverben) mit Schwerpunkt auf dem Ergebnis der Handlung

➤ Handlungen, die kurz zuvor beendet wurden

➤ Handlungen mit Auswirkungen auf die Gegenwart

➤ Handlungen in einem nicht abgeschlossenen Zeitraum

I	**have finished**	the book.
We	**have done**	a test.

➤ keine Umschreibung mit *to do* bei Frage und
Verneinung

Have you	**finished**	the book?
I **haven't**	**finished**	the book.

Present perfect progressive

➤ Handlungen, die in der Vergangenheit begonnen
haben und immer noch andauern mit Betonung auf
dem Verlauf der Handlung

➤ Handlungen, die kurz zuvor beendet wurden mit
Betonung auf dem Verlauf der Handlung

➤ Handlungen in einem noch nicht abgeschlossenen
Zeitraum mit Betonung auf dem Verlauf der Handlung

She	**has been working**	since yesterday.
We	**have been learning**	for two days.

➤ keine Umschreibung mit *to do* bei Frage und
Verneinung

Has she	**been working**	since yesterday.
She **hasn't**	**been working**	since yesterday.

Übersetzungs-Tipp   Bei der Übersetzung vom Englischen ins Deutsche gibt es **keinen Unterschied** zwischen
present perfect simple und *present perfect progressive*:

He	**has repaired**	the car.	He can drive away now.
Er	**hat**	das Auto **repariert**.	Er kann jetzt weg fahren.
He	**has been repairing**	the car for two hours.	
Er	**hat**	das Auto seit zwei Stunden **repariert**.	

Exercise 1 – Present perfect progressive or present perfect?
Fill in the correct forms of the verbs.

1. I don't want to go to the party tonight. I _____ (to work) from three o'clock on, and I'm really tired now.

2. My father _____ (to work) in the same factory for ten years, but he still doesn't earn a lot of money.

3. I _____ (to repair) my father's car for two hours. I'm really exhausted now.

4. Tom _____ (to receive) many letters this week.

5. Jack _____ (to forget) his homework, so he must write an extra translation.

6. Tom _____ (to repair) the car, so he can give you back your hammer.

7. Although Judy _____ (to work) hard for weeks, her English _____ (not to become) better.

8. We _____ (never/to be) in England before, but our teacher _____ (to tell) us a lot about this country.

9. What _____ (you/to do) for the last two hours? – I _____ (to repair) my car.

10. John _____ (not to understand) anything because he _____ (to look) out of the window all the time.

11. Mary _____ (not to arrive) yet although I _____ (to wait) for more than two hours.

12. Although you _____ (to watch) so many films this week, you _____ (not to learn) anything.

13. Although you _____ (to watch) TV all afternoon, you _____ (not to learn) anything.

14. My mother _____ (to tell) me not to hitchhike.

15. We _____ (to work) here quite often, so we know everything about the factory.

16. I _____ (to look) at the problem all over again, but I _____ (not to find) anything new.

17. They _____ (to work) since six o'clock.

18. She _____ (to finish) the job.

19. We _____ (to redecorate) the room all morning.

factory – Fabrik

to earn – verdienen

to receive – bekommen

to hitchhike
– per Anhalter fahren, trampen

Exercise 2 – Present perfect or present perfect progressive? Fill in the correct forms of the verbs (sometimes both are possible).

careful – sorgfältig

1. John _____ (to do) his homework carefully, so he doesn't have to do an extra translation.

to decorate – schmücken

2. The pupils _____ (to decorate) the room for three hours. They are really tired now.

3. We _____ (to work) hard for weeks.

4. Our teacher _____ (to get) on our nerves the whole lesson.

engine – Motor

5. The mechanics _____ (to check) the engine all the time but they _____ (not to find) anything.

6. " _____ you _____ (to see) my father?" – "No, I _____ . I (not to see) him for weeks."

7. The politicians _____ (to think) about the problem again and again, but they _____ (not to reach) an agreement.

agreement – Übereinkunft, Abkommen

important – wichtig

8. I _____ (always/to think) that money isn't important for having a good life.

9. John _____ (to forget) his book again. That's why he must do some extra work.

10. Where _____ all the good times _____ (to go)?

11. I _____ (to think) about you all day long.

12. My parents _____ (to buy) a nice car.

13. She _____ (to try) hard for years, but nothing _____ (to change).

14. For years he _____ (to look) for a partner, but he _____ (not to be) lucky yet.

to be lucky – Glück haben

15. We _____ (to have) breakfast for three hours, so the coffee is cold now.

16. I _____ (never/to like) him.

17. They _____ (to leave) the country because they _____ (cannot/to understand) why they have been treated so badly.

to treat – behandeln

18. She _____ (to have) difficulties with English all her life.

Exercise 3 – Translation.

1. Seit Jahren haben wir Probleme mit den englischen Zeiten.

2. In diesem Jahr haben wir immer wieder Übungen dafür gemacht, aber wir haben überhaupt nichts gelernt.

überhaupt nichts
– not ... anything ... at all

3. Unser Lehrer hat die Probleme nicht sehr gut erklärt und hat uns viel zu schwierige Übersetzungen gegeben.

erklären – to explain

4. Deshalb haben wir versucht, aus englischen Fernsehsendungen zu lernen.

Fernsehsendung – TV-programme

5. Seit Wochen sitzen wir jeden Tag vor der Glotze und schauen uns langweilige Filme an.

Glotze – box
(umgangssprachlich)
langweilig – boring

6. Aber wir haben überhaupt keine Fortschritte gemacht.

Fortschritt(e) – progress

7. Die Filme, die in dieser Zeit gekommen sind, waren viel zu schwer für uns, und deshalb haben wir fast nichts verstanden.

kommen (im Fernsehen laufen)
– to be on

8. Wir haben uns verschiedene englische Bücher gekauft und haben sie auch gelesen, aber der Wortschatz war zu kompliziert und deshalb haben wir nur sehr wenig mitbekommen.

verschieden – several
Wortschatz – vocabulary
kompliziert – complicated
nur sehr wenig – only very little
mitbekommen, verstehen
– to understand
(understood,
understood)

9. Deshalb habe ich seit Wochen versucht, gemeinsam mit meiner Schwester zu lernen, aber weil sie auch seit Jahren Probleme mit der englischen Grammatik hat, ist dabei nicht sehr viel herausgekommen.

herauskommen – to come out
(came, come)

10. Ich habe eingesehen, dass es nur von mir abhängt, ob ich gute Noten schreibe.

einsehen – to realise
abhängen – to depend
Note – mark
gute Noten bekommen/schreiben
– to get, got, got/receive
good marks

The past perfect (simple)

Für das einfache Plusquamperfekt ist sowohl die Bezeichnung *past perfect* wie auch *past perfect simple* möglich. Im weiteren Verlauf wird die Bezeichnung *past perfect* verwendet.

Beispiele

1. Aussagesätze

1. After	I	had (I'd)	seen	the film,	I went to bed.
2. Though	you	had (you'd)	given	me the money,	I was angry.
3. After	he	had (he'd)	left	her,	she went to Japan.
After	she	had (she'd)	left	him,	he flew to Japan.
	It	had	built	a nest	before winter arrived.
4. After	we	had (we'd)	watched	the match,	we went home.
5. Because	you	had (you'd)	told	him a lie before,	he didn't trust you.
6. As they		had (they'd)	seen	the film before,	they were bored.

2. Verneinte Sätze

1. As	I	had not (hadn't)	seen	the film before	I stayed up to watch it.
2. Though	you	had not (hadn't)	given	me the money,	I had enough in my purse.
3. Although	he	had not (hadn't)	left	her flat,	she still went away.
Because	she	had not (hadn't)	left	his flat,	he flew to Japan.
	It	had not (hadn't)	built	a nest	before winter arrived.
4. Because	we	had not (hadn't)	watched	the match,	we went fishing instead.
5. Because	you	had not (hadn't)	told	him a lie,	he trusted you.
6. As they		had not (hadn't)	seen	the film before,	he looked forward to it.

3. Fragen

1. When	had	I	seen	the film?
2.	Had	you	given	him the money before he left?
3.	Had	he	stolen	a bike?
	Had	she	been	to the zoo before?
Why	had	it	built	a nest?
4. When	had	we	looked	out of the window?
5. Where	had	you	spent	your holidays?
6. When	had	they	bought	the car?

Bildung

Das *past perfect* (Plusquamperfekt, 3. Vergangenheit) wird gebildet aus der *simple past*-Form von **to have** (*had* bei allen Personen, auch 3. Person Singular) und dem *past participle* (3. Form) des Verbs:

		simple past-Form von *to have*	+	past participle	
to write:	We	had		written	an essay.
to clean:	He	had		cleaned	his bike.

Bildung

Frage und Verneinung

Da bei der Bildung des *past perfect* bereits ein **Hilfsverb** verwendet wird, darf bei Frage und Verneinung nicht mit *to do* umschrieben werden:

> **Had** they done   their homework before eight o'clock?
> Hatten   sie ihre Hausaufgaben vor acht Uhr gemacht?

He **had** not cleaned   his bike.
Er   hatte   sein Fahrrad nicht geputzt4.

Verwendung

Das *past perfect* wird verwendet

Eine Liste der unregelmäßigen Verben befindet sich auf Seite 6.

Zur Satzstellung und zu Besonderheiten bei Verben mit Präpositionen siehe das Kapitel *Allgemeine Regeln*.

➤ **bei Handlungen, die vor einer in der Vergangenheit abgeschlossenen Handlung stattgefunden haben:**

He   **had done**   his homework   before he went out.
Er   **hatte**   seine Hausaufgaben **gemacht**, bevor er hinaus ging.

As I **had** already **seen** the film,   I didn't go to the cinema.
Da ich   den Film schon **gesehen hatte**, ging ich nicht ins Kino.

➤ **bei Handlungen, die vor einem Zeitpunkt in der Vergangenheit begannen und zu diesem Zeitpunkt noch andauerten:**

Das englische *past perfect* kann hier im Deutschen mit dem Perfekt oder dem Imperfekt wiedergegeben werden. Man kann auch *schon* einfügen:

He   **had been**   in London for two days   when he met Judy for the first time.
Er   **war** (schon) zwei Tage in London (**gewesen**), als er Judy zum ersten Mal traf.

Mary **had had**   the book for two days   before she began to read it.
Mary **hatte**   das Buch (schon) zwei Tage (**gehabt**), bevor sie es zu lesen begann.

Wenn aus dem Zusammenhang hervorgeht, dass eine Handlung vor einer vergangenen Handlung stattgefunden hat, kann statt des *past perfect* auch das *simple past* stehen. Dies ist häufig nach *after*, *when* und *before* der Fall:

After he **was**   in London,   he went to Liverpool.
Nachdem er   in London **gewesen war**, ging er nach Liverpool.

When they **finished** the test,   they gave it to their teacher.
Als sie   den Test **beendet hatten**, gaben sie ihn ihrem Lehrer.

Zeitangaben

Häufig beim *past perfect* verwendete Zeitangaben sind:

➤ after
➤ mit *before* oder *when* eingeleitete Nebensätze, in deren Hauptsätzen dann das *past perfect* steht

Wichtig!

Exercise 1 – Put the following sentences into the past perfect.

1. You stay in a youth hostel.

2. Peter goes swimming.

3. We get away from it all.

4. They don't climb mountains in the winter.

5. We have been here for ten months.

6. Our teachers correct our tests quickly.

Exercise 2 – Fill in the correct forms of the verbs.

to confuse
    – verwechseln, verwirren

to apologise – sich entschuldigen

to happen – passieren

injury – Verletzung
to doubt – bezweifeln

1. After I _____ (to confuse) the English with the Scots, Tom got angry.

2. Before I could apologise, he _____ (to hit) me in the face.

3. When I came back from my trip, I told my teacher what _____ (to happen).

4. In the beginning he didn't believe me, but after he _____ (to see) my injuries, he didn't doubt anything.

5. After I _____ (to see) the doctor, I went to bed.

6. After I _____ (to be) in bed for more than three days, I got bored.

7. So I got up although the doctor _____ (to say) I had to stay in bed.

Exercise 3 – Fill in the correct forms of the verbs.

carpenter
    – Schreiner, Zimmermann

to realize – erkennen, feststellen

argument – Streit
to get rid (of) – loswerden
    (got, got)

After Bill (1) _____ (to finish) school, he (2) _____ (to become) a carpenter. He (3) _____ (to be) a carpenter for ten years when he (4) _____ (to get) the job as a king on an island in the Pacific Ocean. He (5) _____ (to be) there for five years when he realized that the people (6) _____ (not to like) him any more. After an argument they (7) _____ (to get) rid of him.

Exercise 4 – Fill in the correct forms of the verbs.

When Mary (1)   (to come) home from school two months ago,

she (2)   (to see) that someone (3)

(to steal) her bike. After she (4)   (to phone) the police, an

inspector (5)   (to come) around at once and (6)   (to   *at once – sofort*

ask) her some questions. After the inspector (7)   (to get) the

necessary information, he (8)   (to want) to find the criminal.   *necessary – nötig, notwendig*

The inspector, who (9)   (to have) his job for more than

20 years, never (10)   (to have) any problems

in such cases. They (11)   (to find) the criminal after they   *cases – Fall*

(12)   (to look) for him for some weeks.

Exercise 5 – Translation.

1. Obgleich ich Peter gesagt hatte, wo er Nordirland auf der Landkarte finden könne, musste er seine Schwester noch einmal fragen.

   Nordirland – Northern Ireland
   Landkarte – map

2. Seit drei Jahren will er schon dorthin fahren, aber immer wieder hatte er sein Geld für wichtigere Dinge gebraucht.

   immer wieder – time and time again

3. Vor zwei Tagen hat er sich einen Plattenspieler gekauft, den er in einem Vorort seiner Heimatstadt gesehen hatte und auf den er sehr stolz ist.

   Plattenspieler – record player
   Vorort – suburb
   Heimatstadt – home town
   stolz sein (auf) – to be proud (of)

4. Er möchte jetzt gerne in der Wintersaison auf eine der walisischen Inseln fahren, obwohl er nicht weiß, wo er dort wohnen soll, und obwohl dort oft 15° unter Null sind.

   Wintersaison – winter season
   walisisch – Welsh
   unter Null – below zero

5. Gestern hat er einen Reisepass bekommen, den er nicht braucht, weil er ein Bürger des Vereinigten Königreichs ist, und weil Wales nicht von Großbritannien getrennt ist.

   Reisepass – passport
   Bürger – citizen
   getrennt – separate

The past perfect progressive

Beispiele

1. Aussagesätze

1. I	had	(I'd)		been	working		for six hours.
2. You	had	(You'd)		been	watching	the film	since one o'clock.
3. He	had	(He'd)		been	living	here	for ten weeks.
She	had	(She'd)		been	driving		for two weeks.
It		had		been	building	a nest	all morning.
4. We	had	(We'd)		been	learning		a long time.
5. You	had	(You'd)		been	doing	the test	for some time.
6. They	had	(They'd)		been	swimming	in the pool	all afternoon.

2. Verneinte Sätze

1. I	had	not	(I hadn't)	been	working		for six hours.
2. You	had	not	(You hadn't)	been	watching	the film	since one o'clock.
3. He	had	not	(He hadn't)	been	living	here	for ten weeks.
She	had	not	(She hadn't)	been	driving		for two weeks.
It	had	not	(It hadn't)	been	building	a nest	all morning.
4. We	had	not	(We hadn't)	been	learning		a long time.
5. You	had	not	(You hadn't)	been	doing	the test	for some time.
6. They	had	not	(They hadn't)	been	swimming	in the pool	all afternoon.

3. Fragen

1. When	had	I	been	working		for six hours?
2.	Had	you	been	watching	the film	since one o'clock?
3. Where	had	he	been	living		for ten weeks?
Why	had	she	been	driving		for two weeks?
	Had	it	been	building	a nest	all morning?
4. What	had	we	been	learning		a long time?
5.	Had	you	been	doing	the test	for some time?
6. Where	had	they	been	swimming		all afternoon?

Bildung

Das *past perfect progressive* (Verlaufsform des Plusquamperfekts/der 3. Vergangenheit) wird bei allen Personen mit der *past perfect*-Form von **to be** (*had been* für alle Personen) und der **ing-Form des Verbs** gebildet:

Bildung

		past perfect von *to be*	+	ing-Form des Verbs	
to sleep:	He	had been		sleeping	when he arrived.
to sit:	They	had been		sitting	in the room when he came home.

Bei der Übersetzung ins Deutsche wird die *ing*-Form nicht mitübersetzt. Die einzige Möglichkeit, bei der die *ing*-Form *sichtbar* werden kann, ist das Einfügen von *schon*:

He	**had been waiting**	for one hour	when she finally arrived.
Er	**hatte** (schon)	eine Stunde **gewartet,**	als sie endlich ankam.

We	**had been working**	for hours when we saw that everything had been a waste of time.
Wir	**hatten** (schon)	stundenlang **gearbeitet,** als wir sahen, dass alles umsonst gewesen war.

Zu Besonderheiten der *ing*-Form: Vergleiche das Grammatikkapitel zum *present progressive*.

Frage und Verneinung

Da das *past perfect progressive* bereits mit **Hilfsverben** gebildet wird, darf man bei Frage und Verneinung nicht mit *to do* umschreiben:

	Had you **been** writing	a letter?
	Hattest du gerade	einen Brief geschrieben?

He	**had** not **been** singing	in the lesson.
Er	hatte	in der Stunde nicht gesungen.

Zur Satzstellung und zu Besonderheiten bei Verben mit Präpositionen siehe das Kapitel *Allgemeine Regeln*.

Verwendung

Das *past perfect progressive* wird verwendet bei

➤ **der Betonung des Verlaufs einer Handlung:**

Wie schon bei der einfachen Form des *past perfect* wird beim *past perfect progressive* eine Handlung beschrieben, die in der Vergangenheit vor einer anderen Handlung ablief. Im Gegensatz zum einfachen *past perfect* wird jedoch der **Verlauf der Handlung** betont und nicht deren Ergebnis.

Im Deutschen steht oft anstelle des Plusquamperfekts das Imperfekt:

Übersetzungs-Tipp

He	**had been working**	there for hours	when his mother came in.
Er	**hatte** (schon)	stundenlang **gearbeitet,**	als seine Mutter hereinkam.
Er	**arbeitete** (schon)	stundenlang,	als seine Mutter hereinkam.

They	**had been searching**	her for some time	before they found something.
Sie	**hatten** sie (schon)	eine ganze Zeit lang **durchsucht,**	bevor sie etwas fanden.
Sie	**durchsuchten** sie (schon)	ein ganze Zeit lang,	bevor sie etwas fanden.

> **bei wiederholten Handlungen:**
> Das *past perfect progressive* kann auch bei wiederholten Handlungen verwendet werden, die vor einem in der Vergangenheit abgeschlossenen Vorgang auftraten:

Tom	**had been going**	to the same doctor for many years.	
Tom	**war**	jahrelang zum gleichen Arzt **gegangen**.	

He	**had been taking**	pills for a long time,	before he realised they were the wrong sort.
Er	**hatte**	schon lange Tabletten **genommen**,	bevor er erkannte, dass es die falschen waren.

Zeitangaben

Häufig beim *past perfect progressive* verwendete Zeitangaben sind:

Wichtig!

> after
> for
> since
> mit *before* oder *when* eingeleitete Hauptsätze, in deren Nebensätzen dann das *past perfect progressive* steht

Exercise 1 – Fill in the correct forms of the past perfect progressive.

1. John _____ (to live) in London for ten years before he knew where to find good clothes.

2. After I _____ (to live) in the USA for some time, my English became fluent.

   fluent – fließend

3. How long _____ (you/to study) before you found out that being a teacher wasn't the right profession for you?

   profession – Beruf

4. The mechanics _____ (to repair) the car for some time when they saw that the engine didn't work.

   engine – Motor

5. Although she _____ (to tell) me lies, I still liked her a lot.

6. He _____ (to do) his job for more than twenty years when he finally got a payrise.

   payrise – Gehaltserhöhung

7. They _____ (to drink) a lot when they found out that they were at the wrong party.

8. Before the pupils went on the trip they _____ (to study) at the maps carefully.

   careful – sorgfältig

9. He couldn't find the answer although he _____ (to consult) several dictionaries.

   to consult – zu Rate ziehen, hier: nachschlagen

10. Before the politicians got to the solution of the problem, they _____ _____ (to discuss) the matter for a long time.

    solution – Lösung

    matter – Angelegenheit

11. Although the man _____ (to drive) for many years, he still drove terribly.

12. Because he _____ (to live) in England for some time, he got the job.

13. They _____ (to walk) for more than two hours when they finally found a petrol station.

14. The policemen _____ (to try) to find the criminal for weeks without any success.

    success – Erfolg

15. We finally reached an agreement after we _____ (to discuss) the problem all day.

    to reach an agreement – eine Übereinkunft erreichen

16. Ted _____ (to take) the wrong medicine for some time before he realized that he wasn't ill.

    to realize – erkennen

17. How long _____ (you/to learn) Spanish then?

18. I _____ (just/to read) an article about London.

Exercise 2 – Fill in the correct forms of the past perfect progressive.

1. After John _____ (to wait) for Mary for more than two hours, he left the bus stop.

2. We _____ (to listen) to him for some time when we realized that he was only talking rubbish.

3. I _____ (to work) for more than three hours when I saw that everything had been in vain.

4. They _____ (to talk) about the problem when Mr Jones suddenly came in.

5. I was really tired although I _____ (to sleep) for more than twelve hours.

6. We _____ (to watch) the film about Shakespeare when suddenly the TV-set exploded.

7. The pupils _____ (to do) their homework all afternoon.

8. My father _____ (to carry) boxes all morning before he took a rest in the bedroom.

9. He _____ (to climb) the mountain all day before he got to the top.

Exercise 3 – Translation.

1. Nachdem wir den ganzen Nachmittag gespielt hatten, gingen wir wieder nach Hause, weil es zu regnen begann.

    _____

    _____

2. John hatte zwei Stunden lang geübt, bevor er auf die Bühne ging.

    _____

    _____

3. Wir hatten die Fenster schon zwei Stunden lang geputzt, bevor uns unsere Mutter sagte, dass sie es schon vorgestern gemacht hatte.

    _____

    _____

    _____

4. Er arbeitete schon zwei Tage an seinem Computer, bevor er den Fehler herausfand.

    _____

    _____

5. Die Politiker hatten stundenlang über die Arbeitslosigkeit diskutiert, bevor sie zu einer Einigung kamen.

    _____

    _____

to realize – erkennen
rubbish – Müll, Abfall, Unsinn

in vain – umsonst, sinnlos

suddenly – plötzlich

top (of a mountain) – Gipfel

üben – to practise
Bühne – stage

putzen – to clean

Arbeitslosigkeit – unemployment
zu einer Einigung kommen
  – to reach an agreement

Vergleich:
Past perfect (simple)
Past perfect progressive

Past perfect

Past perfect (simple)	Past perfect progressive
➤ Eine Handlung, die vor einer anderen in der Vergangenheit abgeschlossenen Handlung stattfindet. **Der Schwerpunkt liegt auf dem <u>Ergebnis</u> der Handlung.**	➤ Eine Handlung, die vor einer anderen in der Vergangenheit abgeschlossenen Handlung stattfindet. **Der Schwerpunkt liegt auf dem <u>Verlauf</u> der Handlung.**
They **had repaired** the car. So we didn't have to rent one.	They **had been repairing** the car. That's why they were tired.
➤ keine Umschreibung mit *to do* bei Frage und Verneinung	➤ keine Umschreibung mit *to do* bei Frage und Verneinung
They **had** not **repaired** the car. **Had** they **repaired** the car?	They **had** not **been repairing** the car. **Had** they **been repairing** the car?

Bei der Übersetzung vom Englischen ins Deutsche gibt es **keinen Unterschied** zwischen *past perfect progressive* und *past perfect*.   **Übersetzungs-Tipp**

They **had repaired**	the car.		So we didn't have to rent one.
Sie **hatten**	das Auto	**repariert**.	Deshalb brauchten wir keines zu mieten.
They **had been repairing**	the car.		So they were tired.
Sie **hatten**	das Auto	**repariert**.	Deshalb waren sie müde.

Exercise 1 – Fill in the correct forms of the verbs.

Last year the Elliots (1) _____ (to go) to Britain after they

(2) _____ (to spend) most of their previous holidays in southern

Europe. After they (3) _____ (to arrive) in the capital of England,

they (4) _____ (to wonder) why they (5) _____

_____ (not to go) to Spain or Italy again.

The weather (6) _____ (to be) chilly and the sun

(7) _____ (not to shine). The people in the countries where

they (8) _____ (to be) before (9) _____ (to

be) friendly, but the English (10) _____ (not to be) very polite.

The Elliots (11) _____ (not to like) the scenery, either. After

they (12) _____ (to see) the sights of London, they

(13) _____ (to go) to Stratford-on-Avon, where Shakespeare

(14) _____ (to be born). After they (15) _____

_____ (to spend) two weeks in Scotland, they (16) _____

(to fly) to Spain. When they (17) _____ (to leave) the plane, it

(18) _____ (to rain). So they (19) _____

(to swim) home across the Atlantic Ocean. It (20) _____ (to rain)

all the way, but they (21) _____ (not to mind) because

they (22) _____ (to be) in the water anyway.

They (23) _____ (to show) photos of their holidays to

everyone. But after they (24) _____ (to tell) the same stories

all the time, nobody (25) _____ (to visit) them any more.

Exercise 2 – Translation.

1. Wir hatten schon drei Stunden an unserem Computer gearbeitet, als unser Lehrer ins
    Zimmer kam und uns sagte, dass er einen Fehler im Programm gefunden hätte.

    _____

    _____

    _____

2. Obwohl wir das Programm schon seit Jahren verwendet hatten, hatten wir das nicht
    herausgefunden.

    _____

    _____

3. Wir hatten entdeckt, dass es Probleme mit unseren Druckern gab, aber wir dachten
    nicht, dass dies mit unserer Software zu tun habe.

    _____

    _____

Margin glossary:

previous – vorherig, früher

to wonder – sich fragen

chilly – kühl

polite – höflich

scenery – Landschaft

entdecken – to find out
            (found, found)
Drucker – printer

Exercise 3 – Fill in the correct forms of the verbs.

After Mr Jones (1) _____ (to leave) the house yesterday, he

(2) _____ (to want) to know if it (3) _____ (to rain). After he

(4) _____ (to look) up the bright blue sky for more than twenty minutes,

he (5) _____ (to see) that the sun (6) _____ (to shine).

So he (7) _____ (to go) back into the house and (8) _____

_____ (to take) off his coat. When he (9) _____ (to come) out again,

it (10) _____ (to rain) heavily. He (11) _____ (not to

know) what to do. After he (12) _____ (to arrive) at the bus stop, his clothes

(13) _____ (to be) wet through. So he (14) _____ (to

go) back to his house again because he (15) _____ (not to want) to

go to work in wet clothes. When he (16) _____ (to arrive) there he

(17) _____ (to find) out that he (18) _____

(to forget) his keys. So he (19) _____ (to climb) onto the roof and

(20) _____ (to fall) off it immediately. An ambulance (21) _____   ambulance – Krankenwagen

(to take) him to hospital. When he (22) _____ (to lie) in bed, he

(23) _____ (to be) happy because he (24) _____ (to be)

dry again. But his boss, who (25) _____ (to wait) for him all morning,

(26) _____ (to sack) him at once. Mr Jones (27) _____   to sack – entlassen

(to look) for a job since, but so far he (28) _____ (not to find) one.

Exercise 4 – Translation.

1. Letztes Jahr fuhren mein Bruder und ich durch England.

   _____

2. Nachdem wir in London gewesen waren, machten wir einen Ausflug nach Liverpool.   Ausflug (nach) – trip (to)

   _____

3. Weil wir diese Stadt nicht sehr mochten, fuhren wir schnell wieder weg.

   _____

4. Als wir in Dover ankamen, fanden wir heraus, dass das Luftkissenboot schon den Hafen   Luftkissenboot – hovercraft
   verlassen hatte.   Hafen – port

   _____

5. Nachdem wir über drei Stunden gewartet hatten, hatte mein Bruder eine glänzende Idee.   glänzend – brilliant, excellent

   _____

6. Er sprang ins Wasser und schwamm zum Kontinent hinüber.

   _____

7. Seither hat er allen Leuten erzählt, wie gut er schwimmen kann.

   _____

Exercise 5 – Fill in the correct forms of the verbs.

Some time ago there (1) _____ (to be) an extremely good-looking girl named

Janet, who (2) _____ (to have) many boyfriends. She (3) _____

(to be) the star of the local disco. The boys (4) _____ (to love) her but she

(5) _____ (to have) a lousy character. She only (6) _____

(to dance) with the nice boys and (7) _____ (to tell) the others that they

(8) _____ (to be) ugly. After the boys (9) _____ (to

find) this out, they (10) _____ (not to want) to have anything to do with

her any more. She (11) _____ (not to know) what to do. Janet

(12) _____ (to sit) there all alone and nobody (13) _____

__ (to talk) her. After she (14) _____ (to be) frustrated for two weeks she

(15) _____ (to decide) to change. She (16) _____

(to smile) at everyone in the disco, but nobody (17) _____ (to look) at

her any more. Even after she (18) _____ (to behave) more pleasantly

for a long time, still nothing (19) _____ (to change). She

(20) _____ (to begin) to drink alcohol, which (21) _____

(to be) mostly very strong. One night, she (22) _____ (to be) drunk

again and (23) _____ (to run) into a car. She (24) _____

_____ (to be) badly injured and (25) _____ (not to be)

nice any more. And the moral of the story: Nice girls who (26) _____

(to have) a lousy character often (27) _____ (to end) tragically.

Exercise 6 – Translation.

1. Weil wir stundenlang in unserem Zimmer gesessen waren, wollten wir hinausgehen.

   _____

   _____

2. Aber weil es am Tag zuvor ununterbrochen geregnet hatte, war das Gras nass.

   _____

   _____

3. So gingen wir wieder ins Haus zurück, obwohl uns die frische Luft ganz gut getan hätte.

   _____

   _____

4. Wir warteten, bis das Gras trocken geworden war.

   _____

5. Nachdem wir zwei Stunden draußen gespielt hatten, gingen wir wieder ins Haus zurück.

   _____

   _____

local – örtlich

lousy character – mieser Charakter

ugly – hässlich

to decide – beschließen

pleasant – angenehm

stundenlang – for hours

ununterbrochen – non-stop

The going to-future

Beispiele

1. Aussagesätze

1.	I	**am (I'm)**	**going to**	buy	a book	**tomorrow**.
2.	You	**are (you're)**	**going to**	write	a letter	**next week**.
3.	He	**is (he's)**	**going to**	have	a party for my birthday.	
	She	**is (she's)**	**going to**	help	him.	
	It	**is (It's)**	**going to**	build	a nest	**soon**.
4.	We	**are (we're)**	**going to**	sell	our car.	
5.	You	**are (you're)**	**going to**	sleep	in the basement.	
6.	They	**are (they're)**	**going to**	stay	at home for Christmas.	

2. Verneinte Sätze

1.	I	**am (I'm)**	**not**	**going to**	buy	a book	**tomorrow**.
2.	You	**are (you're)**	**not (aren't)**	**going to**	write	a letter	**next week**.
3.	He	**is (he's)**	**not (isn't)**	**going to**	have	a party for my birthday.	
	She	**is (she's)**	**not (isn't)**	**going to**	help	him.	
	It	**is (It's)**	**not (isn't)**	**going to**	build	a nest	**soon**.
4.	We	**are (we're)**	**not (aren't)**	**going to**	sell	our car.	
5.	You	**are (you're)**	**not (aren't)**	**going to**	sleep	in the basement.	
6.	They	**are (they're)**	**not (aren't)**	**going to**	stay	at home for Christmas.	

3. Fragen

1.	When	**am I**	**going to**	buy	a book?	
2.		**Are you**	**going to**	write	a letter	**next week**?
3.		**Is he**	**going to**	have	a party for my birthday?	
	Why	**is she**	**going to**	help	him?	
	Where	**is it**	**going to**	build	a nest	**soon**?
4.		**Are we**	**going to**	sell	our car?	
5.		**Are you**	**going to**	sleep	in the basement?	
6.		**Are they**	**going to**	stay	at home for Christmas?	

Bildung

Das *going to-future* wird gebildet, indem man das ***present progressive* von *to go*** (Vergleiche: Kapitel zum *present progressive*) bildet und den **Infinitiv des Verbs** anfügt:

Bildung		*present progressive* von *to go*	+	Infinitiv des Verbs
to sleep:	I	**am going**		**to sleep.**
to work:	He	**is goin**		**to work.**

Frage und Verneinung

Zur Satzstellung und zu Besonderheiten bei Verben mit Präpositionen siehe das Kapitel *Allgemeine Regeln*.

Da bei der Bildung des *going to-future* bereits ein **Hilfsverb** verwendet wird, darf bei Frage und Verneinung nicht mit *to do* umschrieben werden:
Are you going to buy   the car?
Wirst du   das Auto kaufen?

Verwendung

Das *going to-future* wird verwendet

> **wenn jemand etwas vor allem in unmittelbarer/näherer Zukunft zu tun beabsichtigt:**
> Es kann im Deutschen sowohl durch werden wie auch durch wollen wiedergegeben werden:
> I   **am going to buy**   a car tomorrow.
> Ich   **werde (will)**   morgen ein Auto **kaufen**.
>
> He   **is going to fly**   abroad soon.
> Er   **wird (will)**   bald ins Ausland **fliegen**.

> **bei festen Plänen für die Zukunft:**
> When I grow up,   I **am going to be**   a teacher.
> Wenn ich groß bin,   **werde** ich   Lehrer.
>
> When we get enough money together,   we   **are going to build**   a house.
> Wenn wir genug Geld beisammen haben,   **werden**   wir ein Haus **bauen**.

> **wenn etwas mit Gewissheit/ziemlicher Wahrscheinlichkeit eintreffen wird:**
> We   **are going to have** a nice weekend.
> Wir   **werden**   ein schönes Wochenende **haben**.
>
> They **are going to have** a headache   if they carry on listening to that music.
> Sie   **werden**   Kopfschmerzen **haben**,   wenn sie weiterhin dieser Musik zuhören.

Achtung: Wenn *to go* oder *to come* Vollverb ist, wird häufig statt des *going to-future* das *present progressive* verwendet:

My brother   **is going**   to the disco tomorrow.
Mein Bruder   **geht**   morgen in die Disco.
(Selten: My brother **is going to go**   to the disco tomorrow.)

They   **are coming**   to our part y next week.
Sie   **kommen**   nächste Woche zu unserer Party.
(Selten: They   **are going to come** to our party next week.)

Zeitangaben

Wichtig! Häufig beim *going to-future* verwendete Zeitangaben sind:
> tomorrow, soon, in the future
> next week, next month, next year etc.

Exercise 1 – Fill in the correct forms of the going to-future.

1. My father _____ (to wash) his car in the afternoon.

2. Judy and Jim _____ (to clean) their bikes tomorrow.   bike – Fahrrad

3. What _____ you _____ (to do) next year?

4. Which present _____ he _____ (to buy) for Judy's birthday?   present – Geschenk

5. Jack _____ (to go) to Munich tomorrow.   Munich – (die Stadt) München

6. We _____ (not to do) our English homework for tomorrow.

7. My parents _____ (to buy) a house next year.

8. Where _____ you _____ (to go) in the summer holidays?

9. John _____ (to drive) to Oxford tomorrow.

10. They _____ (not to learn) anything.

11. Jack's sister _____ (not to watch) the film.

12. What _____ you _____ (to do) after school?

13. We _____ (not to have) to write the letters.

14. _____ they _____ (to sing) tonight?

15. She _____ (not to get) the prize.   prize – Preis, Gewinn

16. They _____ (to leave) the town.

17. _____ they _____ (to sell) their house?   to sell (sold, sold) – verkaufen

18. She _____ (not to paint) her room.   to paint – streichen, malen

19. The doctor _____ (to write) a book about diseases.   disease – (Infektions-)Krankheit

20. What _____ you _____ (to do) with the spare tyres?   spare tyre – Ersatzreifen

21. There _____ (to be) heavy rain in a few minutes.   heavy rain – starker Regen
a few – ein paar (wenige)

22. My brother _____ (to watch) a film tonight.

23. The teachers _____ (to go) to the theatre some day.

24. Janet _____ (to visit) her grandma soon.

25. We _____ (not to eat) before dinner.

26. My mother _____ (to do) the washing tomorrow.

27. Jack's friends _____ (to have) a race in the woods.   in the woods – in den Wäldern

28. _____ he _____ (to forget) his homework again?

29. They _____ (to see) the doctor in the afternoon.

30. The mechanics _____ (not to repair) the cars in time.   mechanic – Mechaniker
in time – pünktlich

31. Eric Clapton _____ (to bring) out a new album soon.

32. The discussion _____ (to be) quite interesting.   quite – ziemlich

33. The film _____ (to be) a success.   success – Erfolg

Exercise 2 – Here are some answers, find the questions.
Ask for the words in bold.

to celebrate – feiern

1. _____? – He's going to buy **a car**.

2. _____? – She's going to visit **John**.

3. _____? – **Jack** isn't going to celebrate his birthday.

to arrange – organisieren
wedding – Hochzeit

4. _____? – **My parents** are going to arrange the wedding.

damage – Schaden

5. _____? – He isn't going to pay for **the damage**.

6. _____? – They are going to listen to **the teacher**.

pollution – (Umwelt-)
           Verschmutzung

7. _____? – We are going to talk about **pollution**.

Exercise 3 – Make negative sentences.

to paint – streichen, malen

1. Gilbert is going to paint his room.

   _____

2. The Jacksons are going to buy a new house.

   _____

match – Turnier, Spiel

3. We are going to the match.

   _____

4. They are going to repair their bikes.

   _____

Exercise 4 – Translation.

Schachwettbewerb
   – chess tournament
teilnehmen – to take part (in)
           (took, taken)

1. Ich werde an einem Schachwettbewerb in unserer Schule teilnehmen, weil ich besser als alle anderen bin.

   _____

   _____

2. „Wirst du das grüne oder das rote Auto kaufen?" – „Ich werde das rote nehmen, weil es mir am besten gefällt."

   _____

   _____

heute Nachmittag
   – this afternoon
nirgends – nowhere

3. „Wo gehst du heute Nachmittag hin?" – „Nirgends. Ich werde mir einen Film im Fernsehen anschauen."

   _____

   _____

4. „Wirst du morgen ins Kino oder ins Theater gehen?" – „Ich weiß es noch nicht."

   _____

   _____

The will-future

Beispiele

1. Aussagesätze

1.	I	**will**	**(I'll)**	**have**	a test	**tomorrow.**
2.	You	**will**	**(You'll)**	**fly**	to Italy	**next year.**
3.	He	**will**	**(He'll)**	**be**	sixteen	**next year.**
	She	**will**	**(She'll)**	**have**	her holiday	**in October.**
	It	**will**	**(It'll)**	**rain**		**in a moment.**
4.	We	**will**	**(We'll)**	**visit**	you	**in August.**
5.	You	**will**	**(You'll)**	**have**	problems	**soon.**
6.	They	**will**	**(They'll)**	**search**	you at customs.	

2. Verneinte Sätze

1.	I	**will**	**not**	**(won't)**	**have**	a test	**tomorrow.**
2.	You	**will**	**not**	**(won't)**	**fly**	to Italy	**next year.**
3.	He	**will**	**not**	**(won't)**	**be**	sixteen	**next year.**
	She	**will**	**not**	**(won't)**	**have**	her holiday	**in October.**
	It	**will**	**not**	**(won't)**	**rain**		**yet.**
4.	We	**will**	**not**	**(won't)**	**visit**	you	**in August.**
5.	You	**will**	**not**	**(won't)**	**have**	problems	**soon.**
6.	They	**will**	**not**	**(won't)**	**search**	you at customs.	

3. Fragen

1.	When	**will**	I	**have**	a test	**tomorrow?**
2.		**Will**	you	**fly**	to Italy	**next year?**
3.		**Will**	he	**be**	sixteen	**next year?**
		Will	she	**have**	her holiday	**in October?**
	Why	**will**	it	**rain**		**today?**
4.		**Will**	we	**have**	problems	**soon?**
6.	When	**will**	they	**search**	you at customs?	

Bildung

Das *will-future* wird für alle Personen aus dem Hilfsverb **will** und dem **Infinitiv des Verbs** (ohne *to*) gebildet:

Bildung		*will*	+	Infinitiv des Verbs
to go:	He	**will**		**go**.
to sleep:	They	**will**		**sleep**.

Im formellen Englisch findet man in der 1. Person Singular und Plural neben *will/will not/ won't* auch **shall, shall not, shan't**:

I	**shall/will**	**see**	him tomorrow.
We	**shall/will**	**be**	back soon.
We	**shan't/won't**	**meet**	them before Wednesday.

Frage und Verneinung

Zur Satzstellung und zu Besonderheiten bei Verben mit Präpositionen siehe das Kapitel *Allgemeine Regeln*.

Da das *will-future* bereits mit einem **Hilfsverb** gebildet wird, darf man bei Frage und Verneinung nicht mit *to do* umschreiben:

Will	you	have a test?
Wirst	du	eine Schulaufgabe schreiben?

He	**will** not	sing in the lesson.
Er	wird nicht	in den Stunden singen.

Verwendung

Das *will-future* wird verwendet,

➤ **um ein zukünftiges Geschehen als Gegensatz zur Gegenwart auszudrücken:**

Übersetzungs-Tipp

Wenn der Bezug zur Zukunft aus dem Zusammenhang hervorgeht, kann im Deutschen statt des Futurs das Präsens stehen:

I	**will be**	**back** in a minute.
Ich	**werde**	gleich **zurück sein**.
Ich	**bin**	**gleich zurück**.

My father	**will be**	**angry**.
Mein Vater	**wird**	**verärgert sein**.

(Hier ist das Präsens nicht möglich: *Mein Vater **ist** verärgert* bezieht sich nicht auf die Zukunft, sondern auf die Gegenwart.)

➤ **um ein zukünftiges Geschehen auszudrücken, das vom Sprecher nicht beeinflusst werden kann:**

Übersetzungs-Tipp

Wenn der Bezug zur Zukunft aus dem Zusammenhang hervorgeht, kann im Deutschen statt des Futur das Präsens stehen:

We	**will have**	a test tomorrow.
Wir	**werden**	morgen eine Schulaufgabe **schreiben**.
Wir	**schreiben**	**morgen** eine Schulaufgabe.

I	**will be**	16 next month.
Ich	**werde**	nächsten Monat 16.
Ich	**bin**	nächsten Monat 16.

➤ **um eine Vermutung, Prognose oder Vorhersage über ein zukünftiges Geschehen auszudrücken:**

Es steht vorzugsweise nach Ausdrücken wie *to think/to hope/to expect/to suppose/ to be sure/to be afraid, probably, perhaps, maybe* etc. Wenn der Bezug zur Zukunft aus dem Zusammenhang hervorgeht, kann im Deutschen statt des Futur das Präsens stehen:

He **thinks**	that he	**will leave**	school next year.
Er **glaubt**,	dass er		nächstes Jahr die Schule **verlassen wird**.
Er **glaubt**,	dass er		nächstes Jahr die Schule **verlässt**.
We **hope**	that we	**will be**	better off in August.
Wir **hoffen**,	dass es uns		im August besser **gehen wird**.
Wir **hoffen**	dass es uns		im August besser **geht**.
It		**will be**	cloudy tomorrow.
Es		**wird**	morgen **bewölkt sein**.

Oft verwechseln Schüler das englische *will* mit dem deutschen *wollen*. Diese deutsche Entsprechung ist immer falsch. **Das englische *will* darf nur mit einem deutschen Präsens oder Futur übersetzt werden!** Das deutsche *wollen* wird mit *to want* übersetzt (Ausnahme beim *going to-future*, siehe das vorherige Grammatikkapitel):

Fehlerquelle!

He	**will be**	back in a minute.
Er	**wird**	gleich zurück **sein**.
Er	**ist**	**gleich** zurück.
He	**wants** to **be**	back in a minute.
Er	**will**	**gleich** zurück **sein**.

Mit *when* eingeleitete Nebensätze stehen, auch wenn die Handlung in der Zukunft abläuft, im *simple present*:

Achtung! *when*

He	**will**	be here	**when**	you	**arrive**.
Er	**wird**	hier sein,	**wenn**	du	**ankommst**.

Zeitangaben

Häufig beim *will-future* verwendete Zeitangaben sind:

Wichtig!

➤ tomorrow
➤ soon
➤ in the future
➤ next week, next month, next year etc.

Exercise 1 – Fill in the forms of the will-future.

to set a test (set, set)
 – eine Schulaufgabe schreiben

1. I think our teacher _____ (to set) us a test tomorrow.

2. The holidays _____ (to be) late this year.

probably – wahrscheinlich
New Year's Eve
 – Silvester (Neujahrs-Abend)

3. We _____ probably _____ (to have) a party on New Year's Eve.

4. I think we _____ (to go) out tomorrow night.

to suppose – annehmen

5. They suppose that they _____ (not to pay) anything for the hotel in Switzerland.

6. I _____ (to leave) next Monday.

7. What _____ your father _____ (to say) when he sees your report?

report – Bericht, Zeugnis

to have a fit – ausflippen
lake – See

8. My parents _____ (to have) a fit when they find out that I have driven their car into a lake.

9. I hope my mother _____ (to be) at home tonight.

10. They think they _____ (to have) a test next week.

sure – sicher

11. I'm sure it _____ (not to rain) tomorrow.

12. We _____ (to go) on a trip in September.

13. The match between Bavaria Munich and VfB Stuttgart _____ (to take) place in Munich.

14. There _____ (not to be) any new teachers at our school next year.

Exercise 2 – Translation.

vielleicht – perhaps
reisen – to travel

1. Wir werden nächstes Jahr vielleicht nach Italien reisen.

   _____

2. Ich glaube, dass dort schönes Wetter sein wird.

   _____

wahrscheinlich – probably
Jugendherberge – youth hostel
freie Zimmer – vacancies

3. Wir werden wahrscheinlich in einer Jugendherberge wohnen, wenn es dort freie Zimmer gibt.

   _____

   _____

4. Die Jugendherbergen waren bis jetzt immer sehr billig, aber nächstes Jahr werden sie wahrscheinlich etwas teurer werden.

   _____

   _____

Insel – island
vor – *hier:* off

5. Wenn es in Rom zu teuer ist, werden wir auf eine der Inseln vor der italienischen Küste fahren.

   _____

   _____

genießen – to enjoy

6. Ich bin mir sicher, dass wir unseren Aufenthalt dort sehr genießen werden.

   _____

Exercise 3 – Here are some answers, find the questions.
Ask for the words in bold.

1. _____? – He'll be back **before ten**.

2. _____? – We'll have **a test** soon.

3. _____? – We'll go shopping on **Christmas Eve**.

4. _____? – **Jill** will take the job.

5. _____? – **The teachers** will set the text.

6. _____? – Mary will pay **the doctor**.

7. _____? – **The guide** will probably find the way.   guide – (Fremden-)Führer
probably – wahrscheinlich

8. _____? – We will get on **the train** in time.

9. _____? – TV will be **terrible** in the future.

10. _____? – I will buy **the house**.

11. _____? – The sky will be **cloudy**.   cloudy – bewölkt

Exercise 4 – Translation.

1. Wir werden im Sommer wahrscheinlich nach Rom fahren, nachdem wir in den letzten Jahren unseren Urlaub immer im Norden Europas verbracht hatten.   wahrscheinlich – probably
im Norden Europas – in northern Europe

2. Wir wissen nicht, wie wir dorthin kommen können, aber das macht nichts.   ausmachen – to matter

3. Ich hoffe, dass wir per Anhalter fahren können.   per Anhalter fahren – to hitchhike

4. Obgleich das Wetter in Italien wahrscheinlich sehr schön sein wird, werden wir einen Regenschirm mitnehmen, obwohl ich Zweifel habe, ob wir ihn brauchen werden.   obgleich, obwohl – although
Regenschirm – umbrella
Zweifel haben – to doubt

5. Ich weiß auch nicht, wo wir wohnen sollen, aber ich hoffe, dass irgendwo ein Zimmer frei sein wird.   wohnen – to stay
irgendwo – somewhere

6. Leider werden wir dort auch viele deutsche Touristen treffen.   leider – unfortunately

7. Sie werden vor den Museen Schlange stehen und genauso wie wir alle interessanten Sehenswürdigkeiten sehen wollen.   Schlange stehen – to queue
genauso wie wir – just like us

The future progressive

Beispiele

1. Aussagesätze

1. I	**will**	**(I'll)**	**be**	**taking**	a test tomorrow.
2. You	**will**	**(You'll)**	**be**	**flying**	to Italy next year.
3. He	**will**	**(He'll)**	**be**	**working**	next year.
She	**will**	**(She'll)**	**be**	**spending**	her holidays in Wales.
It	**will**	**(It'll)**	**be**	**building**	a nest.
4. We	**will**	**(We'll)**	**be**	**visiting**	you in August.
5. You	**will**	**(You'll)**	**be**	**discussing**	your problems soon.
6. They	**will**	**(They'll)**	**be**	**searching**	you at customs.

2. Verneinte Sätze

1. I	**will**	**not**	**(won't)**	**be**	**taking**	a test tomorrow.
2. You	**will**	**not**	**(won't)**	**be**	**flying**	to Italy next year.
3. He	**will**	**not**	**(won't)**	**be**	**working**	next year.
She	**will**	**not**	**(won't)**	**be**	**spending**	her holidays in Wales.
It	**will**	**not**	**(won't)**	**be**	**building**	a nest.
4. We	**will**	**not**	**(won't)**	**be**	**visiting**	you in August.
5. You	**will**	**not**	**(won't)**	**be**	**discussing**	your problems soon.
6. They	**will**	**not**	**(won't)**	**be**	**searching**	you at customs.

3. Fragen

1. When	**will**	**I**	**be**	**taking**	a test tomorrow?
2.	**Will**	**you**	**be**	**flying**	to Italy next year?
3.	**Will**	**he**	**be**	**working**	next year?
	Will	**she**	**be**	**spending**	her holidays in Wales?
Why	**will**	**it**	**be**	**building**	a nest?
4.	**Will**	**we**	**be**	**visiting**	you in August?
5. When	**will**	**you**	**be**	**discussing**	your problems?
6. When	**will**	**they**	**be**	**searching**	you at customs?

Bildung

Das *future progressive* (Verlaufsform des Futurs) wird aus dem *will-future* von **to be** (für alle Personen *will be*) und der *ing*-Form des Verbs gebildet:

Bildung

	will-future von *to be*	+	ing-Form des Hautpverbs	
to work:	He	**will be**	**working**	when you arrive.
to sleep:	They	**will be**	**sleeping**	when you come home.

Frage und Verneinung

Da das *will-future progressive* bereits mit einem Hilfsverb gebildet wird, darf man bei Frage und Verneinung nicht mit *to do* umschreiben:

Will	you	**be sleeping**	when I arrive?
Wirst	du	**schlafen,**	wenn ich ankomme?

He	**will**	**be singing**	when you come home.
Er	**wird**	**singen,**	wenn du heimkommst.

Zu Besonderheiten der Bildung der *ing*-Form: vergleiche das Grammatikkapitel zum *present progressive*.

Zur Satzstellung und zu Besonderheiten bei Verben mit Präpositionen siehe das Kapitel *Allgemeine Regeln*.

Verwendung

Das *future progressive* wird verwendet,

➤ **wenn etwas zu einem bestimmten Zeitpunkt in der Zukunft ablaufen wird:**

Im Nebensatz steht dabei meist das *simple present progressive*. Vor allem die mit *when* eingeleiteten Nebensätze stehen, auch wenn die Handlung in der Zukunft abläuft, immer im *simple present*:

He	**will be working**	when you arrive.
Er	**wird (gerade) arbeiten,**	wenn du ankommst.

They	**will be sleeping**	when you meet them at the office.
Sie	**werden (gerade) schlafen,**	wenn ihr sie im Büro trefft.

➤ **wenn etwas in der Zukunft passieren/ablaufen wird, weil dies so üblich ist:**

Im Deutschen ist das Präsens möglich, wenn aus dem Zusammenhang zweifelsfrei hervorgeht, dass die Handlung in der Zukunft stattfinden wird:

Übersetzungs-Tipp

We	**will be spending**	our holidays in Italy as usual next year.
Wir	**werden**	unsere Ferien wie gewöhnlich nächstes Jahr in Italien **verbringen**.
Wir	**verbringen**	unsere Ferien wie gewöhnlich **nächstes Jahr** in Italien.

You	**will be getting**	a letter from him anyway.
Du	**wirst**	ohnehin einen Brief von ihm **erhalten**.
Du	**erhältst**	**ohnehin** einen Brief von ihm.

Zeitangaben

Häufig beim *future progressive* verwendete Zeitangaben sind:

Wichtig!

➤ this afternoon, this evening
➤ later
➤ soon
➤ then

Exercise 1 – Fill in the forms of the future progressive.

1. They ▨▨▨▨▨▨▨▨▨▨▨▨▨▨▨▨▨▨ (to work) when Tom leaves the house.

2. My mother ▨▨▨▨▨▨▨▨▨▨▨▨▨▨▨▨▨ (not to cook) when we come home.

to feed (fed, fed) – füttern

3. Jack ▨▨▨▨▨▨▨▨▨▨▨▨▨▨▨ (to feed) the cows.

4. ▨▨▨▨▨▨▨▨▨▨▨ the band ▨▨▨▨▨▨▨▨▨▨▨▨▨▨▨▨▨ (to play) when we get there at nine o'clock?

5. He ▨▨▨▨▨▨▨▨▨▨▨▨▨▨▨ (to clean) the room.

6. It ▨▨▨▨▨▨▨▨▨▨▨▨▨ (not to rain) when the plane lands.

7. The Jacksons ▨▨▨▨▨▨▨▨▨▨▨▨▨▨▨▨▨ (to have) breakfast when you phone them on a Saturday morning.

8. We ▨▨▨▨▨▨▨▨ still ▨▨▨▨▨▨▨▨▨▨▨ (to sleep) if you arrive before eight o'clock.

9. The pupils ▨▨▨▨▨▨▨▨▨▨▨▨▨▨▨▨ (to take) a test all morning.

10. They ▨▨▨▨▨▨▨▨▨▨ (to talk) about the problem.

11. The football players ▨▨▨▨▨▨▨▨▨▨▨▨▨ (to train) when you arrive.

12. ▨▨▨▨▨▨▨▨ you ▨▨▨▨▨▨▨▨ (to work) during your holidays?

lunch break – Mittagspause

13. You ▨▨▨▨▨▨▨▨▨▨▨ (to decorate) the room over lunch break if you don't finish it now.

14. The students ▨▨▨▨▨▨▨▨▨▨▨▨ (not to listen) to you.

Exercise 2 – Here are some answers, find the questions. Ask for the words in bold.

1. ▨▨▨▨▨▨▨▨▨▨▨▨▨▨ ? – Michael will be talking about **maths**.

2. ▨▨▨▨▨▨▨▨▨▨▨▨▨▨ ? – My sisters will be cleaning **the kitchen**.

3. ▨▨▨▨▨▨▨▨▨▨▨▨▨▨ ? – The boys will be watching **a film**.

to ride (rode, ridden) – reiten

4. ▨▨▨▨▨▨▨▨▨▨▨▨▨▨ ? – **Sandy** will be riding in the morning.

5. ▨▨▨▨▨▨▨▨▨▨▨▨▨▨ ? – I will be helping **my father** all day long.

6. ▨▨▨▨▨▨▨▨▨▨▨▨▨▨ ? – **The Queen** will be opening Parliament.

7. ▨▨▨▨▨▨▨▨▨▨▨▨▨▨ ? – They'll be dining at **the Grand Hotel**.

to rehearse – üben, proben

8. ▨▨▨▨▨▨▨▨▨▨▨▨▨▨ ? – **The musicians** will be rehearsing.

9. ▨▨▨▨▨▨▨▨▨▨▨▨▨▨ ? – We won't be playing **any pop songs**.

10. ▨▨▨▨▨▨▨▨▨▨▨▨▨▨ ? – The men will be working **in the garden**.

artist – Künstler

11. ▨▨▨▨▨▨▨▨▨▨▨▨▨▨ ? – **The artists** will be watching the play.

to attack – angreifen

12. ▨▨▨▨▨▨▨▨▨▨▨▨▨▨ ? – The soldiers will be attacking **the fort**.

13. ▨▨▨▨▨▨▨▨▨▨▨▨▨▨ ? – **The pupils** will be paying attention.

Exercise 3 – Translation.

1. Was werdet ihr gerade tun, wenn wir euch besuchen?

2. Die Kinder werden nicht in ihren Klassenzimmern sitzen, wenn ihr während der Pause in die Schule kommt.

3. Wenn du mich um neun Uhr anrufst, werde ich gerade meine Hausaufgaben machen.

4. Mein Onkel wird sicherlich wieder den ganzen Tag auf den Feldern arbeiten, wenn wir ihn im Sommer besuchen.

   sicherlich – I'm sure
   auf den Feldern arbeiten
   – to work in the fields

5. Du brauchst heute nicht einkaufen zu gehen. Ich fahre sowieso in die Stadt.

   du brauchst nicht
   – you don't have to
   sowieso, ohnehin – anyway

6. Du brauchst heute nicht bei mir vorbeizukommen, weil ich ohnehin lernen werde.

   vorbeikommen – to come over
   (came, come)

7. Die Schüler werden gerade ein Diktat schreiben, wenn der Feueralarm in der dritten Stunde stattfindet.

   Feueralarm – fire drill

   stattfinden – to take place

8. Du darfst uns morgen Nachmittag nicht stören, weil wir dann mit unserem Direktor über unsere Probleme sprechen werden.

   du darfst nicht – you must not
   stören – to disturb
   Direktor – headmaster

9. Wir werden gerade frühstücken, wenn ihr um zwölf Uhr kommt.

10. Die Studenten werden morgen den ganzen Vormittag ihre Abschlussprüfung schreiben.

    Abschlussprüfung – final exams

11. Du kannst mich morgen besuchen, obwohl ich die ganze Zeit mein Auto reparieren werde.

12. Wirst du morgen wirklich den ganzen Tag arbeiten?

The future perfect

Beispiele

1. Aussagesätze

1. I	**will**	**(I'll)**	**have**	**lived**	here	for ten years by 2015.
2. You	**will**	**(You'll)**	**have**	**finished**	the work	when I arrive.
3. He	**will**	**(He'll)**	**have**	**driven**	a car	for nine years by next summer.
She	**will**	**(She'll)**	**have**	**taken**	her exams	by 2014.
It	**will**	**(It'll)**	**have**	**built**	a nest	by the beginning of winter.
4. We	**will**	**(We'll)**	**have**	**taken**	all the tests	by the end of the year.
5. You	**will**	**(You'll)**	**have**	**studied**	enough	by the time the term is over.
6. They	**will**	**(They'll)**	**have**	**visited**	us	by the end of the week.

2. Verneinte Sätze

1. I	**will not**	**(won't)**	**have**	**lived**	here	for ten years by 2015.
2. You	**will not**	**(won't)**	**have**	**finished**	the work	when I arrive.
3. He	**will not**	**(won't)**	**have**	**driven**	a car	for nine years by next summer.
She	**will not**	**(won't)**	**have**	**taken**	her exams	by 2014.
It	**will not**	**(won't)**	**have**	**built**	a nest	by the beginning of winter.
4. We	**will not**	**(won't)**	**have**	**taken**	all the tests	by the end of the year.
5. You	**will not**	**(won't)**	**have**	**studied**	enough	by the time the term is over.
6. They	**will not**	**(won't)**	**have**	**visited**	us	by the end of the week.

3. Fragen

1.	**Will**	I	**have**	**lived**	here	for ten years by 2015?
2.	**Will**	you	**have**	**finished**	the work	when I arrive!
3.	**Will**	he	**have**	**driven**	a car	for nine years by next summer?
	Will	she	**have**	**taken**	her exams	by 2014?
	Will	it	**have**	**built**	a nest	by the beginning of winter?
4.	**Will**	we	**have**	**taken**	all the tests	by the end of the year?
5.	**Will**	you	**have**	**studied**	enough	by the time the term is over?
6.	**Will**	they	**have**	**visited**	us	by the end of the week?

Bildung

Das *future perfect* (2. Futur, 2. Zukunft) wird aus dem *will-future* von **to have** (alle Formen *will have*) und dem **past participle** (3. Form) des Verbs gebildet:

		will-future von *to have*	+	*past participle* des Verbs	
to finish:	He	**will have**		**finished**	the work by two o'clock.
to write:	They	**will have**		**written**	the letter by tomorrow.

Bildung

Eine Liste der unregelmäßigen Formen des *past participle* befindet sich auf Seite 6.

Frage und Verneinung

Da das *future perfect* mit **Hilfsverben** gebildet wird, darf man bei Frage und Verneinung nicht mit *to do* umschreiben:

Will	you	**have** finished	the work	when I arrive?
Wirst	du		die Arbeit beendet **haben**,	wenn ich ankomme?

He	**will**	**have** written	the letter	by the time we need it.
Er	**wird**		den Brief geschrieben **haben**,	bis wir ihn brauchen.

Zur Satzstellung und zu Besonderheiten bei Verben mit Präpositionen siehe das Kapitel *Allgemeine Regeln*.

Verwendung

Das *future perfect* wird verwendet

➤ **bei Handlungen, die zu einem bestimmten Zeitpunkt in der Zukunft beendet sein werden:**

I	**will have finished**	my work **by five o'clock**.
Ich	**werde**	die Arbeit **bis fünf Uhr beendet haben**.

He	**will have written**	the book **in five weeks**.
Er	**wird**	das Buch **in fünf Wochen geschrieben haben**.

Zeitangaben

Häufig beim *future perfect* verwendete Zeitangaben sind:
➤ by Monday, by two o'clock
➤ in ten minutes, in two hours, in three weeks

Wichtig!

Exercise 1 – Fill in the forms of the future perfect.

1. We _____ (to finished) the test by twelve o'clock.

2. They _____ (to inform) the pupils by next week.

3. When you come back, the carpenters _____ (to put) up the roof.

4. The mechanics _____ (to unload) the plane by tomorrow.

5. You _____ (to come) back by two o'clock.

6. Our teacher _____ (not to correct) the English test by tomorrow.

7. I'm not sure if he _____ (to arrive) by two o'clock.

8. The mechanic says that they _____ (to repair) the car only by next week.

9. Where _____ you _____ (to leave) the keys?

carpenter – Zimmermann, Schreiner
roof – Dach

to unload – ab-, entladen

Exercise 2 – Translation.

Ausflug – trip

1. Die Kinder werden ihre Fahrräder geputzt haben, wenn die Eltern von ihrem Ausflug nach Wales zurückkommen.

_____

_____

abfahren nach – to leave for (left, left)
notwendige Informationen – the necessary information
Reisebüro – travel agency

2. Bevor sie nach England abfahren, werden sie die notwendigen Informationen von unserem Reisebüro erhalten haben.

_____

_____

3. Er wohnt nächste Woche schon drei Monate bei uns.

_____

4. Obwohl ich es ihm immer wieder gesagt habe, bin ich mir sicher, dass er die Arbeit bis heute Nachmittag nicht beendet haben wird.

_____

_____

ausgeben – to spend (spent, spent)

5. Ich glaube, dass sie bis zur nächsten Woche ihr ganzes Geld ausgegeben haben wird.

_____

_____

Maßnahmen unternehmen – to take measures
eine Übereinkunft treffen – to reach an agreement

6. Ich werde keine Maßnahmen unternehmen, bevor wir nicht eine Übereinkunft getroffen haben.

_____

_____

The future with the simple present

Handlungen als Teil eines Plans oder Programms

Das *simple present* wird verwendet, wenn zukünftige Handlungen als **Teil eines Fahr- oder Zeitplans** bzw. eines **festgelegten Programms** ausgedrückt werden, wobei diese Handlungen vom Sprecher normalerweise **nicht beeinflusst** werden können. Es steht häufig in Verbindung mit Verben wie *to begin, to end, to start, to arrive, to leave, to land, to take off.*

The plane	**lands**	at 5.45.
Das Flugzeug	**landet**	um 5.45.
We	**leave**	for London **in the morning**.
Wir	**fahren**	nach London **am Morgen** ab.
The term	**starts**	on 9th September.
Das Semester	**beginnt**	am 9. September.

Zukünftiges Geschehen kann auch mit dem *simple present* oder *present progressive* ausgedrückt werden. Zu den Formen dieser beiden Zeiten: Vergleiche die entsprechenden Grammatikkapitel.

The future with the present progressive

Festgelegte, fest vereinbarte Handlungen

Das *present progressive* wird verwendet, wenn zukünftige Handlungen **festgelegt oder fest vereinbart** sind, wie z. B. Termine und Abmachungen. Bei diesen Entscheidungen hat der Sprecher normalerweise mitgewirkt:

I	**am celebrating**	my birthday **after the holidays**.
Ich	**feiere**	meinen Geburtstag **nach den Ferien**.
We	**are seeing**	the doctor **tomorrow**.
Wir	**gehen**	**morgen** zum Arzt.

The future perfect progressive

Der Vollständigkeit halber soll hier noch kurz eine Zeit besprochen werden, die im Englischen nur noch selten verwendet und deshalb auch in den meisten gängigen Schulgrammatiken nicht erwähnt wird: das *future perfect progressive* (die Verlaufsform der 2. Zukunft). Es wird gebildet aus der *future perfect*-Form von *to be* (für alle Personen *will have been*, für die 1. Person Singular und Plural auch *shall have been*) und der *ing*-Form des Verbs. Im Deutschen wird diese Zeit normalerweise mit dem Präsens oder Futur 2 wiedergegeben.

By the end of this month I	**will have been working**	at this school for two years.
Ende dieses Monats	**arbeite**	ich schon zwei Jahre an dieser Schule.
By next March, the students	**will have been studying**	English for two months.
Nächsten März	**studieren**	die Schüler schon zwei Monate Englisch.

Das *future perfect progressive* wird verwendet, um von einem zukünftigen Zeitpunkt aus auf den Verlauf einer Handlung zurückzuschauen.

By next Tuesday he	**will have been staying**	with the Smiths for three weeks.
Nächsten Dienstag	**ist**	er schon drei Wochen bei den Smiths.
My father	**will have been waiting**	for two hours when the plane lands.
Mein Vater	**wird**	schon zwei Stunden **gewartet haben**, wenn das Flugzeug landet.

As he	**will have been travelling** for 24 hours,	he will be tired when he arrives.
Da er	24 Stunden unterwegs **gewesen sein wird**,	wird er müde sein, wenn er ankommt.

Überblick: The future tenses

going to-future

➤ Absicht, in der Zukunft etwas zu tun
➤ Ereignis, das aller Wahrscheinlichkeit nach eintreten wird

| I am | **going to buy** a book tomorrow. |
| It is | **going to rain** soon. |

will-future

➤ zukünftiges Geschehen, das vom Sprecher nicht beeinflusst werden kann
➤ Vermutung über ein zukünftiges Ereignis, Prognose
➤ spontaner Entschluss, etwas sofort oder in Zukunft zu tun
➤ nach Verben wie *to think/know/believe/expect/to be sure* etc.

We	**will have**	a test tomorrow.
I think I	**will go**	out tonight.
I'm feeling bad. I	**will ring**	the doctor.

future progressive

➤ Handlungen, die sich irgendwann in der Zukunft im Verlauf befinden
➤ normalerweise eintretende Ereignisse oder Handlungen, die ohnehin ausgeführt werden

| He | **will be working** | when you arrive. |
| As usual, you | **will be taking** | a test in the first week after Christmas. |

future perfect

➤ zu einem Zeitpunkt in der Zukunft beendete Handlungen

| I | **will have finished** | the work when you arrive. |
| He | **will have saved** | enough money by October. |

simple present

➤ künftige, vom Sprecher nicht beeinflussbare Handlungen als Teil eines Fahr-, Zeitplans oder festgelegten Programms

| The train | **leaves** | at six o'clock. |
| The holidays | **begin** | in August. |

present progressive

➤ durch Vereinbarung festgelegte oder fest beschlossene zukünftige Handlungen

| We | **are having** | a party on the 22nd. |
| I | **am taking** | Jane out, so I can't see you tonight |

Exercise 1 – Will-future or going to-future? Fill in the correct forms.

Tom: "I hope you (1) _____ (to visit) me in June."

Max: "I'm sorry, but we (2) _____ (not to be) on holidays then."

Tom: "When (3) _____ (to take) your holidays?"

Max: "In August. I (4) _____ (to go) to Africa then.

Tom: "What (5) _____ you _____ (to do) there?"

Max: "I don't know. There (6) _____ (probably/to be) a safari park."

Tom: "Oh, I think you (7) _____ (to enjoy) that very much.

Exercise 2 – Translation.

1. Wir werden nächstes Jahr vielleicht nach Italien fahren.

2. Ich glaube, dass das Wetter dort sehr schön sein wird.

3. Die Hotels waren bis jetzt immer sehr billig, aber nächstes Jahr werden sie wahrscheinlich etwas teurer werden.

   wahrscheinlich – probably
   etwas – a bit

4. Deshalb werden wir in einer Jugendherberge am Stadtrand von Rom wohnen, weil dort die Zimmer immer billiger sind.

   Jugendherberge – youth hostel
   am Stadtrand – on the outskirts

5. Wir haben gestern schon unseren Flug im Reisebüro in unserem Einkaufszentrum gebucht.

   Reisebüro – travel agency
   Einkaufszentrum
   – shopping precinct

6. Morgen gehe ich in die Stadt und kaufe mir zwei Shorts und fünf T-Shirts.

7. Mit etwas Glück werde ich etwas Billiges finden, weil ich mein Geld für meinen Urlaub sparen muss.

   mit etwas Glück
   – with a bit of luck
   etwas Billiges
   – something cheap

8. Aber ich glaube, dass das nicht zu schwer sein wird, weil es seit ein paar Wochen Sonderangebote gibt.

   Sonderangebot – special offer

Exercise 3 – Fill in the correct forms of the verbs.

1. My English is really bad. That's why I _____ (to spend) my holidays in America next year.

2. I booked my flight yesterday. I _____ (to leave) Munich at 2.30 tomorrow.

3. French is our new subject this year. We _____ probably _____ (to have) five tests.

4. The tourists hope that it _____ (not to rain).

5. When _____ the train _____ (to leave)?

6. What _____ you _____ (to do) during the football match?

7. What _____ you _____ (to buy) for your brother's birthday?

8. Jason is not very clever. I doubt whether he _____ (to find) the way to the station.

9. We have booked a table in the best restaurant in the city. We _____ (to celebrate) my birthday there.

10. John _____ (to work) the whole afternoon tomorrow.

11. There _____ (to be) a football match on TV tonight.

12. Have you already finished your work? No I haven't. But I _____ (to finish) it by ten o'clock.

13. There _____ (not to be) any flights tonight.

14. The next school term _____ (to last) three months.

15. John has crashed his car. He _____ (to buy) a new one today.

16. The men in the science department have some terrible news: There _____ _____ (to be) an earthquake tomorrow.

17. I talked to my guidance counsellor yesterday. I _____ (to take) Latin next term.

18. I don't exactly know what I _____ (to do), but I'm sure I _____ (to drop) English next year.

19. We _____ (to arrive) in London at 12.34.

20. There _____ (to be) rain all over the country except in the north.

21. I'm convinced that the polls _____ (to give) a good survey.

22. We're sorry, but we can't help you because we _____ (to go) on vacation with our parents tomorrow.

23. You must make up your mind immediately or you _____ (to miss) an excellent opportunity for improving your knowledge.

subject – (Unterrichts)Fach

to doubt – (be)zweifeln

science department – wissenschaftliche Abteilung
earthquake – Erdbeben

guidance counsellor – Beratungslehrer

except – außer

convinced – überzeugt
polls – Umfragen

to go on vacation – in Urlaub (in die Ferien) fahren

to make up one's mind – sich entscheiden
immediately – sofort
opportunity – Gelegenheit
to improve – verbessern
knowledge – Wissen

Exercise 4 – Fill in the correct forms of the verbs.

1. I'm sure I _____ (to finish) the work by tomorrow.

2. What _____ you _____ (to do) if everything goes wrong?

3. When _____ the hovercraft _____ (to leave)?   hovercraft – Luftkissenboot

4. I _____ (to go) downtown. _____ you _____ (to come), too?

5. My boss has invited me to a barbecue. He _____ (to celebrate) his birthday.

6. Jack _____ (to watch) TV all evening tomorrow.

Exercise 5 – Translation.

1. Es wird gleich regnen.   gleich – in a minute

    _____

2. Wir werden uns vor dem Rathaus treffen.   Rathaus – town hall

    _____

3. Weißt du schon, wohin du in den Sommerferien fahren wirst?

    _____

4. Wir werden über das Problem schon° diskutiert haben, bevor er eintrifft.

    _____

    _____

5. Schau mal aus dem Fenster. Es sind überall Wolken am Himmel. Es wird bald schneien.   Wolke – cloud

    _____

    _____

6. Wann fangen eure Ferien an?

    _____

7. Ich habe starke Kopfschmerzen. Ich gehe jetzt zum Arzt.

    _____

8. Gib bitte das Buch nicht her – ich werde es morgen lesen.

    _____

9. Werdet ihr die Arbeit beendet haben, wenn es klingelt?

    _____

10. Wir haben gestern beschlossen, dass wir meinen Geburtstag am letzten Wochenende   beschließen – to decide
    im April feiern werden.

    _____

    _____

° nicht übersetzen

Exercise 6 – Translation.

sich amüsieren
– to enjoy oneself

1. Ich glaube, dass wir uns auf unserer Klassenfahrt nächste Woche sehr gut amüsieren werden.

abfahren – to leave (left, left)

2. Wir müssen schon sehr bald aufstehen, weil unser Zug schon° um drei nach dreiviertel vier abfährt.

rechtzeitig – in time

3. Unser Lehrer hat uns gesagt, dass wir rechtzeitig da sein müssen.

ankommen – to arrive

4. Wir werden in Schottland erst am nächsten Morgen um sieben Uhr ankommen.

Herbergsleute – wardens

5. Ich hoffe, dass die Herbergsleute in den Jugendherbergen nicht wieder° so unfreundlich sein werden wie letztes Jahr.

herum wandern
– to walk around

6. Aber wir werden sowieso den ganzen Tag auf der Insel herumwandern.

7. Hoffentlich regnet es nicht wieder die ganze Zeit.

ohnehin – anyway
Regenmantel – raincoat

8. Aber bis zum Beginn unserer Fahrt haben sich alle ohnehin einen Regenmantel gekauft.

9. Ich werde meinen Mantel morgen mit meiner Mutter in der Stadt kaufen.

10. Ich glaube, dass es dort billiger ist als in unserem kleinen Dorf.

wahrscheinlich – probably
Spinne – spider
beschweren – to complain
(about)

11. Wahrscheinlich wird es in unseren Zimmern wieder schreckliche Spinnen geben, über die sich die Mädchen beschweren werden.

ausmachen, vereinbaren
– to agree
Abschiedsparty – farewell party

12. Wir haben mit unseren Lehrern ausgemacht, dass wir am letzten Tag unsere Ferien mit einer Abschiedsparty beenden werden.

° nicht übersetzen

Exercise 7 – Fill in the correct tenses.

"What (1) .... you .... (to do) tomorrow?" – "I (2) .... (not to know). I think I (3) .... (to go) into town and buy some new clothes." – "But you (4) .... (to buy) some clothes two weeks ago, (5) .... you?" – "You (6) .... (to be) wrong. I (7) .... (not to buy) anything for months because it (8) .... (to be) so difficult to find something good these days. Last week I (9) .... (to run) around in a department store all morning, but I (10) .... (not to find) anything. This (11) .... (to be) a problem all my life." – "Why (12) .... you .... (not to try) Harrods? It (13) .... (to be) an excellent shop." – "I (14) .... (never/ to be) there, but I think I (15) .... (to go) there tomorrow." – "I'm sure you (16) .... (to be) luckier than in the shops so far. And you (17) .... (to have got) enough money, (18) .... you?" – "Yes, I (19) .... My mother (20) .... (to give) me £48 yesterday although my father (21) .... (not to want) to give me so much money. He (22) .... (to be) like that since he (23) .... (to be) a young boy." – "(24) .... (not to be) angry! My father (25) .... (to be) the same" – "All right then. I think I (26) .... (to go) now. Goodbye."

department store – Kaufhaus

Harrods – großes und berühmtes Kaufhaus in London

although – obwohl

Exercise 8 – Translation.

1. John: „Ich nehme an, dass ich morgen mein blaues Kamel bekommen werde."

   ....

   annehmen – to suppose
   Kamel – camel

2. Jack: „Wirklich? Ich habe immer gedacht, dass du schon ein grünes hast."

   ....

3. John: „Das stimmt nicht. Das grüne Kamel in unserem Wohnzimmer ist nicht meines, sondern das meiner Eltern."

   ....

   ....

   sondern – but

4. Jack: „Du hast Glück. Ich will schon seit Jahren ein richtiges Tier haben, aber bis jetzt hatte ich immer° nur langweilige Papageien."

   ....

   ....

   Glück haben – to be lucky
   richtig – real
   Papagei – parrot

5. John: „Und das Känguru in deinem Garten, ist das nicht deines?"

   ....

   Känguru – kangaroo

6. Jack: „Nein, das ist das Haustier des Wärters unseres Zoos. Ich muss im Winter darauf aufpassen."

   ....

   Wärter – keeper
   aufpassen (auf) – take care (of)
   (took, taken)

° nicht übersetzen

Exercise 9 – Fill in the correct tenses.

Jack (1) _____ (just/to tell) me an interesting story. Two weeks ago he

(2) _____ (to fly) to Scotland because he (3) _____ (to

want) to see Nessie, the monster, in a Scottish lake. But nobody (4) _____

(to see) this terrible thing until now. The night before Jack (5) _____ (to

want) to go to the lake, he (6) _____ (to sleep) terribly. He

(7) _____ (to have) bad dreams about ghosts and watersnakes.

This (8) _____ (to be) strange because he (9) _____ (not

to have) any bad dreams until then. The next morning he (10) _____ (to get)

up early. He (11) _____ (to walk) round the lake for more than two hours, but

nothing (12) _____ (to happen). Suddenly there (13) _____ (to be)

a loud noise. Something black and big (14) _____ (to come) out of the water.

Jack's heart (15) _____ (to beat) quickly. Then he (16) _____ (to

begin) to run away. He (17) _____ (never/to be) so frightened all his life.

He (18) _____ (to phone) the police station. The police (19) _____

(to arrive) at once and (20) _____ (to check) the lake for some time. But

they (21) _____ (not to find) anything. Suddenly the

thing (22) _____ (to rise) out of the water again. And everybody could see what

it was: It (23) _____ (not to be) a monster, but a frogman. Jack

(24) _____ (to be) very disappointed now. But he's sure he

(25) _____ (to find) the monster next year. He hopes I (26) _____

_____ (to go) with him, but (27) _____ (not to think) I will.

lake – See

watersnake – Wasserschlange

suddenly – plötzlich

frogman – Froschmann

disappointed – enttäuscht

Exercise 10 – Translation.

1. Nachdem die Römer die Kelten besiegt hatten, gründeten sie viele römische Siedlungen in England.

   _____

   _____

besiegen – to defeat
gründen – to found
Siedlung – settlement

2. Viele Anführer der einheimischen Stämme flüchteten in die Berge, weil sie dort vor den Verfolgungen der Römer sicherer waren.

   _____

   _____

einheimisch – native
Stamm – tribe
flüchten – to flee, fled, fled
Verfolgung – persecution

3. Noch heute kann man viele Überbleibsel aus der Römerzeit besichtigen.

   _____

Überbleibsel – relics
Römerzeit – Roman times

4. Zur Zeit restauriert man viele von ihnen, um den Leuten ein besseres Bild ihrer geschichtlichen Vergangenheit zu geben.

   _____

   _____

restaurieren – to restore
geschichtlich – historical

Exercise 11 – Fill in the correct forms of the verbs.

John: "Do you already (1) _____ (to know) where you (2) _____ (to go) on your next holiday?"

Mary: "I'm sorry, but I (3) _____ (not to decide) anything yet."

John: "But (4) _____ you _____ (not to discuss) your plans with your parents for hours before dinner yesterday?"

John: "Of course I (5) _____ (to be), but we (6) _____ (cannot/ to reach) an agreement so far."

Mary: "I hope you (7) _____ (to decide) where to go by the end of next week."

John: "Well, I'm only sure that I (8) _____ (not to go) with you to Italy again."

Mary: "Why not?"

John: "Because you really (9) _____ (to get) on my nerves last year.

After we (10) _____ (to spend) hours looking at old cathedrals

in Rome, you still (11) _____ (to want/to have) a look at all

the sights in Venice. And after we (12) _____ (to see) almost

everything interesting there, we still (13) _____ (must/to go) to Florence.

Mary: "But (14) _____ (not to be) that wonderful?

John: "Not really. I (15) _____ (not to like) it at all. And I know that I

(16) _____ (not to do) it again."

Mary: "What a pity!"

to decide – entscheiden

agreement – Abkommen, Übereinkunft

Venice – Venedig

Florence – Florenz

What a pity – wie schade

Exercise 12 – Translation.

1. Nachdem die Schüler ihre Schulaufgaben zurückbekommen hatten, waren sie sehr enttäuscht über ihre Noten und beklagten sich über die schwierigen Sätze.

enttäuscht – disappointed sich beklagen, beschweren – to complain

2. Sie hatten den Unterschied zwischen dem past perfect und dem past perfect progressive wochenlang geübt, bevor sie die Schulaufgabe schrieben.

Unterschied – difference wochenlang – for weeks eine Schulaufgabe schreiben – to do a test

3. Aber viele Schüler wissen immer noch nicht, wie man die Zeiten richtig anwendet.

anwenden – to apply

4. Deshalb üben sie seit letzten Montag schwierige Sätze.

5. Seit dieser Zeit langweilen sie sich nicht mehr.

sich langweilen – to be bored

Exercise 13 – Fill in the correct forms of the verbs.

Mother: "Where (1) _____ (you/to be), John? I (2) _____ (to look) for ages. You (3) _____ (to look) terrible!"

John: "Oh, I (4) _____ (to try) to get the progressive forms into my mind in my room for two hours."

Mother: "But (5) _____ (you/not to do) the progressive forms two years ago?"

John: "Of course we (6) _____ . In class 6 we (7) _____ (to talk) about the tenses every day. But I (8) _____ (to forget) everything."

Mother: " (9) _____ (you/to think), your teacher (10) _____ (to give) you a test tomorrow?"

John: "I (11) _____ (not to be) sure. He (12) _____ (only/to give) us one test since the beginning of the year, so there might be another one tomorrow."

Mother: "And how (13) _____ (to be) your last test?"

John: "Oh, it (14) _____ (to be) fantastic. While we (15) _____ (to write), the bell suddenly (16) _____ (to ring) because there (17) _____ (to be) a fire drill and we (18) _____ (must/to stop/to write). So he never (19) _____ (not to give) back the test."

sure – sicher

suddenly – plötzlich

fire drill – Feueralarm

Exercise 14 – Translation.

1. Seit zwei Jahren beabsichtige ich, nach Schottland zu fahren, aber bis jetzt hatte ich nicht genügend Geld.

beabsichtigen
– to want, to intend, to plan
genügend – enough

2. Nachdem mir meine Freundin Bilder von den schottischen Inseln gezeigt hatte, wollte ich sofort eine Reise buchen.

sofort – at once
eine Reise buchen
– to book a journey

3. Ich war begeistert von der Vielfalt der Landschaft, den einsamen Seen und den grünen Wäldern.

ich war begeistert – *hier:* I loved
Vielfalt – variety
Landschaft – scenery
einsamen – lonely

4. Aber ich weiß wirklich nicht, wie ich dorthin kommen soll, und ich zweifle daran, dass mir meine Mutter etwas Geld geben wird.

zweifeln, dass
– to doubt whether

Exercise 15 – Fill in the correct tenses.

Our family (1) _____ (to live) in a town for years. I (2) _____ (not to like) this very much. When I'm older, I (3) _____ (to want/to live) in the country. I (4) _____ (to spend) my holidays on a farm for three years. It (5) _____ (to be) really exciting. One year ago I (6) _____ (to be) on a farm near Colchester. We (7) _____ (to milk) the cows, (8) _____ (to feed) the horses and pigs and (9) _____ (to sleep) in a dirty cowshed even though it (10) _____ (to be) very smelly there. When the weather (11) _____ (to be) nice, we (12) _____ (to ride) in the fields all morning. Next year we (13) _____ (to spend) our holidays on a farm in France. We (14) _____ (to make) the plans for it at the moment. We (15) _____ (to sit) in the dining-room and (16) _____ (to talk) about everything. We (17) _____ (to plan) the trip for several weeks, but nothing interesting (18) _____ (to come) out of it. My brother (19) _____ (to want) to go to the Normandy, my parents to the Cote d'Azur and I would like to go to a place near Spain. But that (20) _____ (to be) the same so far every year. Last year we (21) _____ (to discuss) everything over weeks and then everybody in the family (22) _____ (to go) to a different place.

to milk – melken

cowshed – Kuhstall
smelly – (unangenehm) riechend

Exercise 16 – Fill in the correct tenses.

The Aborigines (1) _____ (to come) to Australia about 40,000 years ago and (2) _____ (to live) there quietly and peacefully till the first European settlers (3) _____ (to arrive) nearly 300 years ago. There (4) _____ (to be) 300,000 Aborigines at that time. But their lives (5) _____ (to change) completely since then. As the settlers originally (6) _____ (to need) the land for farming, they (7) _____ (to push) the Aborigines off their traditional lands. The whites (8) _____ (to destroy) their culture and traditions from then on. The Aborigines today (9) _____ (not to have) much work and virtually nothing (10) _____ (to live) on. Many of them (11) _____ (to become) alcoholics. So Australian Day, which (12) _____ (to be) an Australian public holiday and (13) _____ (to take) place on January 26th every year, (14) _____ (not to be) a holiday for the Aborigines. They hope that in the future the whites (15) _____ (to treat) them better. But unfortunately this (16) _____ (not to happen/probably).

Aborigines
– Ureinwohner Australiens

peaceful – friedlich

originally – ursprünglich

virtually – praktisch

alcoholic – Alkoholiker

unfortunately – leider

Exercise 17 – Fill in the correct tenses.

Two days ago we (1) ⬚⬚⬚⬚⬚⬚⬚ (to go) to the zoo. It (2) ⬚⬚⬚⬚⬚⬚⬚ (to be) a very nice day. We (3) ⬚⬚⬚⬚⬚⬚⬚ (not to have) such a funny day for years. First we (4) ⬚⬚⬚⬚⬚⬚⬚ (to go) to the gorillas' area. Some of them (5) ⬚⬚⬚⬚⬚⬚⬚ (to live) there for more than ten years. We (6) ⬚⬚⬚⬚⬚⬚⬚ (to watch) them for almost an hour and they (7) ⬚⬚⬚⬚⬚⬚⬚ (to jump) and (8) ⬚⬚⬚⬚⬚⬚⬚ (to play) all the time. It (9) ⬚⬚⬚⬚⬚⬚⬚ (to be) really funny. Then we (10) ⬚⬚⬚⬚⬚⬚⬚ (to go) to see the sea lions. The keeper (11) ⬚⬚⬚⬚⬚⬚⬚ (to feed) them. He (12) ⬚⬚⬚⬚⬚⬚⬚ (to throw) lots of fish into the water and the sea lions (13) ⬚⬚⬚⬚⬚⬚⬚ (to catch) them with their mouths. We (14) ⬚⬚⬚⬚⬚⬚⬚ (not to see) anything so funny before.

Later it (15) ⬚⬚⬚⬚⬚⬚⬚ (to begin) to rain. It (16) ⬚⬚⬚⬚⬚⬚⬚ (to rain) all afternoon. We (17) ⬚⬚⬚⬚⬚⬚⬚ (to get) terribly wet. So we (18) ⬚⬚⬚⬚⬚⬚⬚ (to go) to see the rattlesnakes. They (19) ⬚⬚⬚⬚⬚⬚⬚ (to be) very dangerous animals. They (20) ⬚⬚⬚⬚⬚⬚⬚ (to live) in Africa and South America. I hope I (21) ⬚⬚⬚⬚⬚⬚⬚ (never/to meet) one. I'm sure I (22) ⬚⬚⬚⬚⬚⬚⬚ (not to go) on holiday to countries in these continents. Yesterday we (23) ⬚⬚⬚⬚⬚⬚⬚ (to be) back at school again. In our German lesson we (24) ⬚⬚⬚⬚⬚⬚⬚ (to write) something about our visit in the zoo. We all hope that we (25) ⬚⬚⬚⬚⬚⬚⬚ (to go) there again next month because going to the zoo (26) ⬚⬚⬚⬚⬚⬚⬚ (to be) more interesting than sitting in the classroom all the time.

sea lion – Seelöwe
keeper – Wärter

rattlesnake – Klapperschlange

dangerous – gefährlich

Exercise 18 – Translation.

1. Meine Aussprache ist in letzter Zeit immer schlechter geworden, obwohl ich so viel gelesen habe.

2. Ich lese die Sätze nicht gründlich genug, und deshalb klingt alles falsch.

3. Weil ich bessere Noten bekommen will, muss ich das bald ändern.

Aussprache – pronunciation
immer schlechter werden
   – to become worse and
      worse
   (became, become)

gründlich – thorough
klingen – to sound

Exercise 19 – Fill in the correct tenses.

Yesterday John (1) _____ (to drive) his new car for the first time.

After he (2) _____ (to overtake) a lorry, he (3) _____

(to crash) into another car. Somebody (4) _____ (to phone) the police.

The ambulance (5) _____ (to take) him to hospital, where he

(6) _____ (to be) since yesterday. He hopes that he (7) _____

(can/to leave) hospital soon. He (8) _____ (to watch) a film on

TV now, something which he (9) _____ (not to do) for years.

to overtake – überholen (overtook, overtaken)
lorry – Lastwagen

ambulance – Krankenwagen

Exercise 20 – Translation.

1. Vor einiger Zeit haben wir begonnen, über ein neues Grammatikkapitel zu sprechen.

_____

_____

Grammatikkapitel – hier: aspect of grammar

2. Wir haben seit Jahren nichts derartig Schwieriges gemacht.

_____

3. Obwohl uns unser Lehrer alles erklärt hat, haben wir überhaupt nichts verstanden.

_____

_____

4. Deswegen hat er uns in den letzten Wochen viele Arbeitsblätter gegeben.

_____

Arbeitsblatt – worksheet

5. Gestern haben wir eine Übersetzung gemacht, aber wir konnten sie überhaupt nicht.

_____

_____

6. Aber das ist nichts Neues: Wir haben damit schon immer unsere Probleme.

_____

_____

7. Und so müssen wir seit einiger Zeit viel arbeiten, um keine schlechten Noten zu bekommen.

_____

_____

8. Gestern durften wir nicht einmal fernsehen, und nur deshalb, weil wir unsere unregelmäßigen Verben nicht konnten.

_____

_____

unregelmäßig – irregular

9. Wir hoffen alle, dass die Schulaufgabe morgen sehr leicht wird.

_____

_____

Exercise 21 – Fill in the correct forms of the verbs.

Yesterday we (1) _____ (to have) a nice day. The sun (2) _____

_____ (to shine) and it (3) _____ (not to rain) either. We (4) _____

(to be) happy about that because the weather (5) _____ (to be) bad during

the last three weeks. So we (6) _____ (to go) to the zoo with our teacher.

He (7) _____ (to teach) us something about crocodiles and penguins for

several weeks and (8) _____ (to show) us a lot of pictures of them. Two days ago

he (9) _____ (to teach) us something about some strange African animals.

He (10) _____ (just/to return) from there. We (11) _____ (not to

understand) anything although we (12) _____ (to listen) quite carefully and

although we (13) _____ (to be) quiet all the time. It (14) _____

(to be) quite interesting, though. He also (15) _____ (to tell) us something about

South American boars. The bad thing about it (16) _____ (to be) that our

teacher (17) _____ (to give) us a test about all these things next week. We

(18) _____ (to be) a bit frightened about it because we (19) _____

_____ (not to pay) close attention in lessons this week. I'd like to stay home

tomorrow, but my mother (20) _____ (not to like) it very much. That's too bad!

boar – Wildschwein

to be frightened – Angst haben

Exercise 22 – Translation.

1. Vor drei Tagen hat Bayern München sein Fußballspiel gegen Manchester United verloren.

    _____

2. Während des ganzen Spiels spielten die Münchner sehr schlecht und rannten dem Ball
    nicht sehr erfolgreich hinterher.

    _____

    _____

erfolgreich – successful

3. Schon seit Wochen laufen sie sehr langsam und haben in dieser Zeit nicht sehr viele
    Spiele gewonnen.

    _____

    _____

4. Obwohl Bayern München seit Jahren die besten Spieler gekauft hat, ist es nicht immer
    sehr erfolgreich gewesen und hat den Europacup schon seit einiger Zeit nicht mehr ge-
    wonnen.

    _____

    _____

Europacup – European Cup

5. Seit 1972 haben sie an jedem europäischen Wettbewerb teilgenommen, aber sie haben
    den Pokal zum letzten Mal 1980 gewonnen.

    _____

    _____

Wettbewerb – competition
Pokal – Cup

Exercise 23 – Fill in the correct forms of the verbs.

Four days ago we (1) _____ (to go) on a trip to London. We (2) _____ (to spend) the whole afternoon in a Gothic cathedral. We (3) _____ (not to see) anything like it before. There (4) _____ (to be) beautiful sculptures and angels everywhere. We (5) _____ (to look) at all the things carefully, and our teacher (6) _____ (to tell) us some interesting things about the building. After the visit our teacher (7) _____ (to invite) us to a café and we (8) _____ (to have) ice-cream and lemonade there. We (9) _____ (to sit) there all afternoon till it got dark. Then we (10) _____ (to go) home and (11) _____ (to write) a story about the cathedral. Today we (12) _____ (to be) in the classroom and (13) _____ (to talk) about our work. Some pupils (14) _____ (to do) a text of over four pages, but others (15) _____ (to write) only two and half pages. We (16) _____ (to correct) the mistakes now. What a boring lesson! We are sure that our teacher (17) _____ (to give) us a test tomorrow. He (18) _____ (always/to set) tests after trips. I think I (19) _____ (to stay) at home tomorrow.

Gothic – gotisch

sculpture – Skulptur, Plastik

Exercise 24 – Translation.

1. Vor kurzem ging ich in unserer Stadt einkaufen.

   _____

   vor kurzem – not long ago

2. Weil mir einige meiner alten Jeans nicht mehr passten, wollte ich zwei neue kaufen.

   _____

   passen – to fit

3. Ich ging in Judys Modeladen und probierte sieben verschiedene Hosen an, aber keine einzige stand mir wirklich.

   _____

   _____

   anprobieren – to try on
   stehen (kleiden) – to suit

4. Ich habe schon immer Probleme gehabt, die richtige Größe zu finden, weil ich zu dick bin.

   _____

   _____

   Größe – size

5. Deshalb habe ich noch nie eng anliegende Kleidung getragen.

   _____

   eng anliegend – tight
   Kleidung – clothes

6. Seit Wochen versuche ich, etwas Hübsches zu finden, aber bis jetzt hatte ich kein Glück.

   _____

   Glück haben – to be lucky

7. Ich habe schon oft etwas aus einem Katalog bestellt, aber das war meistens noch schlimmer.

   _____

   _____

   Katalog – catalogue

Exercise 25 – Fill in the correct tenses and for or since where necessary.

tired – müde

sure – sicher

quite – ziemlich

It is Monday evening and Tom (1) _____ (to be) really tired now. He (2) _____ (to work) (3) _____ two o'clock. He is sure that they (4) _____ (to have) an English test tomorrow. He (5) _____ (to know) that (6) _____ two weeks, but he (7) _____ (to begin) to learn only yesterday. This year everything (8) _____ (to be) quite hard. In the beginning they (9) _____ (to do) some difficult grammar exercises, and they (10) _____ (to talk) about the present perfect progressive all the time (11) _____ ten days. But he (12) _____ (not to understand) a lot. He (13) _____ (to study) hard with his sister every day (14) _____ one week, but (15) _____ she _____ (to leave) school, she (16) _____ (to spend) her holidays in England only three times and so she (17) _____ (not to know) much about the language now. But (18) _____ that time she (19) _____ (to read) some English books and that's why her English (20) _____ (to become) better. She hopes that her brother (21) _____ (not to have) any problems tomorrow.

Exercise 26 – Translation.

wild – wild
aussterben – to become extinct
         (became,
         become)
sich kümmern – to take care (of)

1. Viele wilde Tiere sind überall auf unserem Planeten ausgestorben, weil wir uns nicht um sie gekümmert haben.

    _____

    _____

annehmen – to think, to suppose
         (thought, thought)
Eisbär – polar bear
Seelöwe – sea-lion

2. Einige Leute nehmen an, dass es bald keine Eisbären, Seelöwen und Pinguine mehr geben wird.

    _____

passieren – to happen

3. Seit Jahren sprechen wir im Fernsehen immer wieder über diese Probleme, aber bis jetzt ist fast überhaupt nichts passiert.

    _____

    _____

sich vorstellen – to imagine
Nilpferd – hippo(potamus)

4. Kannst du dir vorstellen, dass wir im nächsten Jahrhundert Nilpferde und Kamele nur noch im Zoo sehen werden?

    _____

    _____

sammeln – to collect

arm – poor

5. Unser Biologielehrer hat uns seit zwei Jahren jeden Tag etwas über diese Probleme gesagt, und deshalb haben wir seit dieser Zeit Geld für die armen Tiere unserer Erde gesammelt.

    _____

    _____